WRITERS IN THEIR TIME
General Editor: Norman Page

Writers in their Time

Published titles

JOSEPH CONRAD *Brian Spittles*

Forthcoming titles

GEOFFREY CHAUCER *Janette Dillon*
CHARLES DICKENS *Angus Easson*
GEORGE ELIOT *Brian Spittles*
THOMAS HARDY *Timothy Hands*
GEORGE ORWELL *Norman Page*

Series Standing Order

If you would like to receive future titles in this series as they are published, you can make use of our standing order facility. To place a standing order please contact your bookseller or, in case of difficulty, write to us at the address below with your name and address and the name of the series. Please state with which title you wish to begin your standing order. (If you live outside the United Kingdom we may not have the rights for your area, in which case we will forward your order to the publisher concerned.)

Customer Services Department, Macmillan Distribution Ltd
Houndmills, Basingstoke, Hampshire, RG21 2XS, England.

Joseph Conrad
Text and Context

Brian Spittles

MACMILLAN

First published 1992 by
THE MACMILLAN PRESS LTD
Houndmills, Basingstoke, Hampshire RG21 2XS
and London
Companies and representatives
throughout the world

ISBN 0–333–54200–2 hardcover
ISBN 0–333–54201–0 paperback

A catalogue record for this book is available
from the British Library

Phototypeset by Intype, London
Printed in Hong Kong

For Margaret

Contents

Acknowledgements

I would like to thank those people who have helped me personally in the completion of this book: the series editor, Professor Norman Page, who started the whole process; Dr Ruth Whittaker, for showing her usual confidence in me; the helpful library staff at Ruskin College, the University of Oxford English Faculty, and the Bodleian; Rosemary Margaret Martin, who translated from French all the passages not ascribed to other translators; Alied and Joyce; Gillian Hush; Miss Alice Sheridan, CBE, for her enthusiasm, and permission to use the letters of John Pine that are in her possession; and ultimately Margaret Wickett, who contributed most for least reward.

In the course of studying Conrad for nearly thirty years my understanding and appreciation owes an unrepayable debt to the work of many previous scholars. Some of these are: Jocelyn Baines, Charles G. Bell, Val Cunningham, Terry Eagleton, Robert Hampson, Douglas Hewitt, Frederick Karl, Owen Knowles, Zdzisław Najder, Norman Page, Norman Sherry, Ian Watt and Cedric Watts.

The author and publishers wish to thank the following for permission to use copyright material: Cambridge University Press for extracts from *The Collected Letters of Joseph Conrad*, vols I, II and III, eds Frederick R. Karl and Laurence Davies, 1983, 1986, 1988; William Heinemann Ltd for extracts from *Joseph Conrad: Life and Letters*, vols I and II, ed. G. Jean-Aubrey, 1927; Scottish Academic Press Ltd for an extract from 'Song for the Twenty Fourth of May' by John Davidson from *The Poems of John Davidson*, vol. I, ed. Andrew Turnbull, 1973.

Every effort has been made to trace all the copyright holders, but if any have been inadvertently overlooked the publishers will be pleased to make the necessary arrangement at the first opportunity.

Abbreviations

Page numbers in respect of Conrad's novels refer to the following Penguin editions:

Heart of Darkness (1989)
Lord Jim (1986)
Nigger of the 'Narcissus', The (1988)
Nostromo (1990)
Secret Agent, The (1990)
Tales of Unrest (1977)
'Twixt Land and Sea (1988)
Under Western Eyes (1989)
Victory (1989)
Youth (1975)

Compilations of other writing by Conrad are referenced by the following coding:

CD   Zdzisław Najder (ed.), *Congo Diary and Other Uncollected Pieces by Joseph Conrad* (New York: Doubleday, 1978)
CL   Frederick R. Karl and Laurence Davies (eds), *The Collected Letters of Joseph Conrad* (Cambridge: Cambridge University Press)
      Volume I, 1861–1897, published 1983
      Volume II, 1898–1902, published 1986
      Volume III, 1903–1907, published 1988
      Volume IV, 1908–1911, published 1990
LE   Joseph Conrad, *Last Essays* (London: Dent, 1926)
LL   G. Jean-Aubrey (ed.) *Joseph Conrad: Life & Letters*, volumes 1 and 2 (London: Heinemann, 1927)
NL   Joseph Conrad, *Notes on Life and Letters* (London: Dent, 1970)

General Editor's Preface

In recent years many critics and teachers have become convinced of the importance of recognizing that works of literature are grounded in the conditions of their production in the widest possible sense of that phrase – in the history, society, ideas and ideologies of their time, the lives and careers of their authors, and the prevailing circumstances of the literary market-place and the reading public. To some extent this development reflects both a disenchantment with the 'practical criticism' approach that held sway for so long in school, college and university teaching of literature and a scepticism towards the ahistorical biases encouraged by some more recent schools of critical theory.

It is true that lip-service has long been paid to 'background': the English Tripos at Cambridge, for instance, embodied the 'life, literature and thought' formula from its early years. Such an approach, however, tended to treat 'background' as distinct and detachable from literary works and as constituting a relatively minor, marginal and even optional element in the study of a text. What is now perceived to be in question is something more vital and more central: not a loosely defined relationship between certain novels, plays and poems on the one hand and 'history' or 'ideas' on the other, but an intimate informing and shaping of the one by the other. Colonialism in Conrad or Kipling, Christian theology in Milton or Bunyan, scientific discovery in Tennyson or Hardy, politics in Yeats or Eliot: these are not background issues against which the texts can be foregrounded but crucial determinants of the very nature of the texts themselves without which they would be radically different and which profoundly affect the way we understand and value them.

At the same time, as most teachers are ready to attest, even a basic knowledge of the historical and cultural conditions of past, including recently past, generations cannot be taken for granted. To many students, periods as recent as the 1930s or the Great War are largely a closed book, while key concepts of earlier generations such as Darwinism or Puritanism, and major movements such as the spread of literacy and the growth and decline of imperialism, are known in the sketchiest outline if at all.

This series is intended to provide in an accessible form materials that will make possible a fuller and deeper understanding of the work of major authors by demonstrating in detail its relationship to the world, including the intellectual world, in which it was produced. Its starting-point is not a notion of 'background' but a conviction that many, perhaps most, great writers are in an integral sense *in* and *of* their time. Each volume will look afresh at the primary texts (or a selection of them) in relation to the ways in which they have been informed and shaped by both the external and the ideological conditions of their worlds. Historical, political, scientific, theological, philosophical and other dimensions will be explored as appropriate. By understanding more fully the contexts which have made particular works what they are and not other-wise, students and others will be able to bring new understanding to their reading of the texts.

NORMAN PAGE

1
The Unique Background

Joseph Conrad is unique as a writer. Not just as all writers differ from one another, but in the way his life and two careers mark him out as being different from any previous – and perhaps any more recent – novelist in the realms of English literature. Of no other major novelist could another author write the description John Galsworthy, in a letter to his sister, gave of Conrad:

> he is a man of travel and experience in many parts of the world. . . . He has been right up the Congo and all around Malacca and Borneo and other out of the way parts, to say nothing of a little smuggling in the days of his youth.[1]

Galsworthy wrote this in 1893 after his first meeting with Conrad, and they were to become lifelong friends.

At the time of his birth in 1857 the great tradition of the English novel, that Jôzef Teodor Konrad Nałęcz Korzeniowski would ultimately both challenge and develop, was being carried by such writers as Charles Dickens and Elizabeth Gaskell, William Makepeace Thackeray and Anthony Trollope, who had inherited it from Henry Fielding and Jane Austen, and who would pass it on to George Eliot and Thomas Hardy. These were not the only important, or interesting, novelists in English before Conrad began to write, but they are central figures who share one common, dominating, feature: their Englishness. Of course, Irish and Scots novelists also contributed significantly to what is known as English literature – Laurence Sterne and Walter Scott provide outstanding examples – and later Welsh writers too participated in that tradition; but despite their nationality those authors shared in, and largely subscribed to, a British education and culture that was dominated by England. In the year of Conrad's birth it seemed that Britain had overcome much of its strife and uncertainty, and was fundamentally a secure and self-confident political and economic entity – although instability and loss of confidence did occur later.

Few Poles during the period of Conrad's childhood enjoyed the English/British sense of security of national identity, for during most of the nineteenth century Poland was virtually an occupied country. It was pressured from the west by Prussia, the most military of the Germanic States; from the south by the Austro-Hungarian Empire; and from the east by Czarist Russia.

Joseph Conrad came from a family with a long history of patriotic struggle against the forces of occupation. The grandfather from whom Conrad gained his second name, Teodor, won military honours in 1809 fighting against Austria; and in 1830 was again in action, this time in the attempt to end Russian oppression in Poland. He finally died, when his grandson Joseph was five years old, trying to join the Polish insurrection against Russia that occurred in 1863. That spirit of political conflict and aspiration was also evident in Conrad's father, Apollo Nałęcz Korzeniowski, who was exiled by the Russian authorities in 1862 for actions defined as political crimes. In the following year in addition to the death of Joseph Conrad's grandfather one of the boy's uncles was killed in the insurrection, and another sentenced to exile because of his participation in the anti-Russian rising.

It is obvious that Conrad's formative years were a time of political turmoil and violence in which his family were deeply enmeshed. Conrad's family came from aristocratic stock that had fallen socially. A combination of financial carelessness and political idealism, that had embroiled various members in conflict with the Russian forces of occupation, caused that fall; although they remained a well-educated family who never quite accepted their new, and inferior, social status. In fact they did not lose all social prestige. When Apollo married Evelina in 1856 he was an estate manager, and with the help of her dowry leased a farm – in the Ukraine, the south-east area of Poland that was under Russian Czarist government – just before Joseph Conrad was born. That venture, however, lasted only three years, ending again in financial mismanagement. Joseph Conrad grew up as an only child in an atmosphere in which his father was frustrated financially and politically. The latter leading to him being banished in 1862 by the Russian authorities in order to remove him from the political arena in Poland.

Most of the British novelists mentioned earlier were critical, some extremely so, of their society, but they never felt displaced, were never physically exiled from it. Conrad suffered two exiles, both of which served to affect his perception of western European life and culture profoundly.

His first exile, as a boy of four years old, was involuntary – accompanying his father and mother on Apollo's political banishment to a fairly remote area of Russia north-east of Kiev, about 300 miles from their home. They were harsh conditions in which to grow up, as his father's description of the place they were initially sent to illustrates:

> a great three-verst marsh . . . everything rotting and shifting under one's feet. . . . The climate consists of two seasons of the year: a white winter and a green winter. The white winter lasts nine-and-a-half months and the green one two-and-a-half . . . [on their arrival] it had already been raining ceaselessly for twenty-one days.[2]

In the circumstances it is not surprising that in the same letter Conrad's father observed, the 'population is a nightmare: disease-ridden corpses'. Although the family later moved to a less hostile environment Joseph's mother, Evelina, was often ill and died in 1865 when her son was only seven years old. Joseph's father too suffered poor health, and so the boy was then being brought up in a foreign country by a single parent who was impoverished, unwell and a patriot longing to return to his homeland. That ended in 1869 when Apollo also died. Joseph Conrad was an orphan at the tender age of eleven, but that enabled him to return to the family where he was effectively raised by Uncle Thaddeus, his mother's brother.

Conrad's views of political action and idealism, patriotism, sacrifice must have been fundamentally influenced by the havoc and distress these concepts caused to his family, and the sheer physical hardship they inflicted during his formative years. All of these experiences are a long way from any sufferings undergone by British novelists – which is not to argue that they had easy, comfortable lives, but that the scale of their hardships was different, and occurred within a *comparatively* stable political and cultural framework. In moving from the British novelists to Conrad it is necessary for the reader to change perspectives.

Those potentially noble, potentially destructive concepts that drove his family on recur as themes throughout Conrad's work. Writing was also a family trait: his grandfather Teodor wrote a play in verse; and Conrad's own father aspired to being a man of letters. Apollo studied at Petersburg University – that in itself is significant of the power of Russian educational imperialism in the Poland of the nineteenth century – and translated western European writers, including Shakespeare and Dickens. He also wrote poetry and plays. The family was imbued with the literary culture of its time, which was mainly patriotic anti-oppressor in sentiment. Jôzef Teodor Konrad Nałęcz Korzeniowski was given his first two Christian names after his grandfathers, and probably awarded his third name in respect to a fictional character, Konrad Wallenrod – the eponymous hero of an epic, inevitably, patriotic poem. It is a feature of Conrad's fiction, though, that linguistic and structural ironies often make it difficult for the reader to know exactly what the author's attitudes are towards the themes. Although Conrad was brought up in an atmosphere of polemical writing he does not often take a simple propagandist approach to ideas and conflicts. A central facet of Conrad's vision as a writer is the way in which he sees complexity, ambiguity and paradox in situations that the mere polemicist would use simply to illustrate a predetermined theory. His own subsequent honest opinion of his grandfather's Drama, expressed in a letter to Edward Garnett, was that it is 'so extremely dull that no one was ever known to have read it through' (CL, vol. 2, p. 245). In his own work Conrad was determined to avoid both the simple-mindedness and the dullness of conventional epic narratives; which he achieved partly by developing relatively uncommon narrational techniques. The use of a narrator who is also a participating character, in particular Marlow who appears in several works, is one aspect Conrad developed beyond the mainstream of nineteenth century usage; and the use of time in a disorientating manner is a feature of a number of novels and stories.

In *Youth* and *Heart of Darkness*, for instance, the narrative structure is based on an older Marlow telling incidents of his earlier life to an audience of listeners; the main narrator being one of that group. The filtering of the story through memories means that nothing can be taken for granted, as it can be in many earlier novels, that the narrators themselves must be questioned. *Nostromo* is constructed around a very complicated time scheme. In Part the First, for example, the time scheme is circular, denying the traditional convention of a simple linear plot development. Many occurrences are described and analysed, but with the action ending at exactly the temporal point at which it began in the novel. The effect of these devices is to involve the reader intellectually. Conrad's novels cannot be read passively, simply for the plot – the reader has to work quite hard at times simply to understand what is going on. That is part of the challenge of reading Conrad, and also the core of the joy and excitement when some comprehension is attained. Conrad uses the active process of interpretation to question traditional forms and ideas, to challenge conventional attitudes and beliefs.

Conrad's second exile was chosen by him when he was a youth. At the time it was not necessarily a long-term decision but in the event that is what it became, and it led directly to his first career: that of a seaman. As an orphan who had moved about a good deal Conrad was restless and somewhat rootless. He had been taken to the sea at Odessa, and that had fired his imagination; his father had begun to teach him French during their period in exile together, and those two factors fused in young Conrad's desire to escape and begin to form his own life and identity. He left Poland for Marseilles in 1874, at the age of sixteen, and the following year began his career as a sailor in the French Merchant Navy. Four years later Conrad, in the way international sailors often did, drifted into the British Merchant Navy and apparently began to feel some stability seeping into his nomadic existence. It was from this period that he started to gain marine career qualifications, and in 1886 he became a naturalised British subject. In 1895 he formally dropped his Polish name on the publication of his first novel, *Almayer's Folly*. In the following year he married an English woman, Jessie George, and took up permanent residence in England. They had two sons: Borys, who was born in 1898, and John in 1906. Nevertheless Conrad always felt close to Polish troubles, and did revisit the country. When he died in Kent in 1924 the name Korzeniowski was inscribed on his gravestone.

No other major novelist of English literature had quite such a varied life. The experience of Conrad's first career, as a sailor, also marks him out from the mainstream of novelists in the canon of English literature in at least three basic ways: the length of his first career, its nature, and the world perspective it enabled Conrad to bring to English literature.

The majority of the leading British-born novelists had not moved to writing from a totally non-literary career as Conrad had. Of those mentioned earlier, for example, Henry Fielding was engaged with the theatre; Charles Dickens was a reporter for a few years; William Makepeace Thackeray also worked for newspapers; George Eliot was a translator, reviewer and essayist – all occupations related to reading and writing. In addition Laurence Sterne was a clergyman; Anthony Trollope had a public school education and eventually attained a prestigious position in the Post Office. Jane Austen and Elizabeth Gaskell had no formal career as such, but both had physically and financially secure lives in which they were rarely far from a private library. Thomas Hardy did train as an architect, and he was perhaps most removed from contact with the world of letters, but even he published his first novel, *Desperate Remedies*, when he was only thirty years old, and had more or less given up the profession of architect by the time he was thirty-three. Conrad's first novel, *Almayer's Folly*, was published when he was thirty-seven, and his sea-going career lasted for nineteen years. In a way Conrad was returning to an old family concern in becoming a writer. He was, however, a late starter in his own right, later than many other novelists, and came to writing with very different attitudes from those of his grandfather, father, and the majority of other novelists.

The second factor differentiating Conrad from the mainstream was the nature of his first career. This contained two major elements: physical action and acute danger. When Conrad writes about work it is not from a theoretical position, nor does he necessarily rigidly separate mental and physical work. If there was a Victorian Protestant work ethic – and that glib slogan retrospectively applied can cover much poverty of thought – Conrad could hardly be claimed, legitimately, as a subscriber. It is not so much work that is important, but the mental and physical activity involved in it – the energy – that is vital. It is necessary to make a crucial judgement about the two activities, of mind and body. They have to be fused, either one on its own can become sterile. The former can lead to a divorce from practical reality. Decoud's solitude when he is stranded on the Great Isabel engenders:

> The vague consciousness of a misdirected life. . . . His sadness was the sadness of a sceptical mind. He beheld the universe as a succession of incomprehensible images. . . . And all exertion seemed useless.
>
> (*Nostromo*, pp. 413–14)

Chronic inertia leads to stagnation, and in this case death by suicide. But physical activity alone may be ultimately sterile too. Conrad drew, in a *Fortnightly Review* article in 1905 – attacking, incidently, two of the old Polish enemies, Russia and a Prussian-dominated Germany – a parallel between individual people and political States:

> States, like most individuals, having but a feeble and imperfect consciousness of the worth and force of the inner life, the need of making their existence manifest to themselves is determined in the direction of physical activity. The idea of ceasing to grow in territory, in strength, in wealth, in influence – in anything but wisdom and self-knowledge is odious to them as the omen of the end. Action, in which is to be found the illusion of a mastered destiny, can alone satisfy our uneasy vanity.
>
> (NL, pp. 108–9)

Simple action without thought is an illusionary mastering of destiny – mere physical action for its own sake leading to aggression and violence – just as intellectualism divorced from practical action also leads to a condition, or state, of unreality. But the two in fusion are able to generate positive values, for it is energy that is created by the practical and natural yoking of both activities. Aggression is a destructive force; renunciation of the will to use it is a natural and creative force. Conrad argued this in an article in the *North American Review*:

> a fine consciousness is naturally a virtuous one. What is natural about it is just its fineness, and abiding sense of the intangible, ever-present, right. It is most visible in their ultimate triumph, in their emergence from miracle, through an energetic act of renunciation. Energetic, not violent; the distinction is wide, enormous, like that between substance and shadow.
>
> (NL, p. 18)

These are pre-eminently the thoughts of a writer who has had to work practically and intellectually, not simply to earn a wage, but literally as a matter of life and death at sea.

This element – the danger – is the other major aspect of the nature of Conrad's first career. A lot of Conrad's fiction – a great deal more than at first meets the eye – is not particularly concerned with the sea, or only peripherally so, but in order to grasp the whole of his achievement it is necessary for the modern reader to appreciate the quality of sea-going life in the nineteenth century, in which most of the fiction is set although mainly written in the twentieth. The nature of that life permeates most of Conrad's subsequent philosophical ideas.

The danger of a sea-faring life sprang from two basic factors: the relative smallness, and sometimes the unseaworthiness of ships, which left them vulnerable to all manner of accidents; and the unpredictability and potential ferocity of weather conditions. These could be related aspects of experience at sea, and the weather is not a factor over which there is any real control, but its effects were intensified by the state of the shipping.

It is important to realise that the number of commercial sailing vessels outnumbered steamships until just into the twentieth century. The change occurred during Conrad's career as a sailor. In the United Kingdom the numbers of ships registered in 1875, just after Conrad had begun his first career, were: 'sailing vessels 21,291; steam vessels 4,170'. It was not until 1904 that the numerical balance finally tipped in favour of steam, when the statistics were: 'sailing vessels 10,210; steam vessels 10,370'.[3] These were working craft, often plying long routes and carrying a lot of cargo. Over 10,000 sailing ships obviously did not go out of service overnight, and they remained a significant, even if diminishing, aspect of mercantile life well into the twentieth century. It might also be remembered that the figures relate to Britain, which was one of the (if not *the*) leading industrial nations; shipping in some other parts of the world was dominated by sail until much later. These ships were particularly vulnerable to vicissitudes of climate, and to accidents. These might be seen as manifestations of fate, a complex concept that is a recurring theme in Conrad's fiction.

Both those elements of risk were exacerbated, however, by controllable circumstances: the inefficiency of land-based operators, and the greed of some owners. It is because Conrad recognises the subtle interplay between forces that are external to humanity, such as weather, and mankind's actions – the way a crew is treated or a cargo loaded, for example – that his treatment of the theme of fate is complex.

Even human cargo was sometimes transported without consideration. John Pine, for example, wrote to his father of a journey to South Africa:

We arrived safe and sound at Algoa Bay after being in misery 89 days on board the Magaera. When we went out of Plymouth Sound we had nearly four feet of water in us, but we managed to stop the leak after pumping for days and nights. We had the misfortune to have the engine room on fire no less than three times to the great danger of the ship and all our lives. We had nearly 900 souls on board altogether and we were all packed as close as herrings.[4]

Pine's factual observations on the voyage give a perspective of veracity to a story such as *Youth*, in which the *Judea* is submitted to a series of accidents that may appear to be rather melodramatic. That fictional ship also springs a leak that takes several days of ceaseless pumping to withstand, and it suffers a recurrent fire – ordeals of the elements that have a metaphorical, thematic significance, but are also within the truth of Victorian sea-going experience. That John Pine's experience on the *Magaera* was not unique is indicated by his stoical comment in a later letter about another voyage:

I hope, my dear Father, you will excuse this dirty scrawl as I am nearly blinded with coal dust. Our vessel is in a dirty state and we have had shocking accommodation on board of her. If it had been a long voyage, I do not know what we should have done. In fact, it was ten times worse than the Magaera.[5]

Those sort of conditions continued into the twentieth century.

In Conrad's formative sea-going years, the period in which many of his sea stories are set, safety regulations governing ships were inadequate, and even such laws as existed were poorly supervised and implemented. The Plimsoll Line that all ships now carry to help prevent overloading dates from the Merchant Shipping Act of 1876, in which the MP Samuel Plimsoll sought to control shipping owners and operators more closely for the benefit of crews. This was a well-intentioned Act, but one which a later, very conservative, historian dismissed as 'not in itself very effective'.[6] Yet the build up to it in the previous year had been spectacular in the sedate Victorian House of Commons, with Plimsoll – in full flood of indignation – being expelled from the sitting by the Speaker.

Plimsoll had eloquently pleaded with the prime minister, Disraeli, to allow discussion of the Shipping Bill, which the government were abandoning, and 'not to consign some thousands of living beings to undeserved and miserable death'. These were sailors who would drown in unsafe ships. The MP went on to speak 'of shipowners of murderous tendencies' who had friends in the House who ensured measures such as the Shipping Bill were not passed into law. This kind of accusation naturally led Plimsoll into controversy, but he had evidence that some owners did insure an old ship for more than it was worth in the hope that it would be lost at sea. They would then be rid of a vessel that needed expensive repairs, and collect a profit from the insurance company into the bargain. The real losers, of course, were the hapless sailors who drowned. The insurance companies, of which Lloyd's was the main one, had a financial interest in what amounted to large-scale fraud, and they provided Plimsoll with arguments:

> The Secretary of Lloyds . . . does not know a single ship which has been broken up voluntarily by the owners in the course of thirty years on account of its being worn out. Ships gradually pass from hand to hand, until bought by some needy and reckless speculators, who send them to sea with precious human lives . . . every winter, hundreds and hundreds of brave men are sent to death, their wives are made widows and their children are made orphans, in order that a few speculative scoundrels . . . may make unhallowed gains.
>
> (*Hansard*, 22 July 1875)

Plimsoll went on to categorise these people as 'ship-knackers', and to blame them specifically for: 'the following ships – the *Tethys*, the *Melbourne*, the *Nora Greame*, which were all lost in 1874 with 87 lives' (ibid.). This parliamentary speech illustrates the seriousness of the dangers. The *Patna*, on which the eponymous Lord Jim met, and failed, his great test was not an exaggerated example: 'eaten up with rust worse than a condemned water-tank' (*Lord Jim*, p. 53). It is no wonder that Jim expects the ship to sink after the collision that rips a hole in it: 'Have you watched a ship floating head down, checked in sinking by a sheet of old iron too rotten to stand being shored up?' (p. 111). Understanding that he had chosen a career in which such risks were inherent, yet still following it, and knowing men who had survived desperate, potentially fatal, situations gave Conrad a greater perception of life than many other major novelists had experienced.

Conrad also encountered natural elements, in the form of meteorological conditions and the power of the sea, more intensely than land-based writers. Ships in Conrad's fiction are constantly confronting appalling weather; this is partly a verisimilic reflection of the facts of a sailor's life, partly a use of extended metaphor that gives the novels and stories, including those set at sea, universal value. When Charles Dickens crossed the Atlantic he had encountered a storm that he described in his own factual way:

> I could not even make out which was the sea, and which the sky, for the horizon seemed drunk, and was flying wildly about in all directions . . . when everything was sliding and bumping about, and when it did seem difficult to comprehend the possibility of anything afloat being more disturbed, without toppling over and going down. But what the agitation of a steam-vessel is, on a bad winter's night in the wild Atlantic, it is impossible for the most vivid imagination to conceive. To say that she is flung down on her side in the waves, with her masts dipping into them, and that, springing up again, she rolls over on the other side, until a heavy sea strikes her with the noise of a hundred great guns, and hurls her back; that she stops and staggers, and shivers, as though stunned, and then, with a violent throbbing at her heart, darts onward like a monster goaded into madness, to be beaten down, and battered, and crushed, and leaped on by the angry sea; that thunder, lightning, hail, and rain, and wind, are all in fierce contention for the mastery; that every plank has its groan, every nail its shriek, and every drop of water in the great ocean its howling voice – is nothing. . . . Words cannot express it. Thoughts cannot convey it.[7]

Despite his modest disclaimer that the circumstances cannot be described Dickens does so quite vividly. But, imaginative a writer as he was, Dickens the reporter remained here at the level of description. Conrad always pushes such events into a metaphoric sphere too, and an affirmation of the virtues of men who rise to the challenge of nature. The *Narcissus* hits a ferocious storm:

> The lower half of the deck was full of mad whirlpools and eddies; and the long line of the lee rail could be seen showing black now and then in the swirls of a field of foam as dazzling

and white as a field of snow. The wind sang shrilly amongst
the spars, and at every slight lurch we expected her to slip to
the bottom sideways from under our backs. When dead before
it she made the first distinct attempt to stand up, and we encouraged her with a feeble and discordant howl. A great sea came
running up aft and hung for a moment over us with a curling
top; then crashed down under the counter and spread out on
both sides into a great sheet of bursting froth. Above its fierce
hiss we heard Singleton's croak: – 'She is steering'. . . . He
steered with care.

(The Nigger of the 'Narcissus', pp. 64–5)

Although Dickens was one of the great descriptive writers he
experiences the sea literally, simply as it is. This is not solely
because the quotation above is taken from a journal rather than a
novel, it is because, in his own words as a land-based writer, the
experience is beyond 'the most vivid imagination to conceive'. As
a seaman Conrad was able to grasp the circumstances imaginatively, and therefore to extend them into a metaphor of mankind
struggling with the hostile elements. There is more nautical language in the Conrad passage than in the Dickens, and the technical
terms in Conrad's fiction are sometimes considered to make his
work a little inaccessible to the lay reader. Even if the reader does
not know the precise meaning of 'lee rail' the general atmosphere
of the piece can be understood. Conrad knows the technical language, and is exact in his use of it, but he also uses a lot of
imagery. As a landsman Dickens reverts to simile in which the
ship is 'like a monster', whereas Conrad always projects the ship
in the human terms of a sailor, as 'she'. The metaphors are left
for the reader to work out, rather than the more straightforward
simile. The terrible wildness is expressed partly by the 'mad whirl-
pools and eddies', as though the ship herself was losing her sanity
in her fight against the storm. The curious interjection of the 'field
of snow' with which to describe the foam also emphasises the
element of madness, a state of almost illusory perception on the
part of the observer/participant. The sound too is wild, with the
juxtaposition of the wind singing 'shrilly' and the 'feeble and
discordant howl' put up by the sailors in encouragement of their
ship. The crashing of the 'great sheet' of the sea is overcome by
the man's affirmative 'croak' as he controls the vessel despite the
fierceness of the storm. In this case humanity is triumphant over

natural chaos. Conrad uses the sea mainly in order to explore that recurring conflict. It provided a perfect dramatic arena and philosophic metaphor.

It must be appreciated that steamships were also extremely vulnerable to storms, typhoons and hurricanes. There were then no giant tankers or liners of a later age, no electronic aids. Everything had to be done at least in part by hand: although the engines were mechanical even the fuel that fired them, coal, was fed manually. As there was no radar, or computers, all decisions were made by the exercise of an individual's mental, or sometimes instinctive, judgement.

In a 1915 article in the *Daily News* Conrad commented on some of the changes that had occurred in the seaman's craft, and their wider implications:

> More and more is mankind reducing its physical activities to pulling levers and twirling little wheels. Progress! Yet the older methods of meeting natural forces demanded intelligence too; an equally fine readiness of wits. And readiness of wits working in combination with the strength of muscles made a more complete man.
>
> (NL, p. 162)

The final sentence of this passage, and its definition of 'a more complete man', clearly contributes to the earlier argument about the need to fuse mental and physical activity. Later in the article Conrad makes it clear that the word 'Progress!' is being employed ironically, that in this context progress is synonymous with the aggression manifested in the First World War: 'Mines: Submarines. The last word in sea-warfare! Progress – impressively disclosed by this war' (NL, pp. 162–3). Conrad's attitudes, however, are often ambivalent, for he was by no means adamantly against machinery – recognising that it could also be beneficial. In a letter to the brother of an official of the Royal National Lifeboat Institution, for example, Conrad touched on the important subject of coast-based lifeboats: 'what does your brother think of steam-lifeboats? I hate machinery but candidly must own that it seems to me that in most cases steam's the thing for that work' (CL, vol. 2, p. 4). He expressed that view as early in his writing career as 1898, and reiterated the sentiment in a magazine article in 1912 when considering the state of lifeboats that were carried on ships. Conrad argued in the *English Review* that for the sake of safety:

> All these boats should have a motor-engine in them. . . . Doesn't it strike you as absurd that in this age of mechanical propulsion, of generated power, the boats of such ultra-modern ships are fitted with oars and sails, implements more than three thousand years old? Old as the siege of Troy. Older!
>
> (NL, pp. 244–5)

Conrad was never either a consistently straightforward conservative or a convinced progressive. He judged cases individually, on their merits.

His defence, when it occurs, of the older ways of seafaring springs from an interest in the dramatic nature of that life. Conrad's fiction is concerned in part with the vulnerability of the old ships to the forces of nature. This has a thematic, or metaphysical, as well as a verisimilic, or physical, purpose.

Obviously all ships were in a particular state of jeopardy in hostile weather. The newspapers of Conrad's period frequently reported shipping losses – in which fatalities were often incurred – and they were by no means confined to rusty or rotten vessels. For instance, an almost random newspaper report of the period reads:

> the Augusta . . . has been abandoned at sea. The second mate and five seamen were saved. The remainder of the crew were lost . . . the loss of the British steamer Vionis with all hands . . . the English schooner Belle of Devon. . . . Nothing has been heard of the crew . . . The schooner Ocean Bird . . . foundered . . . and all on board were drowned . . . Frederick Whiteheart . . . had died of exposure while lashed to the rigging. Seaman Oliver Kearney . . . swept into the sea by an immense wave and drowned.
>
> (*The Times*, 14 November 1887)

This kind of documented, dispassionate report puts into perspective the sufferings of such fictional ships as the *Nan-Shan* of *Typhoon*, and the *Narcissus*, and their crews. Conrad admired the endurance of men who faced the dangers, who lived always on the edge of life, living with the perpetual presence of death.

Another danger, especially in conditions of bad weather, was that of collision which often resulted in fatalities or extremely serious injuries. There are again a number of illustrations. A strikingly tragic occurrence, for example, involved two ships colliding in fog:

> One of the most appalling collisions which have been recorded since the loss of the ill-fated Northfleet off Dungerness on Jan 22, 1873, when upwards of 200 lives were lost, happened in the English Channel on Saturday night . . . when the screw steamer W. A. Scholton . . . sank with about 130 or 140 souls . . . she had on board 210 passengers and crew all told, and of these 78 are saved, the remainder having, it is supposed, all perished . . . [the ship was holed and] began at once to settle down, and within 15 or 20 minutes sank. Some most heartrending scenes occurred on board. The steerage passengers in particular, men, women, and children, clung to each other and rushed frantically about the decks. . . . The screams of the drowning all round the ship are described as terrible . . .
>
> (*The Times*, 21 November 1887)

Almost twenty years later another disaster of an even greater and more shocking nature occurred to show that even in the twentieth century sea travel was fraught with latent tragedy. In 1912 the most up-to-date ship of its time, the *Titanic*, on its maiden voyage, collided with an iceberg. 1635 people were drowned. A survivor was quoted as reporting: 'the impact was terrific. . . . The stem of the vessel rose into the air, and people ran shrieking from their berths below. Women and children, some of the former naturally hysterical. . . . The weather was extremely cold, and we suffered intensely' (*Daily Herald*, 20 April 1912). These were major news stories because of the numbers involved and in the first case because of the proximity of the accident to the English coast, but the crews of cargo ships across the world not infrequently faced such dangers. The latent imminence of death gave a man a different perspective on life from that held by a relatively secure landsman. In *Youth* the *Judea* is involved in a collision leaving Newcastle docks – nowhere on water is safe – and young Marlow is especially impressed by his old skipper's response in saving his wife from danger. Captain Beard and Mrs Beard escaped into a small boat:

They had been floating about the dock in that mizzly cold rain
for nearly an hour. I was never so surprised in my life.

   It appears that when he heard my shout 'Come up' he understood at once what was the matter, caught up his wife, ran on
deck, and across, and down into our boat, which was fast to
the ladder. Not bad for a sixty-year-old. Just imagine that old
fellow saving heroically in his arms that old woman – the woman
of his life.

(p. 13)

The challenge brings out the best qualities in the sailor. Although
Conrad was often pessimistic about people in the mass he also
celebrated, as here, the virtues that in the *North American Review*
he referred to as the 'indomitable tenacity' of 'mankind' (NL, p.
14).

   This can also be seen in another aspect of life at sea. James
Wait's illness in *The Nigger of the 'Narcissus'*, and the fever Burns
suffers in *The Shadow-Line*, both experienced without the benefit
of proper medical care, were both manifestations of humanity's
unequal struggle against an apparently hostile fate, and an accur-
ate record of the hardships of a seaman's life. W.H.S. Jones in his
autobiography, for instance, recalls a surgical operation carried
out at sea by a ship's captain, as late as 1905, because there was
no trained doctor on board. Gangrene had begun to spread in the
crushed leg of a sailor, and the only hope of saving his life lay in
amputation:

   The cook's meat-saw and knife were hastily sharpened . . . and
   sterilized in a bucket of boiling water. An iron poker was . . .
   placed in the . . . stove to be used for cauterizing the wound . . .
   [the captain] cut through the living flesh, above the knee, and
   bared the bone. Blood spurted from the severed arteries. With
   the red-hot poker the Captain instantly cauterized the cut, and
   stopped the bleeding, as the stench of burning flesh filled the
   forecastle.
      Then, seizing the meat-saw, he quickly cut through the thigh-
   bones, and applied the red-hot poker again, and again . . . pick-
   ing up the putrid severed leg, rushed out of the door and threw
   it overboard.[8]

Clearly Conrad did not exaggerate the hardships of life at sea. It was because the conflict with a potentially malevolent fate did not take place in conditions of equality that humanity's courage, and determination, could be affirmed.

Although many of Conrad's great novels are not predominantly sea stories his time as a sailor contributed profoundly to the formation of his philosophy. Writing to a now unknown reviewer of *The Nigger of the 'Narcissus'* he explained that the ship was an extended metaphor of individual and social life: 'I also wanted to connect the small world of the ship with that larger world carrying perplexities, fears, affections, rebellions, in a loneliness greater than that of the ship at sea' (CL, vol. 1, p. 421). Seafaring epitomised, for Conrad, the essential definition of the individual, of the individual in a group or community, and humanity as a whole in relation to the elemental forces. Conrad never lost his interest in nautical life, and almost at the end of his life restated his uncompromising view of the arena in which mankind struggled with great and hostile forces. In the Foreword to A. J. Dawson's book *Britain's Life-Boats* Conrad wrote of sailors going 'to dispute our homeless fate with the angry seas' (CD, p. 107).

Another factor in Conrad's career at sea that put him in a unique position also relates to his Polishness. When he came to Britain and started writing in English he brought a quite different perspective to bear on western European politics, culture and life. In addition, his life as a merchant seaman sent him to many different parts of the world, a lot of them unseen by other novelists of any nationality. The British writers mentioned earlier all addressed universal themes from a very broad intellectual position, but necessarily from an essentially British, or at least western European, perspective. For Conrad the Far East, South America, central Africa were not peripheral areas, they too were at the core of human experience. Events and experiences there were not of merely secondary interest as measured against the centrality of western European culture, they could bear with direct, and revealing, relevance on the nature of European civilisation. Conrad constantly stressed both the difference of foreign cultures – seeing them in their own right, with their own values, not simply as amusing, or barbaric, variations from European definitions of civilisation – and a possible fundamental unity of human experience.

These facets are often presented through a conflict of cultures. Where British – and French, and German and other – novelists tend to see their culture in comparative isolation (only a very

minor writer would fail to perceive any connections) Conrad often
structures stories and novels around characters from diverse back-
grounds. *Nostromo* provides one example: there are native and
European South Americans, characters from England, France,
Italy, Germany and the United States. Conrad's great Russian
novel, *Under Western Eyes*, is narrated partly by a western 'teacher
of languages' (p.55), who several times expresses his inability to
understand the characters whose story he is narrating:

> Yet I confess that I have no comprehension of the Russian
> character. The illogicality of their attitude, the arbitrariness of
> their conclusions, the frequency of the exceptional, should pres-
> ent no difficulty to a student of many grammars; but there must
> be something else in the way, some special human trait – one
> of those subtle differences that are beyond the ken of mere
> professors.
>
> (p. 56)

This is partly a warning to British readers not to expect the kind
of psychology of character they are used to, not to anticipate
exactly the kind of development of action, of linking of events,
that had become traditional in the English novel.

For Conrad it is not simply a matter of literature, of setting
himself an artistic problem to solve. It involves a grappling with an
alien perspective. British perceptions of Russian history, politics,
attitudes were generally based on the idea that such factors were
essentially the same as in Britain, but just in a different area of
the world. Later, during the Great War, Conrad feared this lack
of understanding would lead the western European powers to
abandon the concept of Polish sovereignty. He argued the case
cogently in 'A Note on the Polish Problem', written in 1916:

> The Poles, whom superficial or ill-informed theorists are trying
> to force into the social and psychological formula of Slavonism,
> are in truth not Slavonic at all. . . . That element of racial unity
> which may be called Polonism, remained compressed between
> Prussian Germanism on one side and the Russian Slavonism on
> the other. For Germanism it feels nothing but hatred. But
> between Polonism and Slavonism there is not so much hatred
> as a complete and ineradicable incompatibility.
>
> (NL, pp. 135–6)

In 1911, at the time of publication of *Under Western Eyes*, Conrad was afraid that western European politicians did not appreciate the true nature of the Russian Slavonic temperament; by 1916 the threat to Poland came from the possibility of the British and French governments in particular committing themselves to a deal to end the war that would ignore Polish sentiments. His concern was not just for his homeland, but that such a solution would not lead to a stable peace: 'No political work of reconstructing Poland either as a matter of justice or expediency could be sound which would leave the new creation in dependence to Germanism or Slavonism' (NL, p. 136). This was written before the Russian Revolution of 1917, of course, and the intervention of the United States in the Great War, both of which changed the situation considerably.

This aspect of Conrad's world perspective can be seen too in his response to western European colonisation of Africa. European humanitarians were certainly against the exploitation of native peoples for the material benefits that ensued to the northern races. Cunninghame Graham wrote an article, 'Bloody Niggers', that expressed their beliefs, and which received magazine publication before Conrad began *Heart of Darkness*, denouncing English imperialism in, and hypocrisy about, Africa: 'So many rapes and robberies, hangings and murders, blowings up in caves, pounding to jelly with our Maxim guns . . . our clergy all dumb dogs, our politicians dazed . . . can England be a vast and seething mushroom bed of base hypocrisy' (*Social-Democrat*, April 1897). Conrad's own summation of imperialism in Africa, based on personal experience, was that it was 'the vilest scramble for loot that ever disfigured the history of human conscience' (LE, p. 17). But these were oppositional, not mainstream establishment, views.

In any event many of the critics of colonialism, such as Graham, understood the problem mainly as an ethical, or ideological, issue concerning the relationship between stronger and weaker groups of people, in which the former have a duty and responsibility to protect the latter. This view was sincerely held by many people, but it could lead to hypocrisy when the language in which the sentiments were expressed was appropriated to cloak exploitation with rhetorical phrases. It is ironic that Kurtz' pamphlet in *Heart of Darkness* for a Belgian missionary society should end with the injunction 'Exterminate all the brutes!' (p. 87). The hypocrisy entailed in the appropriation of humanitarian speech for commercial ends is satirised in the story *An Outpost of Progress*, when a newspaper article:

> discussed what it was pleased to call 'Our Colonial Expansion' in high-flown language. It spoke much of the rights and duties of civilisation, of the sacredness of the civilising work, and extolled the merits of those who went about bringing light, and faith and commerce to the dark places of the earth.
>
> *(Tales of Unrest, p. 90)*

Conrad saw this duplicity, and the hollowness of the moral pretensions, but he also perceived profounder philosophic implications. It is true that the Europeans in Africa were killing the natives, as Conrad's diary of his visit records: 'saw at a camp[8] place the dead body of a Backongo. Shot? Horrid smell . . . Saw another dead body lying by the path in an attitude of meditative repose . . . passed a skeleton tied up to a post' (CD, pp. 8–13). Such scenes are reworked in *Heart of Darkness*. But that alien climate and culture struck back too. The Europeans were killed not so much by Africans as by Africa. Marlow learns that on the French man-of-war shelling the jungle 'the men in that lonely ship were dying of fever at the rate of three a-day' (p. 41). This echoes a colonial truth Conrad heard, and reported in a letter to Karol Zagórski, while he was in Sierra Leone, in May 1890, at the beginning of a scheduled three-year appointment in Africa:

> What makes me rather uneasy is the information that 60 per cent. of our Company's employees return to Europe before they have completed even six months' service. Fever and dysentery! There are others who are sent home in a hurry at the end of a year, so that they shouldn't die in the Congo. God forbid! It would spoil the statistics which are excellent, you see! In a word, it seems there are only 7 per cent. who can do their three years' service.
>
> (CL, vol. 1, p. 52)

Conrad was not reporting mere rumours, for one of the men who had appointed him, Captain Albert Thys, had written of his own experiences in Africa: 'one felt one was faced with an accursed country, a real barrier which seemed to have been created by nature to stop progress'.[9] This kind of experience was ubiquitous.

In the diary of his African journey Conrad records passing an anonymous 'white man's grave . . . heap of stones in the form of a cross' (p. 13), another solitary victim of Europeans' desire to conquer Africa.

It is not, however, only disease and sickness that Conrad shows as the colonists' burden. The clash of cultures can disorientate the European, stripping off the veneer of civilisation and revealing an underlying madness. Kurtz' murderous insanity is one illustration of this, and the ironically titled *An Outpost of Progress* provides another, in which 'the contact with pure unmitigated savagery, with primitive nature and primitive man, brings sudden and profound trouble into the heart' (pp. 85–6) of the European characters. Colonisation, for Conrad, was not a purely ideological matter, nor was he solely concerned with English excesses. As a Pole he had been a victim of foreign rule, and his world perspective gave him the ability to see as early as 1898 that the USA was beginning to emerge as a power with colonial ambitions. In a letter of grim whimsy to Cunninghame Graham he expressed a desire to see the two dominant emerging imperial powers in conflict with one another: 'If one could set the States & Germany by the ears! That would be *real fine*' (CL, vol. 2, p. 81). It is significant that the Occidental Republic in *Nostromo* breaks away from the State of Costaguana with the assistance of the USA. Conrad could also see that the English, with whom his acquaintances were concerned, were not the only conquerors in Africa, that it was a European phenomenon. The madman at the centre of the Belgian Congo is presented as an amalgam: 'All Europe contributed to the making of Kurtz' (p. 86).

Conrad was interested in the philosophic revelations inherent in the imperial experience, rather than simply the ideological aspects. The intimate contact with the primitive and savage, the isolation from the constraining forces of institutionalised civilisation, revealed a truth of human nature. It is latently both barbaric and insecure: capable of inflicting almost inconceivable cruelty on other humans, and always on the brink of ontological crisis and consequent self-destruction. These are profoundly disturbing conclusions because they are less concerned with the immediate evils of imperialism – although Conrad depicted them more vividly than any earlier or contemporary writer – more with their underlying implications, and the questioning of the fundamental values of a civilisation that is capable of undergoing such disintegration.

Conrad made this clear in a letter to Cunninghame Graham. Conrad's life has many paradoxes, and one was his long and close friendship with Graham. He was a radical who became Liberal Member of Parliament for North Lanarkshire, and supported Scottish nationalism and the formation of the Scottish Labour Party – all activities of which Conrad disapproved. Yet Conrad dedicated *Typhoon* to Graham in 1902. They became friends as a consequence of Graham writing to Conrad in 1897 to congratulate him on *An Outpost of Progress*. In subsequently summarising their friendship Conrad showed that he was capable of going beyond political differences to basic human qualities:

> I do not dedicate to C. Graham the socialist or to C. Graham the aristocrat (he is both – you know) but to one of the few men I *know* – in the full sense of the word – and knowing cannot but appreciate and respect – abstractedly [*sic*] as human beings. I do not share his political convictions or even all his ideas of art, but we have enough ideas in common to base a strong friendship upon.
>
> (CL, vol. 2, p. 165)

Although contempt of imperialism had brought them together Conrad and Graham had fundamentally different approaches to it.

Graham, naturally, given his ideological position, believed in the ultimate goodness of human nature and, although he was fervently anti-imperialist, the ultimate efficacy of well-intentioned political action and social organisation. In such arguments imperialism is in itself an evil, and therefore to be condemned, but is also a manifestation of ideological error, which can be redeemed by the workings of beneficent political institutions. Such views were anathema to Conrad's philosophy. His world, and worldly, experience led to a more pessimistic – or realistic – summary of politics, which Conrad expressed in a letter to Graham:

> You with your ideals of sincerity, courage and truth are strangely out of place in this epoch of material preoccupations. . . . In the noblest cause men manage to put something of their baseness. . . . Every cause is tainted: and you reject this one, espouse that other one as if one were evil and the other good while the same evil you hate is in both, but disguised in different

words. . . . Not that I think mankind intrinsically bad. It is only silly and cowardly . . . in cowardice is every evil. . . . But without it mankind would vanish.

(CL, vol. 2, p. 25)

These ideas, embracing the philosophical paradox that mankind survives, not despite of, but because of an essential flaw, recur in various forms throughout Conrad's fiction. Conrad's understanding of these concepts stems from his worldly experience. Their fictional embodiments occur in many areas of the globe, in different historical periods, and in a great diversity of characters and circumstances. For Conrad the practical, wage-earning sailor the truth of character emerges in and through work. He worked across the world with men from many nationalities, races and religions – and by the definition of his trade they were all men. He perceived this idea of the central feature of cowardice – the concept taken in its broadest sense and manifestations – as basic to all human nature, one of the overlapping facets fundamentally uniting the enormous apparent divergence of human experience and cultures. It involves a further paradox too, for against the political scepticism inherent in Conrad's views must be placed his previously mentioned belief in humanity's 'indomitable tenacity'.

Novelists who observe life only within the limits of national boundaries, or social classes, or political affiliations must have a different perception of the nature of experience and character from those who bring a wider vision to their art. People who travel widely, but as passengers and sightseers, not as participants in the affairs of the world, are also likely to draw conclusions that differ from those of people who earn their living by voyaging to, and working in, foreign parts. Those experiences centrally inform Conrad's intellectual grasp of social reality, and the response to it that forms the core of his fiction.

As a seaman Conrad certainly faced the possibility of death at a relatively young age. That seems to make him able to accept unpalatable aspects of existence, to embrace the whole of it. One of the features of his thought in the quotation above is the acceptance of 'mankind' as it stands, that cowardice – and therefore within the thesis, evil – is an unavoidable and unchangeable aspect of humanity. The problem, in Conrad's fiction, is not to attempt to reform a deformed mankind through either moral or political polemic, but to come to terms with the irrevocable truth. Polemicists sometimes have a tendency to see themselves as slightly apart from the mass of people, knowing more, having a higher consciousness than their fellow creatures. This is a theorist's position. Conrad earned his living in a practical way, and a ship's crew is, for all its formal hierarchy, an entity – especially when it is under threat – and it is typical of Conrad's philosophic stance that he does not place himself outside his own observations, or detach himself from the common inadequacies: 'I belong to the wretched gang. We all belong to it. We are born initiated, and succeeding generations clutch the inheritance of fear and brutality without a thought, without a doubt, without compunction' (CL, vol. 2, p. 25). The individual cannot hold a place external to this circumstance, since no single person has any volition in the matter. Every individual, though, can become aware of this reality and attempt to control their destiny in accordance with it.

An important facet of Conrad's uniqueness as a novelist springs from the facts of his exiles. He was a Pole who emigrated to France to earn a living, and ultimately became a British citizen. This meant that as a novelist Conrad wrote in his third language, and as a private correspondent not infrequently used French in quite long philosophical passages. Conrad remained generally aware of the alien nature of his rather curious relationship with the English language. He confessed in a letter of 1898 to being 'shy of my bad English', comically stereotyping himself as a 'b—y furriner' (CL, vol. 2, p. 16). More seriously, in another letter – to an old Polish friend, Marguerite Poradowska, living in Brussels – written at the time of *The Secret Agent*, after twelve years as a professional novelist, he revealed: 'l'Anglais m'est toujours une langue etrangère qui demande un effort formidable pour être maniée' (CL, vol. 3, p. 401). This has been translated: 'English is still for me a foreign language whose handling demands a fearful effort' (ibid.). Nevertheless Conrad had long been drawn to English.

Although he was fluent in French, and was working for a French-language employer, Conrad chose to write his 1890 Congo Diary in English. There are numerous examples of his uncertainty with the language at that stage of his development. The plural of mosquito, for instance, is consistently misspelt 'mosquitos' (pp. 7ff). The influence of French is evident in Conrad's description of uneven ground as 'very accidented' (p. 10), stemming from *accidenté*; and his erroneous spelling 'mentionned' (p. 30) comes from the French *mentionné*; and the construction 'there is 3 islands' (p.

31) is based on the phrase *il y a*. Conrad's native Polish pronunciation comes through in the misspelling of a plain as 'andulating' (pp. 10ff) for undulating. Polish grammar also affects his construction of English, as in the phrase 'there is much more trees' (p. 13). This kind of error very occasionally occurs again later in the fiction. In *Nostromo*, for example, the description of Gould riding a horse runs: 'cantering . . . at his easy swift *pasotrote*' (p. 72), which gives a meaning that is not intended. In the letter admitting the error and explaining what he actually wanted Conrad displayed considerable self-annoyance: 'the mistake is in the word *canter* which I wrote persistently while I really meant *amble*, I believe. I am appalled simply' (CL, vol. 3, p. 176). Some ambiguity remains after the explanation, for '*pasotrote*' means short trot, which is complementary to the 'easy swift' motion, and perhaps closer to 'canter' – the word Conrad thinks he used in error – than to 'amble', the description he thought he intended. Another example of linguistic misunderstanding can be seen in José Avellanos addressing Mrs Gould as 'Emilia, my soul' (pp. 121 and 144), a term that was entirely inappropriate in the context. When it was pointed out to him Conrad was again contrite in his correspondence: 'What misled me was this that in Polish that very term of endearment: "My Soul" has not the passionate significance you point out. I am crestfallen and sorry' (CL, vol. 3, p. 176). Clearly there were occasions when Conrad was thinking in Polish or French while writing in English. Indeed, the articulation in the letter quoted here is not the most perfect form of English.

Conrad also had some trouble with English speech. Edward Garnett, who worked for Conrad's first publisher and encouraged him enormously, observed that when Conrad read aloud to him 'he mispronounced so many words that I followed him with difficulty';[10] and Ford Madox Ford, with whom Conrad collaborated at one period, recalled of Conrad in 1902:

> In speaking English he had practically no idea of accentuation whatever . . . [he] would talk of Mr Cunninghame Graham's book *Success* alternately as *Suc*cess and Suc*cess*, half a dozen times in the course of a conversation.[11]

It seems that Conrad was not totally at ease with the language. He was aware of his own propensity for variant pronunciations. When invited to lecture in the USA towards the end of his life he initially refused because of this factor, writing to his New York sponsor, Elbridge L. Adams, in 1922: 'I will tell you frankly that I am not very anxious to display my accent before a large gathering of people' (LL, vol. 2, p. 283). Even so the reception when he was persuaded to lecture and read in public does not suggest the fashionable New York audience had any real difficulty in understanding him. Conrad, not a boastful man, reported to his wife, Jessie: 'I may tell you at once that it was a most brilliant affair. . . . I had a perfect success. . . . It was a great experience' (LL, vol. 2, pp. 309–10). These reports are doubtless all true, and their contradictory nature perhaps suggests that Conrad's speech was affected by the circumstances in which he was speaking. He never lost his essential foreignness, although he was sometimes able to subdue its more extreme manifestations.

There are two main consequences of the language factor for Conrad the novelist. He sometimes writes in a way that seems to be unEnglish in style; and he had a perception of the *nature* of language that was quite different from any other British writer. The former characteristic annoys some readers, and is perhaps a difficulty it is necessary to overcome in order to enjoy and appreciate the fiction fully. The eminent critic F. R. Leavis, for example, complained in regard to *Heart of Darkness* of repetition and what he considered a straining for effect:

> The same vocabulary, the same adjectival insistence upon inexpressible and incomprehensible mystery. . . . The actual effect is not to magnify but rather to muffle . . . adjectival and worse than supererogatory insistence . . . he asserts with a strained impressiveness.[12]

This, though, is only one view of Conrad's curious style that was certainly different from any of his predecessors and contemporaries.

Partly because Conrad commanded three languages he was specifically aware of both the power and the inadequacies of words. They can move people to great, or terrible, acts; words can also fail to convey meaning and feeling; when ideas and emotions are expressed they may inadvertently be distorted by words; and words can be used deliberately to hide the reality of experiences. On the day of his first son's birth Conrad wrote to

Graham expressing a deep philosophic unease that was related to language:

> we don't know even our own thoughts. Half the words we use have no meaning whatever and of the other half each man understands each word after the fashion of his own folly and conceit . . . thoughts vanish; words, once pronounced, die.
>
> (CL, vol. 2, p. 17)

The language and syntax of Conrad's fiction is never merely deliberately difficult. It is often unusual in form in order to provoke the reader into thought, rather than being used simply to narrate events or describe a scene. Conrad's appreciation, in the letter quoted above, of the link between thinking and language, as early as 1898, to some extent anticipates twentieth century Structuralism.

At about the time he was working on *Youth* Conrad wrote another letter in which he returned to the concerns voiced above:

> pourquoi prêchez Vous au convertis? . . . Il n'y a pas des convertis aux idées de l'honneur, de la justice, de la pitié, de la liberté. Il n'y a que des gens qui sans savoir, sans comprendre, sans sentir s'extasient sur les mots, les repetent, les crient. . . . Et les mots s'envolent; et il reste rien. . . . Absolument rien. . . . Ni pensée, ni son, ni âme. Rien.
>
> (CL, vol. 2, pp. 69–70)

This address to the ideologically committed Graham – incidentally illustrating Conrad's predilection for French – can be translated:

> why preach to the converted? . . . There are no converted to the ideas of honour, justice, mercy, liberty. There are only people who without knowledge, without understanding, without any true conviction, repeat the words, shout them. . . . And the words fly away; nothing remains. . . . Absolutely nothing. . . . Neither thought, nor sound, nor soul. Nothing.

Words themselves cannot create social or existential meaning, though writers cannot help but use them to examine and analyse the realities of experience. Conrad was a novelist who, partly because of his unique background, was profoundly concerned with the values and limitations of language. One of the crucial factors, and difficulties, in reading his fiction is the necessity to think closely about the relationship between diction and context: narration and apparent description, and the associative meanings, conceptual connotations and possibilities of words.

2
Conrad as Crucible

Conrad's working life as a novelist spans a crucial period in British society and English literature. His career overlaps those of such central, and different, writers as the great Victorian novelist Thomas Hardy, and the twentieth century experimentalists D. H. Lawrence, James Joyce and Virginia Woolf. Conrad's first novel, *Almayer's Folly*, was published in 1895, one year before Hardy's ultimate novel, *Jude the Obscure*; the bulk of his fiction was published before Lawrence's great new novels, as he referred to them, *The Rainbow* (1915) and *Women In Love* (1921); and Conrad's final completed novel, *The Rover*, was published in 1923, only one year after Joyce's extraordinary *Ulysses* and Woolf's first experimental novel *Jacob's Room*.

His artistic achievement was to take a major role in transforming the nineteenth century classic realist novel, which was mainly based on a reliable, authoritative and chronological narrative development, into a twentieth century modernist artifact challenging received notions of reality. Conrad also wrote a good many essays and articles on a wide variety of subjects, as well as being a prolific private correspondent. He ventured into play-writing too, although with no success, either commercially or artistically, and also made a single, unsuccessful attempt to write a film script. If his early collaborator Ford Madox Ford is to be believed Conrad made only one, extremely brief, attempt to write poetry, round about 1902.

Conrad is rightly known predominantly as a great novelist. Nevertheless his output of non-fiction is both interesting in its own right, and a revealing entry into the novels. The subjects covered include politics, philosophy, science, literary criticism, artistic and aesthetic theory – all areas that his own fiction embraces. His essays, newspaper articles and letters also show Conrad's keen interest in, and perception of, the important national and international events of his time, some illustrations of which have already been cited in chapter 1. Conrad the former seaman never closeted himself in an aesthete's ivory tower.

Conrad's essays and articles show that his interest in the sea as a setting for some of his fiction was not the result of mere nostalgia on his part: he retained an interest in seafaring developments throughout his life, even going to sea during the Great War of 1914–18, at the age of fifty-eight, to observe the activities of the British Navy. That Conrad was not simply embedded in the past is also illustrated by the fact that in 1916 he flew for the first time. That was very early in the history of aviation, which was then almost entirely a young man's activity. The first cross-Channel flight had occurred only six years earlier, in 1910, and aeroplanes were hardly out of the experimental stage. The adventurousness, and curiosity, of Conrad was particularly emphasised by the fact that he flew in a hydroplane, taking off from and landing on the sea (they were later known as flying-boats), a concept that had been developed into an actual machine only four years previously. Conrad described the plane, and his experience in climbing into it, in his essay 'Flight':

> [it] seemed as big as a cottage, and much more imposing. . . . The close view of the real fragility of that rigid structure startled me considerably, while Commander O. discomposed me still more by shouting repeatedly: 'Don't put your foot there!' I didn't know where to put my foot. There was a slight crack; I heard some swear-words below me.
>
> (NL, p. 211)

Despite the apparent frailty of the machine Conrad enjoyed the flight and 'its mysterious fascination, whose invisible wing had brushed my heart' (p. 212). Flying was an aspect of progress of which he fully approved, responding to its romantic features, the idea of man and machine in touch with, and controlling, the elemental forces.

At that time planes were relatively small and very unsophisticated, flown by only one or two people. A plane the size of 'a cottage' is obviously going to give a different experience from a present 500-seater flying restaurant, which is controlled mainly by computer. These are factors in Conrad's response, for part of his scepticism regarding progress as applied to ships was that they had become too big, and liners especially had developed into luxurious floating hotels. In an essay for the *English Review*, 'Some Reflections on the Loss of the *Titanic*', the ship launched as unsinkable that had sunk with the loss of over 1600 lives on her maiden voyage, Conrad explained that the fashion for sheer enormity had outstripped the technology of shipbuilding:

> I could much sooner believe in an unsinkable ship of 3,000 tons than in one of 40,000 tons. It is one of those things that stand to reason. You can't increase the thickness of scantling and plates indefinitely. And the mere weight of this bigness is an added disadvantage.
>
> (NL, p. 219)

Larger vessels need a different construction technology based on lighter yet stronger materials, which at that time were not available. Conrad's whole approach to life has such a practical thread in it. Impractical characters, like unpractical shipbuilders, ultimately create disaster.

In this case Conrad clearly sees the reasons why bigger liners are being built despite the safety hazards. He added satirically that if the ship had been smaller: 'she could not have had a swimming bath and a French café. That, of course, is a serious consideration' (ibid.). In a subsequent essay Conrad indicated one of the reasons for his scepticism about progress – which in view of his enthusiasm for the new technology of aviation he was obviously not against simply for its own sake. He remarked on the 'crestfallen attitude of technicians' in the aftermath of the *Titanic* catastrophe:

> They are the high priests of the modern cult of perfected material and of mechanical appliances [for navigation], and would fain forbid the profane from inquiring into its mysteries. We are the masters of progress, they say.
>
> (NL, p. 230)

Scientific and technical advance, however, does not occur in a socio-economic vacuum, as Conrad realised somewhat prophetically, and rather against the prevailing mood of his time. He argued that the motivation towards the gigantic ship:

> isn't a servant of progress in any sense . . . [but] is the servant of commercialism. . . . For progress, if dealing with the problems of a material world, has some sort of moral aspect. . . . The men responsible for these big ships have been moved by

considerations of profit to be made by the questionable means of pandering to an absurd and vulgar demand for banal luxury.

(NL, p. 234)

This argument clarifies an apparent paradox regarding the concept of progress by distinguishing between genuine and valid scientific endeavour, and the obsessive impulse towards greed.

Conrad's essays and articles illustrate that his interest is always in philosophic issues rather than mere physical details. He wrote about the sea not simply as a phenomenon he knew, but because it provided him with a perfect metaphor for humanity's vulnerability, and for its struggle against overwhelming forces. Even as prosaically an entitled article as 'Protection of Ocean Liners', which appeared in the *Illustrated London News* in 1914, brought out this point. In writing of a recent collision at sea in fog in which a passenger ship, the *Empress of Ireland*, had been sunk with considerable loss of life, Conrad observes:

As long as men will travel on the water, the sea-gods will take their toll. They will catch good seamen napping, or confuse their judgement by arts well known to those who go to sea, or overcome them by the sheer brutality of elemental forces. It seems to me that the resentful sea-gods never do sleep, and are never weary; wherein the seamen who are mere mortals condemned to unending vigilance are no match for them.

(NL, p. 251)

The idea of mankind trying to assert its own values, and the validity of its life, in the face of a hostile fate is a recurring theme in the novels.

In an article, 'Well Done', written in appreciation of the Royal Navy for the newspaper the *Daily Chronicle* just before the end of the Great War, the sea is described as:

uncertain, arbitrary, featureless, and violent . . . its wrath . . . is endless, boundless, persistent, and futile . . . Its very immensity is wearisome. . . . The greatest scene of potential terror, a devouring enigma of space.

(NL, p. 184)

Conrad could here be writing about life itself, as he perceived it at times. But he sees too, in the same article, the positive features of human existence: 'our lives have been nothing if not a continuous defiance' (p. 185). It is the kind of affirmation with which Conrad concluded his essay on the loss of the *Titanic* six years earlier:

> material may fail, and men, too, may fail sometimes; but more often men, when they are given the chance, will prove themselves truer than steel, that wonderful thin steel from which the sides and bulkheads of our modern sea-leviathans are made.
>
> (NL, p. 228)

Since he was writing physically of sailors Conrad meant 'men' literally, but as he intended most of his work to be understood metaphysically too 'men' in this context signifies humanity as a whole. The defiance of a malignant fate by both men and women characters is a recurring feature of his fiction, and is illuminated to some extent by the essays and articles.

Although Conrad was prolific in various forms of prose, and some passages of his fiction have a poetic cadence and rhythm, he apparently wrote only a very few words of poetry. Interestingly this single, uncompleted poem was written in French:

> Riez toujours! La vie n'est pas si gaie,
> Ces tristes jours quand à travers la haie
> Tombe le long rayon
> Dernier
> De mon soleil qui gagne
> Les sommets, la montagne,
> De l'horizon . . . [1]

It is not easy to translate, but an acceptable version might run:

> Keep laughing! Life is not so happy,
> These melancholy days when across the hedgerow
> Falls the long last ray
> Of my sun which reaches
> The summits, the mountain,
> From the horizon . . .

Conrad wrote these unpublished words around 1902 in the company of Ford Madox Ford, when they were collaborating, for commercial reasons, on writing novels. Of the poem Ford commented: 'There was a line or two more that the writer [Ford] has forgotten. That was Conrad's solitary attempt to write verse.[2] It expresses the gloomy Pole aspect of Conrad's work, but even as a fragment lacks the vigour of conflict between opposing situations, ideas, attitudes and states of mind that his prose contains.

The collaboration did not succeed either. It produced three novels: *The Inheritors*, *Romance* and *The Nature of a Crime*, which were published between 1901 and 1906. All three are artistically inferior to Conrad's best solo work, and it is difficult to argue with Norman Page's judgement that: 'to regard these works as part of the corpus of Conrad's fiction is perhaps stretching the point a little'.[3] Certainly they lack the thematic complexity, the ambiguity and paradox, that characterises Conrad's most controlled style.

Paradoxically, Conrad's dramatic texts display a similar absence of essential tension, one of the main features of good theatre. Conrad's plays were based on his own fiction, and it was possibly a fundamental error that he did not attempt to conceive a work specifically for the stage, rather than producing what were essentially adaptations. The plays were: *One Day More*, a relatively early one-Act play based on his short story 'Tomorrow'; and over fifteen years later, in 1920, *Laughing Anne*, adapted from 'Because of the Dollars'; and a stage version of his 1907 novel *The Secret Agent*.

One Day More received only three performances in 1905. The whole business caused Conrad considerable anguish, although he was pleased that Britain's most successful dramatist of the time, George Bernard Shaw, praised the play. Conrad's general summation of the experience, in a letter to Galsworthy, was ambivalent:

> I don't think I am a dramatist. But I believe I've 3 or even 5 acts somewhere in me. At any rate the reception of the play was not such as to encourage me to sacrifice 6 months to the stage.
>
> (CL, vol. 3, p. 272)

Conrad seems to suggest that he was too constrained by the one-Act format, but it did take him a long time to recover sufficiently to actually try a full-length play. His later plays were no more successful. The dramatisation of *The Secret Agent* ran for only one week in 1922, *The Times* summarily categorising the author as 'a

great novelist, but not yet a great dramatist' (3 November 1922).
Conrad, in writing to an American acquaintance, Elbridge L.
Adams, revealed his sourness in a remark on the subject of failure:

> I have had an experience of it lately in the non-success of my
> play which was put on at the Ambassadors Theatre and was
> withdrawn at the end of a week. It was very disagreeable . . .
> it deserved a better reception.
>
> (LL, vol. 2, p. 284)

One Day More and *Laughing Anne* were published in 1924; and all
three plays were published posthumously in 1934 under the generic title *Three Plays*. They have not been revived on stage. During
this late period Conrad also had ambitions to write a screen-play
for a film version of his 1906 story 'Gaspar Ruiz'. He eventually
produced this in collaboration with his literary agent James Pinker,
although it was never filmed.

This dramatic aspect of Conrad's work illustrates another paradoxical element of his attitudes. Despite the failure of his first play
script, and his belief that he was capable of being a dramatist,
Conrad actually disliked the theatre. At the very time, in 1897, he
was considering a collaboration on a play with Stephen Crane, the
author of *The Red Badge of Courage* who had become a friend of
his, Conrad admitted:

> I haven't seen a play for years. . . . I have no notion of a play.
> No play grips me on the stage or off. Each of them seems to
> me an amazing freak of folly. They are all unbelievable. . . . The
> actors appear to me like a lot of *wrongheaded* lunatics. . . . They
> are disguised and ugly. To look at them breeds in my melan-
> choly soul thoughts of murder and suicide – such is my anger
> and my loathing of their transparent pretences. There is a taint
> of subtle corruption in their blank voices, in their blinking eyes,
> in the grimacing faces, in the false light in the false passion.
>
> (CL, vol. 1, pp. 418–19)

The production of *One Day More* in 1905 confirmed all Conrad's
worst fears. As long as twelve years after that experience he wrote
in bitter recollection to Christopher Sandeman: 'I have a secret
terror of all actors . . . since they murdered for me a one-act play
I wrote once . . . and had some illusions about' (LL, vol. 2, p.

191). This was, of course, before his second assault on the career of playwright. At the same time he reassailed the theatre he also broached the screen-play. A similar contradiction can be seen in Conrad's attitudes: as an apprentice screen-writer he observed 'The Movie is just a silly stunt for silly people'.[4] Even taking into account the fact that he was writing, against his better judgement, simply for money, as he admitted to Richard Curle: 'and also write a cinema scenario of "Gaspar Ruiz". I am ashamed to tell you this – but one must live!',[5] this seems a curious statement from someone attempting to write for the medium.

This unsuccessful aspect of Conrad's artistic life partly illustrates a basic paradox: that he could be simultaneously both radical, or progressive, and conservative. He was never entirely satisfied with being solely a novelist, and wanted to move into new areas of writing – partly because throughout his writing life Conrad was worried about finances, and always hoped to find a new market for his work, but also because he was intrigued by the artistic challenge and the possibility of expressing his vision of life and society in a new form. Although Conrad dismissed film as 'silly' it is perhaps more significant that he took any professional notice of it at all. Popular cinema, after all, has not been very intellectually demanding at any time; and film did not make any large-scale impact in Britain until Conrad was half way through his writing career. He could have been forgiven for simply ignoring it. The fact that around the age of sixty Conrad was prepared to embark on a new writing venture suggests a progressive spirit. His conservatism is shown by the textual way in which he approached theatre and cinema. He thought in terms of adaptations, of the artistic security gained from working on a text he had already created. Also, the novels or stories chosen tended to be quite old works: thirteen years in the case of *The Secret Agent* play, and fourteen in the instance of the film script for 'Gaspar Ruiz'. There is often a strong ambivalence discernible in Conrad's attitudes – he both disliked, and was interested in, new media; he wanted to venture into uncharted artistic waters, yet was apprehensive of doing so.

One of the main reasons these scripts fail is that they reduce the fiction to its basic plot. When they are broken down Conrad's story-lines are often rather melodramatic. It is the use of such techniques as narrative complexity, changing point of view, time shifts, and the metaphoric use of diction and atmosphere and objects, that help to elevate the novels and stories into great and powerful art. The performance scripts provide dialogue without any philosophic context, speech which merely moves on the action, but does not provide the complex analysis of motive, for example, that is found in the books. *The Times* review of the stage version of *The Secret Agent* previously referred to summarised the defects succinctly: 'Mr Conrad has tried, we think, to bring too much of his novel onto the stage. The result is a play with a certain excess of talk' (3 November 1922). Conrad seemed to have some, possibly prophetic, understanding of the difficulties when recounting later in life his first encounter with the idea of the stage. In 1897, while Conrad was still in his infancy as a novelist, Stephen Crane suggested that they should collaborate on a play. The idea did not come to fruition, and Conrad's subsequent judgement on their discussions was that 'the action, I fear, would have been frankly melodramatic' (LE, p. 168).

This problem of transposition to another medium was not one that Conrad alone failed to solve. Subsequently at least thirteen of his works have either been filmed, or have provided the basis of a screen-play, some more than once. The first of Conrad's works to form a basis for a screen-play was *Victory*, as early as 1919. This novel has been the most filmed of Conrad's fiction, with four versions in all. A silent *Lord Jim* in 1925 was followed by a prestigious 1965 remake starring Peter O'Toole; *The Secret Agent* formed the basis of Alfred Hitchcock's most famous early film, *Sabotage*, in 1936; Francis Coppola's 1979 *Apocalypse Now* was claimed to be a Vietnam version of *Heart of Darkness*, with Marlon Brando in the role of the latter-day Kurtz. Even this abbreviated list shows Conrad's work having a formidable influence in the cinema.

None of the films, however, attain the complexity or subtlety of the original novels. *Apocalypse Now*, for example, presents a compelling view of the horror of war, and the Vietnam campaign in particular, but in it the ideas are concerned with only the physical world. It is as though a radical, materialist writer such as Cunninghame Graham had written the script. Conrad's horror is certainly physical and political, but it is also immaterial and metaphysical. It is not simply a matter of governments being bad, or individual people being malevolent, rather, for Conrad, that kind of horror is in the very nature of humanity and its existence, not to be facilely combated simply by having more altruistic politicians or people having better intentions.

One of the problems of the films is that they tend to present
the story-lines in a more or less chronological way, through
straightforward mainstream camera techniques. These factors put
the emphasis on suspense, on simple interest in the plot. This
makes the works much easier to follow as films than as novels,
but the elusiveness of tone is lost, and the uncomplicated and
chronological narrative denies an essential artistic and intellectual
quality – the very characteristic that made Conrad's novels so
seminal.

Early in his career as a writer Conrad moved away from the basic
nineteenth century notion of an objective, omniscient narrator –
a figure generally detached from the action, having full knowledge
of all events and complete understanding of all characters. There
were notable exceptions in the nineteenth century to this narrative
position, but it was certainly the dominant one when Conrad
began writing in the 1890s. The short story *Youth* was written in
1898, and marks the first appearance of the narrator/character
Marlow. Although it is not especially complex in form it does
introduce two technical aspects that were to recur throughout
Conrad's fiction.

The action involves Marlow, and is told by him from his own
point of view. It is, however, slightly more complicated than that
for it is not Marlow's voice that actually carries the narrative. It is
related by an anonymous listener, who explains that Marlow 'told
the story, or rather the chronicle, of a voyage' (p. 9). This creates
some distance in the relationship of writer and reader, a gap that
requires two characters to fill. There is a further distancing,
through the time scheme: 'It was twenty-two years ago' (p. 10)
that the incidents narrated occurred. The lapse of time, and the
refraction of the remembered events, create a framework in which
the narrative may not be wholly trustworthy. This does not mean
the narrative is a deliberate lie, or even exaggeration – and it may
in fact be absolutely true – but that in relation to the tale told
directly by an omniscient narrator, without intermediary or
memory, the story-line of *Youth* is not completely and automatically unquestionable. Memory is not necessarily objective, and in
this case Marlow is recalling his youth, 'I was just twenty' (p. 10),
which is often a deceptive operation. The narrative emphasises
both the relativity of time in retrospect, and the glow that may be
cast on events in remembrance: 'How time passes! It was one of
the happiest days of my life' (p. 10). Those sentiments from the

beginning of the story resonate at its conclusion: ' "Ah! The good old time – the good old time. Youth and the sea. Glamour and the sea!" . . . the romance of illusions' (p. 39). The effect of the techniques is to encourage the reader to challenge, rather than simply accept, what is written. This transforms reading from a passive to an active process, and may be seen as Conrad's first step towards pushing the novel as an artistic form into modernism, providing the groundwork on which such authors as Joyce and Woolf were able to build.

Youth is a short, and not in fact very complex, story, but it forms the basis from which Conrad developed modernist techniques: confronting the perception of his readers, making reading part of the creative process. *Heart of Darkness* utilises the same narrative and time forms, but extends them into profounder areas. One example is that the central cry of the novel, Kurtz' summation – 'The horror! The horror!' (p. 111) – is never explicated. It may refer to his own experiences of 'abominable terrors . . . abominable satisfactions' (p. 113), to the excesses of colonialism, to the nature of existence itself, to anything else – and none of these are mutually exclusive – but the text is not definitive. In the vast majority of nineteenth century novels, in any novel with an omniscient third-person narrator who knows and understands everything, an interpretation might, and probably would, have been given. This would limit the interpretive possibilities, and involve the reader less in the processes of understanding. This is not to argue that Conrad is *per se* a better writer than his predecessors, merely that he is different, producing a different kind of text. That more ambiguous text formed the basis from which the great twentieth century modernist novels were developed.

Marlow is used as an indirect narrator in other novels too, appearing, for instance, in both *Lord Jim* and *Chance*, two quite different works in which his role as participating character is more peripheral. Complex narrative and time techniques are not dependent on Marlow's presence, for they are also used in novels in which he does not appear. *Nostromo* is mainly related by an omniscient narrator in the traditional manner, although there are occasions when a subjective narration is used, as in the section Captain Mitchell narrates. The main technical feature of the novel, however, is the structural control of time. The time movement of Part the First has already been noted in chapter 1 above, but the whole way in which information is released is important and not necessarily chronological. The lighter on which Nostromo and Decoud leave, for example, is sunk on page 263, and the latter character takes no further active part in the action, yet his death is not described until page 416. This emphasises the structural and thematic connections between Decoud's death and Nostromo's rebirth. During that gap Nostromo returns to Sulaco, where everyone believes him to be dead. His metaphoric resurrection occurs after the long swim from The Isabel rocks to the shore, after which: 'Nostromo woke up from a fourteen hours' sleep . . . with the lost air of a man just born into the world' (p. 347). At this point the precise nature of the rebirth is not known, but it is to be as a rich man. That wealth is ironically forced on Nostromo by the nature of Decoud's suicide, for the latter drowns himself weighted by four ingots of the silver they had been commissioned to save on behalf of the Sulaco separatists. Because of his reputation for scrupulous reliability Nostromo is trapped by the missing ingots; he feels he cannot return the treasure without them because he would be suspected of having stolen them. The only solution is to steal the remainder of the treasure by not revealing its hiding place. The chapter describing Decoud's death ends:

> The Capataz looked down for a time upon the fall of loose earth, stones, and smashed bushes, concealing the hiding-place of the silver. 'I must grow rich very slowly,' he meditated, aloud.
>
> (p. 417)

The time structure clearly links the death of one character and the rebirth of another. The irony, a central feature of Conrad's work, is pushed further when on his own death-bed Nostromo claims that by taking the four ingots Decoud betrayed him, and that as a consequence, 'The silver has killed me' (p. 460). This is true in more than one sense, and again the novel ends ambiguously with none of the characters knowing the truth.

Conrad went on developing these techniques, using them to heighten the irony and deepen thematic complexity, through the convoluted time scheme of *The Secret Agent* (1907) and the double narrative of *Under Western Eyes* (1911). For some critics one of Conrad's greatest achievements is *Victory*, published in 1915, which also has an intricate structure demanding close analysis. Frederick Karl, for instance, has written of it: 'the book was indeed a culmination . . . we see Conrad working toward an artistic vision . . . He displayed both craft and courage'.[6] Stories such as 'The Secret Sharer' (1912) and 'The Shadow-Line' (1917) use a narrator who is a participating character in order to explore the ambiguities of subjective perceptions of illusion and reality.

Most of these works pre-date the experimental novels of Lawrence, Joyce and Woolf. Early in his writing career Conrad challenged the sensibilities and expectations of readers, not providing chronological sequences of events that could be tied neatly together in a conclusion that did not allow of argument; not working through a wholly trustworthy and knowledgeable narrator who acted as a kind of friendly guide through the morass of plot. Conrad's novels are not necessarily cosy experiences, they can be as bewildering and disorientating as those of later modernists. Conrad struck an experimental seam early, and continued to work it throughout most of his novelist's life, although it did not until late bring him commercial recognition and security. Part of Conrad's greatness lies in his integrity to the art of the novel, and his own philosophic ideas, despite public apathy or bewilderment. Perhaps his essential greatness, though, lies in the fact that he took nineteenth century forms of story-telling and novel-structure and recreated them. The point of doing this is that some of the older certainties had been undermined, or even destroyed, and in a world that had to embrace uncertainty – willingly or otherwise – ambiguity and paradox seemed more appropriate than simple resolutions and conclusions. Conrad's fiction provides a bridge from the nineteenth century to the twentieth. Old forms and assumptions are challenged, and new ones emerge from the process. Raymond Williams observed in 1958:

> we tend to look at the period 1880–1914 as a kind of interregnum. It is not the period of the masters. . . . Nor yet is it the period of our contemporaries, of writers who address themselves, in our kind of language, to the common problems that we recognize.[7]

Conrad has, since then, come to be recognised as a master of that period, a time that was less a rather dull interregnum than a fiery crucible in which the relative security of the Victorians was fused with the hostile universe of 'our contemporaries'.

3
Conrad in Context

If the period in which Conrad mainly wrote was not an interregnum, a simple waiting for the Great War to change everything in 1914, but a time in which a new consciousness was forged, then it was a time in which an essentially twentieth century awareness had to embrace changes in commerce as well as art. Writers have to eat, and families have to be provided for, as Conrad the husband and father realised. Discussion of art that ignores the processes of production, including the financial considerations, is liable to become detached from a reality of which the artists themselves are always aware. Conrad may have perceived himself at the centre of the forging of the modern consciousness, but he never forgot his financial problems, and the need of a writer to have a reading public.

In the 1890s, as in our own day, there was a reciprocal influence between technology and commerce. In the mid-Victorian period, when the long three-decker novel was the most popular form, the cost of paper and the relative slowness of printing kept the cost of books high: a novel could cost the equivalent of two weeks full wages. In 1873, for instance, at a time when labourers were earning anything between four and thirteen shillings (20–65p in decimal terms) a week – and that entailed working nine hours a day, every day except Sunday – a *cheap* bound edition of George Eliot's *Middlemarch* went on sale at a price of one guinea (£1.05p). Twenty years later cheaper paper had been developed, and so too had linotype type-setting which was ten times faster than previous methods, and that cut the labour costs of printing considerably. The length of novels had generally, although not entirely, been reduced too. All these factors meant that the same labourer could have bought Conrad's first novel for nearer a couple of days' pay, than two weeks' wages.

The fact that more novels were being bought directly by the public lessened the hold of the private circulating libraries, the most influential of which, Mudie's Select Library, had been founded in 1842. These had exerted an enormous influence on early and mid-Victorian literature. While prices of books were high – and a guinea or so for a novel was by no means cheap even for a middling-class reader – the libraries were an important link between writer, publisher and reader. They more or less guaranteed a market, but because of that dictated the terms of the product. Novels of 500 pages or more were not unusual, and that, on the whole, enforced particular kinds of characterisation and narrative development: multiple, interwoven story-lines, for example, of the kind Dickens and Eliot mainly used; that compelled the use of a multiplicity of characters; which again referred back to the methods of depicting character – externally described, and very visual, so that readers could place individuals in the overall scheme and distinguish between a plethora of characters, some of whom would reappear after long absences from the action.

Novelists who wanted to experiment – Dickens, Eliot and Hardy all succeeded in doing so – had to achieve their ends within the conventional framework, which although not absolutely rigid was extremely limiting. By the 1890s the combined effects of changing technology, the pressure of The Incorporated Society of Authors, which had been founded in 1883 to advance writers' commercial interests, and the influence of contemporary French experimental novelists such as Maupassant and Zola, culminated in a confrontation with Mudie's and the other libraries. In the outcome, the popularity of shorter six shilling (30p) novels with the reading public meant the end of the old style libraries. Although private libraries continued to exist, and to be reasonably profitable for their owners, their power never again equalled that of the earlier Mudie's. This left writers more free to experiment in both form and content, but it also exposed them to the hostility or apathy of public taste. Conrad experienced the former, and for half his career suffered the latter. Nevertheless, had he begun writing in the 1870s, rather than becoming a merchant seaman, Conrad would have found experimenting with the novel an even more difficult, and financially unrewarding, task.

An important aspect of the earlier Victorian literary scene that survived, in fact expanded towards the end of the century, and into the twentieth, and which helped Conrad enormously, was that of magazine serialisation. It was a practice that many of the major Victorian novelists followed. Novels were printed as serials before being produced as a bound book. This enabled the writer to receive payment as s/he worked, rather than having to finance anything up to two years work before receiving any money. It also virtually guaranteed the publication of the completed text, and therefore a little further income.

In the earlier period serialisation was to some extent tied in with the private circulating libraries, but after their power had diminished the magazine serial became a central forum for experimental expression. If one text appearing in any particular magazine was not popular it was unlikely to affect sales disastrously, so a liberal and forward-looking editor could afford to take occasional risks. The literary magazine was a popular journal for the novel-reading public, and many different titles appeared weekly, fortnightly, monthly or quarterly, giving the author a wide choice of possible markets. Conrad published fiction in, amongst others, *Cosmopolis*, the *Illustrated London News*, *London Magazine*, *Pall Mall Magazine*, *Harper's Magazine*, and most importantly at the beginning, *Blackwood's Magazine*. The names alone indicate something about these publications: they had a metropolitan, with a tendency towards cosmopolitan, leaning; and they emanated from entrepreneurial publishing houses that were essentially family concerns.

At that time most publishing firms were still family businesses, or at least controlled by the members of a single family. Until the 1880s these businesses, on the whole, were run as paternalistic organisations which argued that they knew best the writer's commercial interest. As a consequence many authors felt their work was undervalued and underpaid, and that was one motivation behind the founding of The Incorporated Society of Authors. Mid-Victorian and earlier novelists, except for the few who were in a powerful enough position to negotiate a better contract – such as George Eliot during her most prestigious period – usually received a single lump sum payment for the copyright of a manuscript. Anthony Trollope, writing in 1877 to the aspiring Thomas Hardy, advised: 'the royalty system is best, if you can get a publisher to give you a royalty',[1] but publishers paying an author a lump sum then stood to gain all the profits from long-term sales for themselves, so they were reluctant to negotiate royalty contracts. A main weakness of the novelist's bargaining position, especially at the beginning of a career, was indicated by Trollope's qualification, in the same letter, of his advice that the royalty system was best: 'if you are not in need of immediate money'.[2] Peter Keating has concisely summarised the position:

The full royalty system, by which an author receives an agreed percentage of the published price of every copy of a book sold, and therefore retains a direct financial interest in the success or failure of his work, was hardly known in Britain before the 1880s.[3]

Indeed, when Conrad's first novel, *Almayer's Folly*, was published in 1895 he received a single payment of £20 from Fisher Unwin, so that practice did not end, although it was weakened, before Conrad began his writing career.

Conrad was happy to accept a payment that was low even at that time, in order to get into print. He wrote to Marguerite Poradowska: 'J'ai ecrit que j'acceptais ces conditions. . . . J'ai pris ce que l'on m'offrait car vraiment le fait même de la publication est de grande importance' (CL, vol. 1, p. 177). Karl and Davies translate this as: 'I wrote accepting the terms. . . . I have taken what they offered me because, really, the mere fact of publication is of great importance' (CL, vol. 1, pp. 177–8). In fact Conrad was offered a form of royalty, although not on particularly advantageous terms. In any event he was in the trap Trollope had outlined to the young Hardy. Conrad described, again to Marguerite, his interview with his publisher: 'Il m'a dit franchement que si je voulais prendre une part dans le risque de la publication je pourrai participer au profits' (CL, vol. 1, p. 179). This has been translated: 'He told me frankly that if I wished to share in the risk of publication, I could participate in the profits' (ibid., p. 180). Unwin apparently justified his offer on commercial terms. Conrad reported him, although Unwin did not speak in French and Conrad's version cannot necessarily be taken as a literal account, as explaining that:

> Nous vous payons très peu . . . mais considerez cher Monsieur que vous êtes un inconnu et que Votre livre appelle a une public très limité. Puis il y a la question du gout. Le Public le goutera-t-il? Nous risquons quelque chose aussi.
>
> (CL, vol. 1, p. 179)

Translating Unwin's words back into English, he said something like:

> We are paying you very little . . . but, remember, dear Sir, that

you are unknown and your book will appeal to a very limited
public. Then there is the question of taste. Will the public like
it? We are risking something also.

(ibid., p. 180)

Despite Conrad's acceptance of the reasonableness of the arguments at the time he later changed publisher and became acerbic
towards Unwin.

Conrad was then still a full-time sea-captain, and the income
was less important than the breakthrough into print, but Unwin's
remarks in the autumn of 1894 make it clear that Conrad was
entering a demanding commercial world. By the autumn of 1896
Conrad felt in a strong enough position to reject an offer from
Unwin of £50 plus a small royalty for a volume of short stories:

As to my demands, which You might think excessive it's just
this: I can't afford to work for less than ten pence per hour. . . .
I don't like to give up anything I have taken hold of and intend
to stick to scribbling. . . . After all my work has some value.

(CL, vol. 1, p. 308)

The capitalised 'You' displays Conrad's pique. Conrad was
encouraged in this stance by Edward Garnett, despite the fact that
he was a reader for Unwin, and by the publication of the short
story 'The Idiots' in the magazine *Savoy* in the month in which he
wrote the letter above.

The author was still not in control of the marketplace, but the
ability to place texts with magazines strengthened the negotiating
position, and it is not insignificant that in the following year, 1897,
several of Conrad's stories appeared in magazines. The most major
of these pieces was *The Nigger of the 'Narcissus'*, which was printed
initially in the *New Review*, and published shortly afterwards in
book form by the house of William Heinemann. By that time
Conrad's sea career had ended, somewhat indeterminately, and
he was reliant on writing for his income. That was, and remained
for many years, comparatively small, so that he lived in some
financial distress until *Chance* in 1913. Nevertheless Conrad had
made enormous strides within three years of his first novel's publication: his work was being printed in magazines, he had changed
his publisher and had begun to develop some power of nego-
tiation, and although some critics were hostile to his fiction Conrad

was receiving encouragement from many people he admired, and whose judgement he trusted.

The next important commercial development in Conrad's career again occurred through contact with a magazine. Conrad completed his extraordinary *Heart of Darkness* early in 1899, and it was serialised in three instalments in the very prestigious literary monthly *Blackwood's Magazine*. Three years later Blackwood's published it, together with *Youth* and *The End of the Tether*, in a single volume book form. This form of dual publication became usual for Conrad's fiction almost until the end of his life – in fact his unfinished novel *Suspense* appeared as serial and then book the year after Conrad's death. Shortly after the first appearance of *Heart of Darkness*, in 1899, Conrad committed his commercial future to the hands of J. B. Pinker, a literary agent; and after that changed publishers – Blackwood, Heinemann, Dent, Methuen – according to conditions.

Literary agents as a type were another phenomenon to emerge from the changes that took place in the 1880s and 1890s, and so were still a relatively new breed when Conrad began writing. Before the 1880s some writers had powerful personalities who negotiated on their behalf – George Eliot's partner, G. H. Lewes, for instance, insisted on her gaining a form of royalty from *Middlemarch* – but they were not professional agents whose sole employment was to place manuscripts with publishers and arrange contracts, and whose own livelihood depended on their success on behalf of authors.

Until he became Pinker's client Conrad had depended largely on the individual patronage of admirers who happened to have a position of some, although not ultimate, influence in the publishing world. Edward Garnett, as a reader for Unwin, encouraged Conrad and went far beyond his professional duties in order to introduce Conrad's fiction to other possible buyers when his own employer was not interested. One of these was David Meldrum, literary adviser to Blackwoods, and he also worked hard behind the scenes to get Conrad the best possible treatment. On one occasion in 1899, for example, Meldrum wrote to Blackwood pleading that Conrad was a special case who needed, and deserved, nurturing both artistically and financially:

It surprises me that he can get along at all. His long story costs two years' work. He *may* get £400 out of it, not more. And we see what he does besides his long story – two or three short ones each year, bringing in at the most £100. That means that his total income from his work doesn't exceed £300. . . . I think it very splendid of him to refuse to do any pot-boiling and hope, for him and for ourselves too, that it will pay him in the long run.[4]

Conrad's own self-judgement of his business affairs was not flattering. He wrote to Pinker:

My method of writing is so unbusiness-like that I don't think you could have any use for such an unsatisfactory person. I generally sell a work before it is begun, get paid when it is half done and don't do the other half till the spirit moves me.

(CL, vol. 2, p. 195)

Pinker took up the challenge with considerable success – he later worked for D. H. Lawrence too – and eventually became a close friend of Conrad's. He represented Conrad's interest consistently, despite his irascible client's uncooperativeness for quite a long period, until he died, only two years before Conrad's own death. The role of supportive non-writers in the work of any literary artist is likely to be important, as Conrad himself acknowledged in the case of his agent, in a letter to the collector of his manuscripts, John Quinn, in 1916:

Those books owe their existence to Mr Pinker as much as to me. For fifteen years of my writing life he has seen me through periods of unproductiveness, through illnesses, through all sorts of troubles. . . . Pinker was the only man who backed his opinion with his money, and that in no grudging manner.[5]

When Pinker died in 1922 Conrad again paid tribute, in a letter to his American publishers, to his influence:

I need not tell you how profoundly I feel the loss of J. B. Pinker, my friend of twenty years' standing, whose devotion to my interests and whose affection borne towards myself and all belonging to me were the greatest moral and material support through nearly all my writing life.

(LL, vol. 2, p. 266)

The note of genuine self-deprecation that occurs in some of the quotations above does not perform complete justice to the amount of work Conrad frequently put into his writing. But it does seem that he was a poor manager of finances.

Even with Pinker's help the combination of a relatively low income and a lack of financial organisation sometimes left Conrad at the mercy of his friends' generosity. Nevertheless a great debt is owed by literature to Conrad's artistic integrity. He always refused to compromise in the novels simply in order to indulge mass taste and make money. There was a trait at the core of Conrad's personality that went against such attitudes, and it is not surprising that his deliberate attempts to court popularity were both outside his real writing interest – they were his collaborations, the unsuccessful plays and film script – and failures in the field of demotic culture. Conrad's achievement in, and for, the novel was recognised by discerning readers, and they manifested their belief in his importance by persuading various official bodies to make financial grants to Conrad.

In 1902 Conrad was granted £300 by the Royal Literary Fund, three years later the Royal Bounty awarded him £500, and in 1911 he was given a pension of £100 from the Civil List. It might be felt that acceptance of such Establishment patronage confirms the view of Conrad as essentially conservative in politics, although critically so in details – however, D. H. Lawrence, in his most politically radical period, also received similar payment – but Conrad was not a man to be bought. Conrad felt he was pushed into accepting these sources of income for purely practical reasons, but later he became financially more viable and refused a number of prestigious offers of public honour. These culminated in his refusal of a knighthood in 1924. As it happened this offer came from the first Labour Party prime minister of Britain, Ramsay MacDonald, and it might be argued that Conrad's erstwhile Polish aristocratic, anti-democratic, background made him reject the approach because of the source from which it originated. That, however, would be to ignore the fact of Conrad's earlier rejections of public honour. In the previous year he had declined an honorary degree from the University of Cambridge, which was not the action of either a vain man or a political reactionary, and that was consistent with his previous refusals. In 1923 he confided to Frank Doubleday, his New York publisher:

I ought to tell you of the offers I had by the Universities of
Oxford, Edinburgh, London and Durham, of an honorary
degree, which I have declined. This is between ourselves.

(LL, vol. 2, p. 297)

Conrad explained that although gratified by the recognition con-
ferred 'I am perfectly determined to have nothing to do with any
academic distinction' (LL, vol. 2, p. 298). Karl has justifiably
argued that the reason for Conrad's refusal of all honours is:

> that the acceptance of such distinctions was not consistent with
> what he was and what he had been in his work. He resisted
> association with such traditional awards because they distracted
> the reader from what he really was – an author proving himself
> in the sole way he could, on paper, in the privacy of his own
> room, working along the lines of what was uniquely his.[6]

Conrad's attitudes had no basis in political stances, or false mod-
esty, but in his artistic integrity.

Conrad constantly struggled in the marketplace conditions in
which he worked. He was able to ignore mass best-seller taste
and continue to experiment with form, and explore philosophic
issues in the content of his fiction, but only at the expense of
complete financial security and independence. Lawrence and
Joyce followed a similar pattern along their own different paths,
and Woolf would have been put in the same situation had she
attempted to be an experimentalist without the support of
additional sources of income from outside her writing. Conrad,
though, was eventually able to take advantage of two sources of
finance denied, on the whole, to his literary predecessors.

In 1911 an American collector, John Quinn, agreed to purchase
Conrad's original manuscripts. This, of course, was money in
addition to that Conrad received from actual publication. The
relatively wealthy American collector is now a well-known
phenomenon, American universities in particular having built up
very important literary collections, but the type really stems from
the early twentieth century. Conrad was glad of the extra income,
which was more or less guaranteed for life as the deal encom-
passed future as well as existing manuscripts, and Quinn was a
genuine admirer of his work; there was, however, a commercial
aspect that ultimately caused Conrad some distress, and formed

a model perhaps for other writers of the period who had begun to exploit the same avenue of additional finance. In 1923, with Conrad's reputation at its peak, and shortly after his successful visit to the USA, Quinn decided to auction his collection of the writer's manuscripts. It is interesting to note, in respect of the wider commercial implications, that the same sale included the manuscript version of Joyce's *Ulysses*. Quinn made an immense profit, which Conrad estimated at 1000 per cent. The prices paid were the highest ever at that time for the work of a living author. The practice of collection, whether or not pursued for monetary gain, was another factor that intervened in the changing relationship of author and publisher, further complicating the old mid-Victorian patrician basis.

In this particular instance Conrad expressed his bitterness about being treated as a commodity in this way. In a letter about the auction Conrad wrote to his New York publisher:

> Did Quinn enjoy his triumph lying low like Brer Rabbit, or did he enjoy his glory in public and give graciously his hand to kiss to the multitude of inferior collectors who never, never, never, dreamt of such a coup? . . . there are a good many also whom nothing will persuade that the whole thing was not a put-up job and that I haven't got my share of the plunder.
>
> (LL, vol. 2, p. 324)

There is perhaps here a tone revealing the old aristocratic blood of Conrad's grandfather, a supercilious satire of *parvenu* collectors as a whole as a species of lower humanity.

An author's products are commodities, and Conrad could not validly protest about being treated like a tradesman, since a writer is basically that in the world of commerce. He was happy to take the payments when times were lean, and if that became a good economic investment for the collector, Quinn might have argued it was fair return for the risk. If Conrad's reputation had remained at its 1911 level Quinn may not have made a profit. The indignity of having one's manuscripts traded at public auction had become part of being a writer in the twentieth century. Where Conrad did appear to have a valid complaint against the collector was in his claim that Quinn had promised not to disperse the manuscripts, but to ensure they were retained as a complete collection. Conrad wrote to Garnett shortly after the sale in a tone of tired resignation:

'Yes, Quinn promised to keep the MSS. together – but the mood passes and the promise goes with it.'[7] Had Quinn sold the papers as such he would have undoubtably raised far less money. Ultimately, though, writers have to live with commercial realities.

Paradoxically Conrad did benefit indirectly himself, as he recognised to Doubleday:

> it is a wonderful adventure to happen to a still living (or at any rate half-alive) author. The reverberation in the press here was very great indeed; and the result is that lots of people, who had never heard of me before, now know my name, and thousands of others, who could not have read through a page of mine without falling into convulsions, are proclaiming me a very great author.

> (LL, vol. 2, p. 324)

The ironic tone reveals how little Conrad relished this kind of fame. He desperately needed to be taken seriously as a novelist, but never wanted to become a mere celebrity, as his refusal of public honours also shows.

The other new source of income, which Conrad was among the first of the great writers to tap, came from film rights. As early as 1919 he received over £3000 for these. In view of the number of films based on his work that were subsequently made it was a modest enough amount, but as an injection of capital for an individual it was considerable, more than enough, for example, to buy a decent suburban house. Although it is difficult to see Conrad, with his rather misanthropic need for privacy, actually living in suburbia this is a useful measure by which to gauge the value of money at that time, when such houses averaged around £2000.[8]

As the century went on novelists began to realise that the film rights to their books could be worth more than the publishers' royalties. This inevitably changed the direction of fiction aimed at a more popular market. Some authors wrestled, with more or less success, to serve the two masters of literature and film, attempting to write serious novels that might also provide the basis of film scripts. In passing it is perhaps not altogether surprising that the initial wave of these were from the USA: Scott Fitzgerald, John Steinbeck, Ernest Hemingway, for example. It is certainly a factor that could not have concerned Conrad's Victorian pre-film predecessors.

Conrad came into writing professionally on the crest of transition. Most of these subsequent developments were made possible by the changes that occurred in the 1880s and 1890s. Some of
them have been outlined above, and they mainly came about in
an evolutionary, gradual way. In addition, however, it is difficult
to underestimate the importance of changes in education, which
were the result of deliberate government policies and decisions.

A number of systems of widespread education did exist in Britain by the middle of the nineteenth century, but for the great mass
of people schooling, formal or informal, did not go beyond an
elementary level. Three Acts of Parliament in particular – there
were several in all – during the second half of the Victorian period
consolidated schooling and increased literacy.

In general before 1870 the responsibility for providing formal
education had been left to voluntary bodies, most of which had a
specific religious base. One of the purposes of Forster's 1870 Education Act was 'to complete the present voluntary system, to fill
up gaps' (*Hansard*, 17 February 1870). It achieved this partly by
expanding government influence in education, and by giving local
authorities the right to enforce compulsory schooling. Not all
authorities took up that right, but sufficient did to make a difference to the overall literacy level of the mass of young people.

In any event Mundella's Education Bill ten years later introduced
compulsory schooling between the ages of five and thirteen
throughout the country. In 1891 the right of free education was
made universal. A process of improvement in educational provision is evident throughout that generation, although history
should never be seen as a simple smooth transition from a state
of relative barbarism to one of comparative civilisation. It is one
thing to pass an Act of Parliament, quite another to provide and
distribute the resources to enable its spirit to be put into practice.
The historian Pauline Gregg has observed that six years after the
introduction of compulsory schooling:

> There were then still many thousands of children over five who
> had 'never been inside a schoolroom'. The reasons attendance
> fell 'lamentably short' of provision of school places were partly
> the uneven distribution of schools, partly the continued growth
> of certain areas and the failure of school boards to keep up with
> the growing requirements of an expanding population . . . [and]

the continued evasion by parents of the 'school-board man' whenever there was money to be earned by their children.[9]

It is important to appreciate the vacillations of historical processes; nevertheless the overall result was to create a mainly literate society by the 1890s, and that was a significant aspect of the transitional society into which Conrad came as a writer.

It was also an increasingly politically democratic society in the sense of an expanding franchise. The effect of the 1867 Reform Act was that the number of men entitled to vote – no women had such a right until 1918 – in the 1868 General Election was treble that of those holding suffrage in the 1865 election. Again the process towards greater democracy is characterised by oscillation, but the general trend is marked by the introduction of secret ballots in 1872, and a further extension of the franchise in 1884. The culminative effect was manifested in the election to parliament of three Independent Socialists in 1892, one of whom was Keir Hardie who in the following year became chairman of the newly formed Independent Labour Party.

The movements towards more widespread education and franchise occurred simultaneously, and that was not mere coincidence. The population of Britain was growing rapidly – at the rate of between 3 and 4 million people every decade between the 1861 census and that of 1911, from approximately 23 million people at the former date, to almost 41 million by the latter. The increase was especially fast in urban areas, and it was thought that one way of stopping the towns and cities from becoming ungovernable, unmanageable areas of barbarity was to involve the people more fully in citizenship. In introducing his Education Bill to the House of Commons in 1870 Forster claimed that he was doing so:

> with the hope of doing great good, by removing that ignorance which we are all aware is pregnant with crime and misery, with misfortune to individuals, and danger to the community. . . . The question of popular education affects not only the intellectual but the moral training of a vast proportion of the population.
>
> (*Hansard* 17 February 1870)

Forster was clear about what he saw as the connection between lawlessness – and therefore, in the context, misery – and lack of education. He went on to argue the link between responsible democracy and adequate schooling:

> I am one of those who would not wait until the people were educated before I would trust them with political power . . . but now that we have given them political power we must not wait any longer to give them education.

(ibid.)

The subsequent extensions of systematic education were based on these premises: that education would create more responsible individuals, and help to channel parliamentary democracy along controllable lines.

One result of the eventual emergence of a dependable mass market of literate people, as the effects of increased schooling accumulated over time, was the foundation of the modern popular press, characterised by large-circulation morning dailies. Newspapers had been popular before the 1890s, but on the whole they were either specifically radical – such as the *Poor Man's Guardian* – and bought mainly by the politically conscious working class; or very establishment – such as *The Times* – and published mostly for the ruling classes. The demotic scandal-paper, such as *The News of the World* which was first printed in 1843, was a weekly publication. There were also a great many magazines emanating from particular religious sects: the *Christian Observer*, for which the young Mary Anne Evans, before she became George Eliot, wrote is one example.

These were, however, of a different calibre from what might be called the modern popular press. They usually had a fairly specific, relatively small, target readership which had a reasonably high level of literacy. Those publications were not cheap to buy either. The cheap press of the 1880s and 1890s was literally that, with even the most expensive priced at 2d (less than 1p). Although not a morning daily but a weekly magazine, *Tit-Bits*, founded in 1881, set the journalistic model for the newspapers of the 1890s, with no paragraph longer than two sentences, and no sentence containing more than nine words. It demanded minimum concentration from readers, and was aimed at that broad band of the newly, and functionally, literate public who had no interest in pursuing anything much more than gossip.

Evening newspapers began to gain popularity, and in 1896, the year following the publication of *Almayer's Folly*, the *Daily Mail* appeared as the first of the new daily morning national news-papers. Its style has been analysed by the eminent historians Cole and Postgate:

> Serious matters were banished from its columns – thoughtful leaders, long Parliamentary reports, connected accounts of con-ditions at home or abroad or underwritten and restrained news were equally forbidden. Their places were taken by news items which were disconnected, short, sensational, inaccurate, and in one famous case . . . mere fabrications.[10]

The popularity of this approach, pitched just at the right level for a public that could indeed read in a technical sense, but was not interested in developing that skill beyond its basic application, is shown by the fact that the *Daily Mail* was the first newspaper to sell one million copies of an edition. This landmark, achieved in 1900, stimulated in the three following years the appearance of similar newspapers: the *Daily Express*, the *Daily Mirror*, and the *Daily Sketch*.

Not all the new readers created by the succession of Education Acts simply read crass journalism. One of the reasons for the changes in book publishing during the last two decades of the Victorian period was the diversification of the marketplace. As literacy increased so too did the number of levels at which it provided a commercial foothold. The private circulating libraries had served a fundamentally homogeneous reading public, people with a similar level of education and overlapping economic, social and general interests. By the time Conrad was being published that homogeneity had fragmented. The disintegration of the prime Victorian monolithic readers' market opened up the possibility of a diversity of smaller markets. Not all the reading classes wanted pulp news or trivial fiction, and the existence of a level of discern-ing and adventurous readers – even if relatively small in numbers – just about gave writers of experimental and philosophic fiction a commercially viable readership. It was into this maelstrom of transition that Conrad arrived and began to claim his place.

As the circumstances had not existed in quite this way in Britain before, and because of Conrad's peculiar international back-ground, there was no direct overwhelming British artistic influence on his work – which is one of its remarkable characteristics. His father had translated Dickens into Polish, and Conrad had read some of the novels. There are certainly Dickensian echoes in *The Secret Agent* – the atmosphere of Victorian London, the diligent policeman, the humorous treatment of serious themes, the independent life of inanimate objects, for example – but it is difficult to trace direct influences across the body of Conrad's fiction. He also read Captain Marryat, Thackeray, Trollope, Galsworthy and H.G. Wells, as well as the plays and poetry of Shakespeare and Byron, and the American novels of Stephen Crane and James Fenimore Cooper, but again it is not easy to see these writers' presence in Conrad's work.

The English author with whom Conrad was most frequently compared, especially in his early writing days, was Rudyard Kipling. Of *The Nigger of the 'Narcissus'* one reviewer wrote: 'Mr Conrad has in this book introduced us to the British merchant seaman, as Rudyard Kipling introduced us to the British soldier' (*Illustrated London News*, 5 February 1898). The comparisons, though, often made value judgements, which could be either complimentary or unfavourable. This dichotomy can be seen in two reviews of *An Outcast of the Islands*: 'There is an extraordinary vitality and virility about the book. . . . It is as masculine as Kipling, but without that parade of masculinity which Kipling loves' (*Manchester Guardian*, 19 May 1896). This view can be compared with: 'Kipling is a master of rapid delineation of character, of vivid directness of style . . . Conrad, on the contrary, is diffuse. He spreads his story over a wilderness of chapters and pages' (*National Observer*, 18 April 1896). Conrad himself was ambivalent towards Kipling's work. Although he did write to Aniela Zagórska of his contemporaries, 'Among the people in literature who deserve attention the first is Rudyard Kipling' (CL, vol. 2, p. 138), there is in fact no evidence of a positive influence. On the whole Conrad was disparaging towards Kipling, and if there is an influence it is that Conrad felt impelled to write against the kind of celebration of imperialism that Kipling favoured.

The English-language novelist Conrad came to admire most, in fact, was Henry James. Like Conrad he was naturalised, rather than native, British, having come from the United States. In 1905 Conrad praised James as a 'great artist and faithful historian', and in summarising his art concluded:

One is never set at rest by Mr Henry James's novels. His books

end as an episode in life ends. You remain with the sense of
the life still going on; and even the subtle presence of the dead
is felt in that silence that comes upon the artist-creation when
the last word has been read. It is eminently satisfying, but it is
not final.

(NL, p.19)

This deliberate refusal to absolutely resolve unresolvable issues is a
factor that applies centrally to Conrad's own fiction. Nevertheless,
there is little evidence that James as a writer directly influenced
Conrad. They were friends, but the subject matter of Conrad's
work is far from that of James', as too are the philosophic attitudes.

Conrad's fiction, perhaps not surprisingly in view of the influence of Russia on his life, has also been compared to that of
Dostoevsky. David Daiches, for instance, takes a not uncommon
critical stance in asserting that in *Under Western Eyes* Conrad was:
'writing his most Dostoevskian novel which has been clearly
influenced by the Russian novelist'.[11] There are similarities
between this novel and *Crime and Punishment* in particular, but the
question of influence is more subtle than that. Conrad actually
disliked Dostoevsky's novels, criticising them in a letter to Garnett
for being 'like some fierce mouthings from prehistoric ages' (LL,
vol. 2, p. 140). Dislike does not, of course, automatically mean
there was no influence, but it is then likely to be in the nature of
repudiation of the other author's works. Whatever the status of
Under Western Eyes in this respect it is not easy to see the mark of
Dostoevsky in Conrad's canon as a whole. That is Conrad's most
Slavic novel – with its secret societies, conspiracies, institutionalised fear and violence, tyrannous government, political assassination – and seems to have been written partly because Conrad
thought western Europeans in 1911 did not appreciate what he
saw as the true nature of Russia and Russians.

Conrad's dislike of Dostoevsky's novels can be seen in part
as a manifestation of his general hatred of things Russian, but
paradoxically he admired Dostoevsky's contemporary Turgenev.
In implicitly comparing the two Russians in 1917 Conrad wrote of
Turgenev's:

essential humanity. All his creations, fortunate and unfortunate,
oppressed and oppressors, are human beings, not strange beasts

in a menagerie or damned souls knocking themselves to pieces
in the stuffy darkness of mystical contradictions.

(NL, p. 47)

These latter references are certainly to Dostoevsky's fiction, but
the praise of Turgenev cannot be read simply as the acknowledge-
ment of a conscious artistic influence, although that does not
necessarily rule out an unconscious one.

Conrad did have a long admiration for Turgenev's work. In
1900 he wrote to Graham referring to Turgenev's stories as 'really
fine . . . worth reading' (CL, vol. 2, p. 255); and seventeen years
later Conrad expanded his appreciation of Turgenev to Garnett:

> so great and at the same time so fine . . . the clearest vision
> and the most exquisite responsiveness, penetrating insight . . .
> unerring instinct for the significant, for the essential in human
> life and in the visible world.
>
> (LL, vol. 2, p. 192)

These are all qualities that occur in Conrad's own fiction: particularly the focusing on a point of physical detail that can be expanded
into a significant metaphor, and one that encapsulates a metaphysical idea. The realism of surface detail is transformed into metaphoric and universal truth.

Whatever unconscious force Turgenev's work may have exerted
on Conrad the acknowledged influences are French. Conrad read,
in French, the novelists of the middle period of the nineteenth
century, Balzac, Flaubert, Hugo; the later Zola, Daudet and Maupassant; and his own contemporaries Proust, Gide and Anatole
France. An early reviewer, James Payn, commented on a seem-
ingly unlikely duality of influences on Conrad: 'In his realism he
almost equals Zola. . . . At times there is the same sort of poetic
power . . . that is manifested by Victor Hugo' (*Illustrated London
News*, 5 February 1898). In fact Conrad was not impressed by Zola's
social realism, but liked his predecessor in a form of naturalism,
Balzac. It was later recorded that stylistically: 'Conrad held that a
habit of good cadence could be acquired by the study of models.
His own he held came to him from constant reading of Flaubert.'[12]
Ford wrote this, however, twenty years after his close friendship
with Conrad had cooled, and the extent to which a writer in
French can influence the style of a native Pole writing in English

is a moot point. In 1918 Conrad himself was ambivalent towards Flaubert. Writing to Hugh Walpole, who had just produced a study of him, Conrad asserted: 'One can learn something from Balzac, but what could one learn from Flaubert? He compels admiration, – about the greatest service one artist can render to another' (LL, vol. 2, p. 206). In the same letter the admiration is defined in terms of 'the rendering of concrete things and visual impressions', which possibly links with Conrad's appreciation of Turgenev's instinct for the significant, essential and visible.

Flaubert's detachment does appear to have worked through to Conrad's own artistic stance, but not necessarily as a direct influence. The clearest force at the time Conrad began writing was Flaubert's most impressive disciple, Maupassant. Even before he became a professional author Conrad was informing Poradowska, in 1894:

> Je lis Maupassant avec delices [sic] . . . J'ai peur que je ne sois trop sous l'influence de Maupassant. . . . Ça n'a l'air de rien mais c'est d'un compliqué comme mécanisme qui me fait m'arracher les cheveux.
>
> (CL, vol. 1, pp. 169–83)

which Karl and Davies translate as:

> I am reading Maupassant with delight . . . I fear I may be too much under the influence of Maupassant. . . . It seems nothing, but it has a technical complexity which makes me tear my hair.
>
> (CL, vol. 1, pp. 171–85)

Four years later Conrad wrote to Garnett in praise of Maupassant's novel *Bel-Ami* again stressing the technical complexity achieved: 'that amazing masterpiece . . . The technique of that work gives to one acute pleasure. It is simply enchanting to see how it's done' (CL, vol. 2, p. 62). In those formative years Maupassant influenced Conrad as both a practitioner and a theorist. In his 1887 essay 'The Novel' Maupassant argued of the serious novelist:

> The skill of his plan will not therefore consist in emotion or charm, in a beguiling opening or a thrilling catastrophe, but in the ingenious grouping of changeless little facts from which the real meaning of the work will emerge . . . he must know how

to eliminate from the innumerable small daily events all those that do not serve his purpose, and throw into relief in a special way all those that might have remained unnoticed by unobservant onlookers, and which give the book its meaning and value as a whole.[13]

Conrad too eschewed overt melodrama, even when describing very dramatic events, concentrating instead on elaborating the metaphysical value of small, but significant, physical actions and characteristics. The emphasis here, as in the earlier quotations, is on a novel's structure, the ingenious grouping of little incidents that reveal the work's essential meaning. In this context structure is defined as the selection and juxtaposition of episodes.

Conrad's own critical essay on Maupassant focused on some of these points, revealing the depth of his concern with them. He argued that the perfection of a Maupassant story was in 'the vision of its true shape and detail' (NL, p. 28), and that the technical structure carries the author's integrity of perception and ideas:

> He is merciless and yet gentle with his mankind . . . he looks with an eye of profound pity upon their troubles, deceptions and misery. But he looks at them all. He sees – and does not turn away his head. As a matter of fact he is courageous.
>
> Courage and justice are not popular virtues.
>
> (NL, p. 29)

This is almost as good a self-summation as it is possible to achieve. Conrad too fused austerity of vision with compassion, and was not afraid in the novel to stand uncompromisingly against the easy popularity gained by following the fads and fashions of public taste. He held to a philosophically severe course. In a lifetime that experienced the achievement in Britain of almost universal adult suffrage, of the first Labour prime minister and women MPs, of compulsory schooling; and also went through the trauma of the Great War, saw the foundation of Stalinism in Russia and the seeds of incipient fascism spread in Italy and Bavaria, Conrad's severity of vision was truer to his time than that of any other novelist.

4

The African Arena

Heart of Darkness was Conrad's first profound work: challenging to its readership artistically, philosophically and politically. The framing of events as a narration within a narrative is not a simple storyteller's device, it allows the creation of deliberate thematic ambiguities, a critical historical perspective and a tone of ironic detachment. The anonymous narrator who retails Marlow's story warns that it – and therefore the novel – will not be of the conventional sort that other storytellers, and novelists, provide. The novel contains a new kind of content that requires a different form of expression:

> The yarns of seamen have a direct simplicity the whole meaning of which lies within the shell of a cracked nut. But Marlow was not typical . . . and to him the meaning of an episode was not inside like a kernel but outside, enveloping the tale which brought it out only as a glow brings out a haze, in the likeness of one of these misty halos that sometimes are made visible by the spectral illumination of moonshine.
>
> (p.30)

This is a clear indication that the novel will not be like other novels, that the form – the shell – is part of the meaning and has to be understood as well as the events described. A new form is necessary because the novel is not a mere reflection of a tangible, and known, reality, but an exploration of different types of realities.

This concept is carried in the novel partly by the shifting ideas of dream, nightmare and palpable reality; which are reinforced by images of light and dark. For instance, Marlow's experiences in Africa are a 'choice of nightmares' among 'greedy phantoms' (p.110); and after he has returned to Brussels – the initial reader's reality of a substantial European city, not unlike London – Marlow is still haunted by the memory of Kurtz: 'a shadow insatiable of splendid appearances, of frightful realities; a shadow darker than the shadow of the night . . . the heart of a conquering darkness' (p.116). Unlike a phantom a shadow does have a reality, but it is not palpable; and whereas shadows are normally formed by darkness within light in the case of Kurtz and Africa the shadow is a darker pattern of darkness. The reader cannot simply bring a comprehension of life in late Victorian Britain to the novel, and interpret it as normal experiences might be interpreted.

In traditional novels the reader is usually required to understand events and motives only in terms of a known reality. A fictional town such as Eliot's Middlemarch, or an area like Hardy's Wessex, may have certain particular local characteristics, but they can be related to towns and areas known to a wide variety of readers' general experiences. Those localities are in a sense everywhere, at least everywhere likely to be understood by the mainstream of the British reading public. That was the way the vast majority of earlier novels were written – which is not to denigrate the method, for both Eliot and Hardy, amongst others, wrote great novels within it.

Conrad, though, was at pains to detach his fiction from that framework. In his Preface to an earlier novel, *The Nigger of the 'Narcissus'*, Conrad had declared a manifesto:

> My task which I am trying to achieve is, by the power of the written word to make you hear, to make you feel – it is, before all, to make you *see*. That – and no more, and it is everything.
> (p.xlix)

By italicising *'see'* Conrad emphasised that he was not referring merely to physical sight, or to the visualising of scenes in literature imaginatively – although that is an aspect of fiction – but that he was using the word in the sense also of comprehending, of seeing and understanding, of perceiving. For fiction to render a new, different, challenging perception of the world, and of experience, 'is everything'.

As a foreigner with a very finely developed perception of his own, Conrad realised that he did not necessarily see events in the same way as the majority of the British, or indeed western Europeans as a whole. He was writing at a time of expanding colonisation, and having experienced the effects of imperialism was sceptical about its benefits, during a period when such activities were more celebrated than questioned. The literary culture into which Conrad came as a naturalised Briton mainly reflected, and supported, the ideological assumptions behind the idea of Empire. His task was to apply a different perspective to those concepts that were taken for granted and permeated the attitudes of most readers. The early Far East books were set in an area of the world that was not at the centre of the British political consciousness; but Africa was, and Conrad had personal experience of what Europeans were actually – as opposed to theoretically – doing to Africa, and of what the dark continent did to them, which was much less publicised than the glories of imperial adventure. In order to create this new perception Conrad needed a different form, a novel that required the reader to actively think about, rather than just passively accept, the text. The enormity of the leap required of the reader, and the absolute centrality of the issues raised, cannot fully be appreciated without some understanding of what Africa really meant at the time *Heart of Darkness* appeared.

Although it is set in the Belgian Congo, where Conrad's own experiences occurred, the novel was relevant to British conquest in Africa too, and in the 1890s that was a sensitive subject. *Heart of Darkness* was serialised between the reconquest of Sudan and the final Boer War, with its volume publication occurring just after the bitter and traumatic campaign against the Boers had been concluded. National consciousness of Britain's place in Africa was high, and intensified by the knowledge that the country was in competition there with other western European powers. Africa was the arena of the time for international political, economic, and occasionally military, conflict.

In 1884, for example, the British general, Charles George Gordon, and his troops were besieged for almost a year in Khartoum, in northern Africa, by rebelling indigenous Sudanese, and suffered a defeat that entailed the death of Gordon himself in 1885, and the loss of control over the area. The whole matter was generally considered a disaster to British imperial pride, prestige and material interests. It was so serious that a Motion of Censure on the government was put forward in the House of Commons in February 1885:

the course pursued by Her Majesty's Government in respect to the affairs of Egypt and the Soudan, has involved a great sacri-

fice of valuable lives and a heavy expenditure . . . without any
beneficial result.

(*Hansard*, 27 February 1885)

The terms of criticism suggest that loss of life and considerable
expense would have been justified if British prestige and power
had been re-established.

In the event it was 1898 before Kitchener's army reoccupied
Khartoum, bringing the area back into the ambit of the British
government. This was considered a suitable avenging of the death
of Gordon, and it also achieved the re-establishment of British
power in the region. The mood of celebration that greeted the far-
off events of September 1898 was epitomised in the headlines of
the *Daily Telegraph*, which published special war editions proclaim-
ing: 'Great Victory', 'Dervish Army Totally Routed', 'Heavy Losses
of the Enemy' (4 September 1898); and carried a detailed report
under the banner 'Most Picturesque Battle of the Century' (5 September 1898). Whether or not the participants experienced it that
way the reporter did not inform his readers, but it illustrates
the tendency to turn contemporary events in Africa into instant
mythology. Electronic technology was in its infancy and virtually
the only reports were in newspapers, and because of the distances
involved these were often not available until two or three days, or
more, after their occurrence. There was an air of slight uncertainty,
unrealness about the events, but simultaneously a national feeling
of identification with the idea of the British Empire that provided
fertile ground for the creation of legend out of fact.

This happened in literature too. For example, Kipling wrote a
poem based on the expedition to relieve Gordon's troops in Khartoum, the title of which, *Fuzzy-Wuzzy*, refers to the colloquial name
of the enemy. Part of it runs:

So 'ere's *to* you Fuzzy-Wuzzy, at your 'ome in the Soudan;
You're a pore benighted 'eathen but a first-class fightin' man;
We gives you your certificate, an' if you want it signed
We'll come an' 'ave a romp with you whenever you're inclined.
. . .
Then 'ere's *to* you, Fuzzy-Wuzzy, an' the missis and the kid;
Our orders was to break you, an' of course we went an' did.
We sloshed you with Martinis, an' it wasn't 'ardly fair;
But for all the odds agin' you, Fuzzy-Wuz, you broke the square.[1]

The British army of the time in Africa frequently fought pitched battles by forming into a square, the holding of which often led to victory, but if the enemy broke it part of the square was exposed to disastrous attack from the rear. 'Fuzzy-Wuz' proved his fighting credentials by achieving that feat in particular battles, despite facing the latest make of Martini-Henry rifles. The tone of patronisation to an inferior, ''eathen', culture is carried partly through the idiomatic, ungrammatical speech of the common-soldier narrative voice, partly by the way the unfamiliar Sudanese is projected through known concepts, a man with a 'missis and the kid'. The African may well have a wife and child, but the colloquial expression tends to portray him as also going to the pub for a game of dominoes, and generally enjoying a 'normal', in this context, British, culture.

It is this very perception of the different in terms of the known that Conrad fundamentally undermines. In the contrast, for instance, between the pilgrims and the cannibals it is the former, the known, Europeans, who become alien to civilised behaviour; while the latter, the unknown element, are accepted on their own terms, within the bounds of their own civilisation. The group Marlow refers to as the pilgrims are white men who at the Central Station:

> wandered here and there with their absurd long staves in their hands, like a lot of faithless pilgrims bewitched inside a rotten fence. The word 'ivory' rang in the air, was whispered, was sighed. You would think they were praying to it. A taint of imbecile rapacity blew through it all . . . I've never seen anything so unreal . . . [as] this fantastic invasion.
>
> (p.52)

There is a good deal of irony here: they carry 'staves' like medieval pilgrims, and appear to pray; but their staves are 'absurd', they are 'faithless', and their prayers are to, or about, 'ivory'. Pilgrims traditionally have a motivating impulse of goodness impelling them on their pilgrimage, which is literally a holy journey involving a degree of self-sacrifice. These characters are motivated solely by greed, and will sacrifice anyone else who is an obstacle to their desires. In theory a pilgrimage is a spiritually creative force, as imperialism nominally creates better conditions for the conquered peoples. In fact both are destructive forces, even self-destructive

– the members of another group of European traders/conquerors, the Eldorado Exploring Expedition, for example, are apparently destroyed by their colonial greed. Because of their greed the pilgrims 'slandered and hated each other' (p.54).

The description 'imbecile rapacity' perhaps suggests subhuman intelligence allied with a predatory motivation, associating the pilgrims less with spirituality than with animalistic appetites. An echo of this occurs in the way the fate of the other group of invaders is later reported:

> the Eldorado Expedition went into the patient wilderness, that closed upon it as the sea closes over a diver. Long afterwards the news came that all the donkeys were dead. I know nothing as to the fate of the less valuable animals.
>
> (p.66)

There are two techniques here that are recurrent in the structure of Conrad's fiction. The laconic satire, which is not made explicit by a narrative voice, but in which the men are implicitly less valuable than the donkeys; and the way in which the incident provides a specific illustration of a generalisation Marlow makes earlier. That occurs shortly after his arrival on the African continent: 'I foresaw that in the blinding sunshine of that land I would become acquainted with a flabby, pretending, weak-eyed devil of a rapacious and pitiless folly' (p.43). The pilgrims exhibit their 'pitiless folly' by shooting at Africans at almost every opportunity on the journey up-river, a trait that is prefigured when they are waiting for the essential, because practical, rivets:

> There was an old hippo that had the bad habit of getting out on the bank and roaming at night over the station grounds. The pilgrims used to turn out in a body and empty every rifle they could lay hands on at him. . . . All this energy was wasted.
>
> (p.59)

This kind of action is presented as typically European. On his way to the Congo Marlow encounters:

> a man-of-war anchored off the coast. There wasn't even a shed there, and she was shelling the bush. . . . In the empty immensity of earth, sky, and water, there she was, incomprehensible,

firing into a continent. . . . There was a touch of insanity in the
proceeding . . . the men in that lonely ship were dying at the
rate of three a-day.

(pp.40–1)

The essential self-destructiveness of the action is expressed by the
fact that no Africans, hostile or otherwise, were in 'the bush', for
'There wasn't even a shed there', and it is the European military
sailors who are dying. The pattern of predatory, pitiless, insane
actions permeates the novel – putting both the military engage-
ments, and the emissaries of European trade and commerce, in a
quite different perspective from the one that was politically and
culturally pervasive.

That is emphasised by the contrast in the novel between these
Europeans and the very worst characters the British imagination
could encompass: the cannibals. Despite being 'very hungry'
(p.75) they are not rapacious, although their culture may have
allowed them to be, and Europeans would have expected it of
them:

> Why in the name of all the gnawing devils of hunger they didn't
> go for us – they were thirty to five – and have a good tuck in
> for once, amazes me now. . . . I saw that something restraining,
> one of those human secrets that baffle probability, had come
> into play there . . . [they] had no earthly reason for any kind of
> scruple. Restraint! I would just as soon have expected restraint
> from a hyena prowling amongst the corpses of a battlefield. But
> there was the fact facing me . . . an unfathomable enigma.
>
> (p.76)

Restraint is a central concept in the novel, and a quality nominally
ascribed to civilised Europeans – in this case ironically appropriated by the cannibals. Marlow is conveying the expectations of
almost any western observer – which is part of his narrative function. Another feature of this is that unlike the omniscient narrator
of conventional novels Marlow does not know everything. He has
areas of ignorance, such as the exact fate of the Eldorado Exploring
Expedition and the inner motivation of the cannibals. There are
realities of which any individual will always be ignorant, which is
an important aspect of the new perception projected in the novel.

It is implicit in this context that most readers of the novel will not know the full truth about imperialism in Africa.

This raises a significant epistemological issue. People can know only what they are told, or what they are able to deduce and perceive from the information, attitudes and ideas they are given. An almost random example of a magazine approach to colonialism can be seen in Sir Richard Temple's response to Victoria's Diamond Jubilee, 'The Reign of Queen Victoria'. He compares the vast empires of the past – those of Darius of Persia, Alexander the Great of Macedonia, Philip of Spain, Peter the Great of Russia, Napoleon – and concludes that none of them equalled the vastness of Victoria's. Moreoever, the Victorian additions to the British Empire:

> have never fallen into the lap of Britain by chance or luck – they have been ever striven for and won by the valour and enterprise, by the blood and sweat, of her sons, belonging to the civil as well as to the military professions. They have been consolidated and rendered fruitful by the genius of her administrators.
>
> (*Cosmopolis*, June 1897)

This perception was held implicitly by the majority of Britons. The strength of the empire, it was felt, rested on the cornerstones of trade, military presence, administration and religion. It was essentially beneficial to the 'pore benighted 'eathen' and his 'missis', and since it cost the British so much courage and hardship was virtually a form of international altruism. There is no rapacity or imbecility in Temple's reality. Conrad's views of empire, and his characterisation of the representatives of trade, and 'the civil . . . professions', are not likely to be taken seriously by anyone with Temple's perception of Africa. In fact the reader may see them as an insult to her/his national pride, to which they are certainly subversive.

The Boer War of 1899–1902 set up a furore of xenophobia fired by the most vociferous politicians and elements of the press. Conrad's reservations about imperialism ran against the grain. On the whole our culture today has grave reservations about colonialism, and in retrospect it is difficult to appreciate just how strong public feeling became about it and the conflict with the Boers, and therefore the extent to which Conrad's work subverted the dominant ideology.

The Dutch had begun to colonise southern Africa in the seventeenth century, and the Boers – farmers of mainly Dutch ancestry – were, by the late Victorian era, largely the descendants of earlier colonists. The southern area of Africa was a huge territory, which the British had begun to occupy from the early nineteenth century, but after 1886 conflict was intensified by the discovery of gold in Boer-governed regions, to which large numbers of British were then attracted. In October 1899 the Boer Republics invaded the British Province of Natal, provoking a full-scale war. Many newspapers carried a full page of war reports and analysis every day. Philanthropic appeals were immediately set up on behalf of refugees, wounded soldiers, and also the troops in action, as a letter emanating from the 'Lady White Fund' illustrates:

> All classes have combined with enthusiasm to do their utmost . . . to help me in sending to those men who have not been wounded and who have gone through the past trying weeks at Ladysmith some articles of clothing, tobacco, papers, and cigars to reach them about Christmas time.
>
> (*The Times*, 18 November 1899)

Although the organisation was aristocratic the 'All classes' was probably not entirely rhetorical. The war was at the forefront of the national consciousness.

After the resounding victory in Sudan only thirteen months previously a mood of confidence pervaded early expectations, and even initial military setbacks were considered merely temporary embarrassments. In December 1899, however, in what became known as Black Week, the British suffered a number of defeats that sobered military and civilian spirits. The British High Commissioner for South Africa, Sir Alfred Milner, writing in a private letter to a friend, Mrs Toynbee, admitted 'disaster after disaster has come upon us'.[2] Whilst another friend of Milner's, Bertha Synge, wrote to him describing the mood in the capital of the Empire:

> In my life-time this state of tension is unique. The war affects all, rich and poor alike . . . we are all plunged in gloom. . . . Imagine the rush for papers . . . reading the telegrams with breathless anxiety. . . . Carriages stopped at the corners for papers to be bought – bus conductors rushed with handfuls of

pennies as deputation for their passengers . . . intense gravity
prevailed . . . nothing is spoken of save the war.[3]

Some of those newspapers were sombre, others attempted to miti-
gate the catastrophes with such headlines as 'British Troops' Brav-
ery' (*Morning Post*, 12 December 1899). The historian John Wrench
has retrospectively interpreted the situation in dire terms: 'Even
as late as February (1900) Buller [a British commander] was again
defeated at Spion Kop by the Boer forces. Not since the Crimean
War had the Empire faced such a disaster.'[4] It appears that Synge's
description of London reflected that of the nation in general,
although not every individual's response.

The genuine darkness of the collective mood, as it was expressed
by Synge, is shown when it is compared to the joy of a victory
five months later. The relief of Mafeking, in May 1900, after over
seven months of siege by the Boers, was probably of greater
symbolic than military significance. News of the event, however,
was received with almost unprecedented public displays of spontaneous rejoicing. As the information was released in London
there were immediate celebrations:

London simply went wild with delight . . . crowded and
jammed with an excited throng of cheering, shouting, gesticulat-
ing, happy people . . . the cry was taken up on the omnibuses
and the people came clambering down in hot haste to hear
the news . . . the streets became thicker with people cheering,
shouting and singing . . . the Lord Mayor was surrounded by
a crowd of no fewer than 20,000 madmen, all yelling: 'Mafeking
is relieved!' or singing 'God Save the Queen'.

(*Daily Mail*, 19 May 1900)

This all occurred as the news was reported. In the evening a kind
of celebratory anarchy broke out, which the same edition of the
paper described under the headline 'Wild Frenzy That Surpasses
Description'.

The importance of events at this time can partly be judged by
the way at least two aspects have passed into the popular cultural
consciousness. It was while Baden-Powell was besieged at Mafeking that he conceived the notion of the Boy Scout movement, one
purpose of which was to be training in self-reliance; in a sense,
the development of abilities to withstand siege conditions. The

battle for Spion Kop, a hilltop battery of the Boer artillery, also caught the popular imagination. The British were in fact defeated, but subsequently saw it as an honourable battle withdrawal that enabled them to win the war. The words Spion Kop passed into the common language with many football grounds in England – it was a time of tremendous expansion for the game – naming one of their terraces in honour of the battle: the term having subsequently been abbreviated to the Kop. A few years later a racehorse was named Spion Kop, and became a popular Derby winner. These sporting instances depict how deep public interest was in the Boer campaign.

Cunninghame Graham, as a socialist, was opposed to the war on principle. By the end of Black Week, in which the disasters in Africa had dominated all the newspapers, and apparently all common conversation, Conrad was writing to him: 'I am so utterly and radically sick of this African business' (CL, vol. 2, p.228); and to Garnett the following month that, 'This imbecile war has just about done for me' (ibid., p.242). Conrad, not for the only time, was going against mainstream sentiment – but he had prophetically perceived the likely drift at the very outbreak of hostilities. As soon as news of the Boers' invasion of Natal was received Conrad wrote to Graham:

> Now with this idiotic war there will be a bad time coming for print. All that's art, thought, idea will have to step back and hide its head before the intolerable war inanities. . . . The whole business is inexpressibly stupid.
>
> (CL, vol. 2, pp.206–7)

The kind of inanity Conrad feared is illustrated by an almost random selection of headlines from the *Daily Mail*, the largest selling newspaper of the day, from the following weeks: 'Boer Treachery', 'Party under Flag of Truce Fired On' (11 November 1899); 'Boer Spies in London', 'Superb Heroism of Two Handfuls of Men' (16 November 1899). Conrad wrote to Sanderson complaining of the press and 'the hysterical transports of some public organs' and their 'infernal scribblers' (CL, vol. 2, p.211). His depression early in the Boer War was not doctrinaire, emanating from preconceived political theories of socialism or pacifism, but based on commonsense and a knowledge of what happens in times of war.

In fact Conrad's attitudes to the war were ambivalent. Although not condoning colonisation, neither did he categorically condemn it. The ambiguity emerges in *Heart of Darkness* when Marlow is looking at the map of Africa on the wall of the Brussels' office:

> a large shining map, marked with all the colours of a rainbow. There was a vast amount of red – good to see at any time, because one knows that some real work is done in there, a deuce of a lot of blue, a little green, smears of orange, and, on the East Coast, a purple patch, to show where the jolly pioneers of progress drink the jolly lager-beer.
>
> (p.36)

Such maps were commonplace during the whole Empire period, the different colours denoting the various European colonies. The blue probably represented the French, green Portuguese, orange Dutch, and the purple German. Red signified British, and there are two main interpretations of Marlow's remarks. The uncritical original reader might have taken his comments at face value: the British Empire was justified because real work was done in it, and by implication the imperialism of other countries had no justification. A more recent view is that Marlow's thoughts are ironic – and there is certainly a good deal of irony in the novel – so that no true validity should be allowed to them. Marlow, however, does speak as an inexperienced Englishman of his time, so there is no reason why he should not think as one. But because Marlow expresses a conventional view does not necessarily mean there is no truth in it, any more than such an attitude should be unquestionably accepted. If Marlow's ideas are presented within the structure of an interpretive dialectic, in which they may be fully accepted or totally rejected, perhaps the reality lies in a synthesis: some truth, some falsehood. The narrative voice can be neither automatically trusted nor distrusted.

A few days after Black Week Conrad wrote to a cousin, Aniela Zagórska, who was living in Brussels, where anti-British sentiment on the issue was high, the Belgians being one of the European nations vying for power in Africa:

> Much might be said about the war. My feelings are very complex . . . that they [the Boers] are struggling in good faith for their independence cannot be doubted; but it is also a fact

that they have no idea of liberty, which can only be found under the English flag all over the world. . . . This war is not so much a war against Transvaal as a struggle against the doings of German influence. It is the Germans who have forced the issue . . . Canada and Australia are taking part in this, which could not influence their material interests. Why? Europe rejoices and is moved because Europe is jealous and here in England there is more real sympathy and regard for the Boers than on the Continent, which proclaims its compassion at the top of its voice.

(CL, vol. 2, p.230)

It was in fact the first war in which some (the predominantly white-populated) countries in the British Empire participated with a collective identity. Also, by the end of the war many professional commentators were to agree with Conrad's political analysis of the attitudes of the continental powers. Conrad's opinion was written in 1899; in regard to the peace negotiations two and a half years later a commentator tartly observed:

The value of German comments on the restoration of peace in South Africa is questionable, seeing that to a very great extent they represent the reflections of impotent malice, disappointment, or despairing resignation. . . . No State was so eager to encourage the fatal Boer ideas of independent nationality as Germany was.

(*The Times*, 3 June 1902)

Although British newspapers were generally anti-Boer at the time, Conrad was probably right in perceiving an underlying feeling of conciliation towards them. This might be seen in the eventual peace settlement, which some, although not all, historians have interpreted as magnanimous, Ensor and Wood respectively typically recording 'the generosity of its terms',[5] and 'the remarkable humanity of the peace terms'.[6] Wood sees 'the mildness of the terms'[7] manifested in the fact that the Boers were not subjugated, a view he substantiates with the observation that many of South Africa's subsequent political leaders have been of Boer descent. Conrad did not accept that all British imperialism was beneficial to those colonised, but in the letter to Zagórska he shows both an understanding of the Boer position and an acceptance that British colonialism was less despotic, on the whole, though not in every instance, than that of other countries.

Conrad tended to reject simple views of issues. He could not embrace Graham's socialist pacifism – having earlier told Graham 'I am not a peace man' (CL, vol. 2, p.158) – or Kipling's justification of the war as a moral crusade, to which Conrad responded in another letter to Graham:

> There is an appalling fatuity in this business. If I am to believe Kipling this is a war undertaken for the cause of democracy. C'est à crever de rire. [It's enough to make you die laughing.]
>
> (CL, vol. 2, p.207)

A factor that makes Conrad difficult to understand at times is his ability to stand outside both left- and right-wing categorisation. He did not approve of colonisation, but he saw it in a historical perspective. Events in Africa stemmed from material greed and lust for power – but for Conrad those attributes were not merely the product of nineteenth century capitalism: the Czarist Russia that had colonised southeastern Poland, with the subsequent disintegration of the Korzeniowski family, was politically and economically closer to medieval feudalism than to modern industrialism. The desire to dominate was not, for Conrad, the simple manifestation of a particular economic system, but an aspect of human organisation. Strong societies often do oppress and exploit weaker ones.

In *Heart of Darkness* there are references to England itself having once been a dark place that attracted alien conquerors:

> the Romans first came here, nineteen hundred years ago – the other day . . . darkness was here yesterday. Imagine the feelings of a commander of a fine – what d'ye call 'em? – trireme in the Mediterranean, ordered suddenly to the north . . . Imagine him here – the very end of the world, a sea the colour of lead, a sky the colour of smoke . . . precious little fit to eat for a civilized man . . . cold, fog, tempests, disease, exile, and death.
>
> (pp.30–1)

Structurally this parallels the experience of northern European man in the dark continent, as Africa was known at the time.

Imperialism is part of a historical process to which countries may be subjected at one time, and may exercise against others at another period. If ambitious nations are fated to rise and fall – and none has risen without having subsequently fallen – then an aspect of the fate of conquerors is eventually to be conquered. In the extract above the relativity of time is emphasised, 'nineteen hundred years ago' and 'yesterday' are given the same value, are part of a linked experience. It is an aspect of human nature, and of its organised form, society, for Conrad, that it will explore and conquer even when that experience is unpleasant and dangerous. That cannot be changed by a mere change of government, as Graham, representative of the political left, advocated; nor should it be given specious moral justification as Kipling, representative of the political right, attempted.

Despite Conrad's personal belief in the relative efficacy of the British Empire, he also realised its inadequacies. The fact that *Heart of Darkness* is set in the Belgian Congo does not mean, within the structure of the novel, that the British are exonerated from responsibility.[8] There is, for example, the ambiguity of Marlow's thoughts on the map, and although Marlow does not comment on them, there are several signifiers of, at least peripheral, if not central, British involvement. Marlow himself, of course, is one of these. Also, the African to whom Marlow gives a biscuit 'had tied a bit of white worsted round his neck' (p.45). This is another insoluble mystery of which the narrator/participant cannot have, or discover, knowledge. There is no rational reason for the piece of cloth within the verisimilitude of the novel. This is emphasised by Marlow's own response to it: 'Why? Where did he get it? Was it a badge – an ornament – a charm – a propitiatory act? Was there any idea at all connected with it?' (p.45). It seems totally inexplicable, but it does have a thematic purpose; which is indicated by Marlow's final observation on it: 'It looked startling round his black neck, this bit of white thread from beyond the seas' (p.45). It was brought into Africa 'from beyond the seas', and is not just any piece of thread, being specifically 'worsted'. In the late Victorian period that signified English manufacture. The explication that baffles Marlow is that the white thread involves British trade in the exploitation of the young man with: 'sunken eyes . . . enormous and vacant, a kind of blind, white flicker in the depths of the orbs, which died out slowly' (p.45). He is the victim of a blind rapacity, dying in the depths of 'some Inferno' (p.44), a hell he cannot comprehend, and the flicker in his orbs prefigures the moment of dying illumination Kurtz later experiences. In a way Kurtz also has a link with the thread, for 'His mother was half-English' and he 'had been partly educated in England'. In helping to put Kurtz' 'sympathies . . . in the right place' (p.86) England had again contributed to the pattern of exploitation in Africa. Moreover, Kurtz himself had donated an additional character from Britain to the dark continent in the form of 'an English half-caste clerk' (p.64).

A further British connection with the Belgian Congo is Marlow's discovery of the English book *An Inquiry into some Points of Seamanship*. He finds it 'Some fifty miles below the Inner Station' in 'a hut of reeds' which 'was unexpected' (p. 70), in a place far from any ostensible British influence. Certain features are again focused on: the unexpectedness of the book in that context, the fact that it was English, and pre-Victorian since Towson was a Master in 'His' Majesty's Navy, and the 'white cotton thread' (p. 71) that holds its leaves together. It represents an old British presence in Africa, yet it has been renewed, for the thread is still clean despite the dirtiness of the pages. Since Marlow finds it quite a long way up-river it is far from the sea, and therefore its subject matter is particularly incongruous in the circumstances. These factors draw attention to it as a significant detail. In the nightmarish, phantasmagoric world of the Congo the 'sixty years old' book gives the practical seaman Marlow 'a delicious sensation of having come upon something unmistakably real' (p. 71). Despite its being out of date it appears more real to Marlow than his present experiences. He eulogises that reality because he is unsure of the one in which he is participating.

As a participant Marlow is not always able to objectively analyse the significance of events, or to appreciate ironic aspects. He is unable to comprehend the full signification of another British artifact that occurs in the present reality of the River Congo. It has a specific (ironic in the context) purpose too. The contents of the boat's pilot-house are verisimilically detailed: 'It contained a couch, two camp-stools, a loaded Martini-Henry leaning in one corner, a tiny table, and the steering-wheel' (p. 79). There is nothing in this description that any reader of adventure stories would find unusual – except that the casually introduced weapon leaning in a corner is not just a rifle, but specifically a 'Martini-Henry'. The weapon is referred to again in this particular way when it is

put to use, ironically by an African against Africans, when the
helmsman 'had dropped everything, to throw the shutter open
and let off that Martini-Henry' (p. 81). This is the same 'Martini'
Kipling celebrated the efficiency of in his poem *Fuzzy-Wuzzy*,
quoted earlier. It is a rifle manufactured in England, and used by
the British army. The way in which it is introduced into the pilot-
house catalogue, casually but specifically, draws attention to it,
especially for the readers of the time who might have been expected to know – as Kipling obviously assumes they do – what a
Martini-Henry was, and where it came from. There is an echo of
all this when the owner of Towson's manual, the Harlequin, later
asks Marlow for 'a few Martini-Henry cartridges', and goes off:

One of his pockets (bright red) was bulging with cartridges, from
the other (dark blue) peeped 'Towson's Inquiry', etc., etc. He
seemed to think himself excellently well equipped for a renewed
encounter with the wilderness.

(p. 104).

The Harlequin appropriately balances the dialectic of construction,
in the form of learning, and destruction, represented by the Martini-Henry cartridges. This thesis/antithesis may be synthesised in
the English origins of both.

Perhaps the colours of bright red and dark blue also suggest a
political synthesis, that conservative and radical, or liberal, ideas
and attitudes are connected in a closer way than simply by their
apparent opposition to one another: possibly through an element
of symbiosis. Both Marlow and Kurtz are sent to the dark continent
partly as representatives of self-appointed, and genuinely well-
meaning, philanthropic enlightenment. Marlow's aunt, an 'excel-
lent woman', who gets him the African job, sees him as: 'one of the
Workers, with a capital – you know. Something like an emissary of
light, something like a lower sort of apostle' (pp. 38–9). Kurtz
was entrusted with making a report for 'most appropriately, the
International Society for the Suppression of Savage Customs' (p.
86). There is certainly an irony in this, which is carried by Marlow's
observation that it was most appropriate. The Europeans are sav-
agely rapacious, and in the event Kurtz succumbs to the savage
customs – implicity of cannibalism, 'inconceivable ceremonies of
some devilish initiation' (p. 84) – because he had 'no restraint' (p.
108), while the 'savages', actual cannibals, do have restraint and

are 'fine fellows . . . men one could work with' (p. 67). It is the Europeans who are not interested in work, a paradox the enlight-ened 'Workers' such as Marlow's aunt failed to grasp.

In fact there were British missionaries in the Congo. This was highlighted by a dispute that gained wide newspaper coverage earlier in the decade in which *Heart of Darkness* first appeared. A Mr Glave died in the Congo and there was a subsequent conflict over his possessions in which the British government became involved. A letter in *The Times* from 'The Missionary in Charge of the Station where Mr. Glave is Buried' explained that he had left no written Will, but:

> within two hours of his death, Mr. Glave told me his wishes concerning his papers and effects in the event of his decease . . . [later] Mr. Glave was delirious for the first time during his fever, and he never regained consciousness . . . Mr. Glave had requested me to take charge of his effects and papers, and allow me to carry out his wishes concerning them.
>
> (*The Times*, 3 January 1896)

There may be an echo of this case in the way Kurtz dies and Marlow becomes the custodian of his papers and last wishes. Kurtz falls into fevers, in which 'The wastes of his weary brain were haunted by shadowy images' (p. 110), until his final surren-der. When Marlow returns to Brussels there is also some dispute over Kurtz' papers:

> A clean-shaved man, with an official manner and wearing gold-rimmed spectacles, called on me one day and made inquiries, at first circuitous, afterwards suavely pressing, about what he was pleased to denominate certain 'documents'. I was not sur-prised, because I had had two rows with the manager on the subject out there. I had refused to give up the smallest scrap . . . and I took the same attitude with the spectacled man. He became darkly menacing at last . . . He withdrew upon the threat of some legal proceedings . . . another fellow, calling himself Kurtz's cousin, appeared two days later, and was anxi-ous to hear all the details about his dear relative's last moments.
>
> (p. 114)

These conflicts over Kurtz' possessions contribute to the Europe/

Africa dichotomy, but for the original reader they may have also recalled the arguments over the papers of the late Mr Glave. All documents written in the midst of the African experience had potential official, political and commercial significance, and clearly it had been felt that Glave's personal observations may have had value in those areas. In any event, if Kurtz is a reference to the Glave case it was a reminder that the British were not entirely absent from the exploitive horrors of the Congo.

Another point concerning the implication of Britain in the Congo arena is related to the curious narrative structure of the novel. Before Marlow begins his narration the initial narrator describes how he, the Director, the Lawyer and the Accountant were waiting for the tide to turn: 'The Accountant had brought out already a box of dominoes, and was toying architecturally with the bones' (p. 28). These characters, although it is not yet evident, are involved, if only indirectly, in the exploitation the story exposes. The word the rapacious pilgrims reiterate, the god to which they appear to be praying, is 'ivory' (p. 52); and Kurtz' fame is based partly on the fact that he 'Sends in as much ivory as all the others put together' (p. 47). Dominoes had become a popular game, and though cheap ones were produced from wood the Accountant's would have been made of ivory, a factor emphasised by the description of them as 'bones'. That the audience of Marlow's narrative is involved in the very process of exploitation he outlines is a form of retrospective irony, since the reader does not know at that stage what the story will be about. As both the audience in the novel, and the original reader of it, are recipients of Marlow's tale they are related groups – they were also likely to be connected in terms of social class and culture – therefore the involvement of the audience of characters is implicitly projected onto the readership. The reader too is implicated in the rape of Africa.

The image of bones is a recurrent one in the novel. The young man to whom Marlow gives a biscuit is described as 'black bones' (p. 44), a paradox – since all bones are white, whatever the colour of the skin covering them – that focuses attention on the thinness of the maltreated African, who looks like bones without flesh; it is also a thematic echo of the Accountant's ivory dominoes. The very reason Marlow is appointed to command the ship up the Congo is that his predecessor, Fresleven, was killed, and when Marlow later discovers his skeleton he finds 'the grass growing through his ribs was tall enough to hide his bones' (p. 35). This image also links with one of Brussels, the 'whited sepulchre' in which there was 'a dead silence, grass sprouting between the stones' (p. 35). The concept of an accountant building architecturally, with ivory bones in the form of domestic dominoes, is redolent with conceptual associations. As Roger Webster has argued, the images fuse:

> to form a complex set of ideas which is hard to unravel . . . to suggest the corpse of capitalism but in ways which the characters are unaware of and which the reader has to discover through hidden associations.[9]

One distinct idea is that no European is entirely innocent of the horrors of the imperial adventure.

Achieving the expression of this concept is one aspect of Conrad's desire to encourage the reader to reperceive reality, to '*see*'. In the absence of much pictorial documentary evidence – film was very much in its infancy, and even photography had not advanced technically sufficiently to allow spontaneous shooting – and with relatively few people having travelled outside Europe, or even Britain, literature was a major medium through which readers perceived imperialism. Adventure novels were extremely popular, and Conrad's early work was often put into that category. An early reviewer who lacked perception recommended the novel specifically because it 'contains plenty of adventure' (*Daily Telegraph*, 26 November 1902), without quite realising the nature of that adventure. The adventure writers were usually pro-imperialist, or at the most critical merely around the edges of it. Rider Haggard was a very popular contemporary of Conrad, and his novel *King Solomon's Mines* a typical example of the genre. The expression of Conrad's own, sceptical, perception of Africa had to take into account that many of his readers' comprehension of the dark continent had been formed, at least in part, by Haggard's projection of it.

Where ivory is, for Conrad, a source of greed, and an excuse for the exercise of aggressive and mindless power, in *King Solomon's Mines* it is presented as a perfectly natural commodity for legitimate accumulation:

> We had killed nine elephants, and it took us two days to cut

out the tusks. . . . It was a wonderfully fine lot of ivory. I never
saw a better, averaging as it did between forty and fifty pounds
a tusk.[10]

There is no irony in this account, no detached objectivity between
novelist and narrator, and in broader considerations no criticism
within the novel's structure. It is simply a celebration of literal
accumulation, materialism and destruction.

In such stories as these the indigenous population in general,
with occasional exceptions, fall into one of two basic stereotypes:
loyal and brave servants or helpers; or enemies, with a variation
that they may be either courageous or cowardly. In *King Solomon's
Mines* the European character Good is rather vain, and this characteristic puts him into danger of being trampled by an elephant.
As Good stumbles when being pursued by it:

> Khiva, the Zulu boy, saw his master fall, and brave lad as he
> was, turned and flung his assegai straight into the elephant's
> face . . . the brute seized the poor Zulu, hurled him to earth . . .
> and *tore him in two.*
>
> (p. 39)

The boy's loyalty is specifically to 'his master', the imperilling of
his own life can be, in the context, interpreted as a recognition
and acceptance of racial and cultural inferiority. The Zulu is
ennobled by a sacrifice to a higher being. After Haggard's character
Good has been saved the other Europeans manage to shoot the
elephant. Good reacts predictably: 'he rose and wrung his hands
over the brave man who had given his life to save him'. The final
epitaph over the Zulu is: 'he is dead, but he died like a man!' (p.
39). The gratitude Good feels towards the Zulu for his sacrifice is
elided into an inverse posthumous gratitude: Khiva, it seems,
might be grateful that Good gave him the chance to attain human
nobility. The pointless death of the African helmsman who lacked
restraint is reported differently by Marlow:

> in the very last moment, as though in response to some sign we
> could not see, to some whisper we could not hear, he frowned
> heavily, and that frown gave to his black death-mask an incon-
> ceivably sombre, brooding, and menacing expression.
>
> (p. 82)

In the structure of the novel the dying of the helmsman prefigures that of Kurtz, and like the later event it lacks nobility. The mystery of death does not confirm any obvious value of life, but makes it too more mysterious, more inexplicable. The narrator cannot know the dying thoughts of the African, and makes no attempt to imply what they might have been.

Haggard's Africans, even when threatening, are physically noble creatures: 'very tall and copper-coloured . . . some of them wore great plumes of feathers and short cloaks of leopard skins' (p. 70). These perfections of nature say they are going to kill the Europeans, but do not carry out the action because they are impressed by Good's ability to remove and replace his dentures. The warriors ask for 'Pardon', which is granted significantly 'with an imperial smile' (pp. 73–4). This is an imperialism based less on brute force than on supercilious patronising. When Marlow gets ashore he encounters a different kind of African:

> Six black men advanced in a file, toiling up the path. They walked erect and slow, balancing small baskets full of earth on their heads. . . . Black rags were wound round their loins, and the short ends behind waggled to and fro like tails. I could see every rib, the joints of their limbs were like knots in a rope; each had an iron collar on his neck, and all were connected together with a chain.
>
> (pp. 42–3)

None of Conrad's contemporaries could write with such power and precision, and very few would have described such a scene at all. Marlow here represents the late Victorian reader. He sees, perceives the scene, with the responses of a practical Englishman who believes, at this stage in the novel, in the conventional wisdom of his society regarding imperialism. The visual facts that are recorded need no interpretation, an omniscient author telling the reader what to think may have been counter-productive, a practical man simply observing allows the ideas to emerge. The shell, the form, of the episode expresses its meaning, as the narrator of Marlow's tale said it would (p. 30).

The diction is an important aspect of the form. These Africans walk 'erect', but not because they are proud warriors, as Haggard's are, rather because they are beasts of burden having to balance the 'baskets full of earth'. The animal suggestion is reinforced by them apparently having 'tails'. This occurs because they are not dressed in fine native costume of leopard skins, but in dirty rags.

They are maltreated animals too, thin enough to show every rib and joint, and also suffering from iron collars and a chain, signifying the worst kind of Victorian treatment of criminals.

All these features of the ignoble African are emphasised by the next group Marlow encounters:

> Black shapes crouched, lay, sat between the trees leaning against the trunks, clinging to the earth, half coming out, half effaced within the dim light, in all the attitudes of pain, abandonment, and despair. . . . They were dying slowly . . . nothing but black shadows of disease and starvation . . . bundles of acute angles sat with their legs drawn up . . . I stood horror-struck.
>
> (pp. 44–5)

Here Marlow does make a personal response, but it is not specifically ideological or political, merely the reaction of a decent human being. These Africans have ceased to be human, they are reduced to 'shapes', 'shadows', 'angles', which cannot even be seen clearly. They hardly exist at all, seeming part of the jungle, of the earth itself. They signify 'pain', 'abandonment', 'despair', 'disease', 'starvation' – the European bequest to the dark continent. Dark in this context because of the evils colonialism has brought. These Africans are quite different from the specimen Haggard's narrator describes as 'a desperate savage six feet five high, and broad in proportion' with 'mighty muscles' (pp. 154–6), who is nevertheless defeated and slain in hand-to-hand combat with an English aristocrat. The natives Marlow encounters are not killed so cleanly, but are starved to death by a merciless and mindless administration. That is a feature of the imperial adventure the vast majority of Conrad's original readers would have had difficulty in accepting, yet which he has to find a way of expressing in *Heart of Darkness*. Although Conrad was never simply and straightforwardly anti-colonial, perceived in this context the novel is a profoundly radical critique of the imperial adventure.

Looking at the scenery of part of colonised Africa in *King Solomon's Mines* the narrator admits 'language seems to fail' him when he attempts 'to describe the extraordinary grandeur and beauty' of 'the majestic sight' (pp. 54–5). The characters are significantly on a mountain, aloof from the reality of the scenery, although without realising it. Marlow is on the river, oppressed by the jungle that closes in around his boat: 'The woods were unmoved, like a mask – heavy, like the closed door of a prison – they looked with their air of hidden knowledge, of patient expectation, of unapproachable silence' (p. 96). Marlow feels imprisoned by something menacing, a kind of primitive understanding and expectancy lying in wait, knowing that the Europeans will not all be able to withstand the jungle's claustrophobia. He is given glimpses of an opening-out, but they are always thwarted. Even dawn has its promise frustrated:

> When the sun rose there was a white fog, very warm and clammy, and more blinding than the night. It did not shift or drive; it was just there, standing all around you like something solid. At eight or nine, perhaps, it lifted as a shutter lifts. We had a glimpse of the towering multitude of trees, of the immense matted jungle . . . then the white shutter came down again.
>
> (p. 73)

Haggard's characters certainly encounter hardships, but they can be endured and overcome. Marlow is tormented by something he cannot control, a hostile fate that will ultimately overcome all Europeans. In *King Solomon's Mines* the elements do become friendly. Fog and cloud in that novel are not consistently blinding and claustrophobic, but are also described as a 'gauze-like mist' and a 'fleecy envelope' (p. 55).

In *King Solomon's Mines* the country opens out, in *Heart of Darkness* it closes in. It is a significant difference. Haggard's characters see a:

> glorious panorama . . . league on league of the most lovely champaign country. Here were dense patches of lofty forest, there a great river wound its silvery way . . . a vast expanse of rich . . . grass land, whereon we could just make out countless herds of game or cattle. . . . The landscape lay before us as a map, wherein rivers flashed like silver snakes, and Alp-like peaks rose in grandeur, whilst over all was the glad sunlight and the breath of Nature's happy life.
>
> (pp. 67–8)

For Marlow there was no 'glad sunlight' illuminating and warming. In his experience 'The sun was fierce' (p. 40), and 'blazing' (p. 73), burning rather than nurturing. The simile of the 'silver snakes' illustrates how this landscape is projected romantically, the flashing of the rivers linking with the glorious grandeur. Everything is ordered, patterned, and seen as beneficent, and the Europeans are unlikely to destroy such practical beauty. Indeed, as Brian Street has observed of Haggard's novel in relation to the narrator's view of nature: 'such beauty is modified somewhat by Quartermain's comments . . . however beautiful the view, it needs man to make it complete'.[11] It is all there to be used, which in the context means colonised, exploited.

Heart of Darkness in part uses such images as a starting point, but works away from them. Looking at the coloured map in the Brussels office, for example, Marlow notes that: 'Dead in the centre . . . the river was there – fascinating – deadly – like a snake' (p. 36). This reptile is not silvery and beautiful, it is more like a threatening serpent, associated with death.

Marlow is not attracted to its beauty, but rather, in the nature of a victim, he is hypnotised, fascinated, by a metaphoric creature that is closely linked to death. Biblically, Adam and Eve forfeited their immortality by succumbing to the temptation offered by the serpent; and in the novel Marlow has been given the job because of the murder of Fresleven, and Kurtz dies shortly after Marlow meets him, and is buried 'in a muddy hole' (p. 112) on the bank of that river. The difference between Kurtz' muddy hole and Haggard's glorious panorama signifies a fundamental difference of vision between Conrad and most of his novelist contemporaries.

Ultimately the conventional perception of Africa was of a continent bountiful with nature's gifts, and therefore needing Europeans to cultivate, organise and utilise that richness. Haggard's narrator recalls:

> The brook, of which the banks were clothed with dense masses of a gigantic species of maidenhair fern interspersed with feathery tufts of wild asparagus, sang merrily at our side, the soft air murmured through the foliage of the silver trees . . . It was a paradise.
>
> (p. 70)

This is indeed a description of a medieval or renaissance Eden. There is perhaps an ideological implication that the colonisation of Africa is a way for Europeans to return to the paradise Adam and Eve lost. Such an idea would clearly justify imperial claims.

In *Heart of Darkness* the parallels drawn between the contemporary adventurers and the earlier Romans invading northern Europe indicate that the novel's main concerns are philosophic, but in terms of actual history. The invaders are all men out of place, disorientated in circumstances in which they are aliens, carrying 'the germs of empires' (p. 29). The concept of 'the seed of common-wealths' (p. 29) corresponds to the dominant comprehension that imperialism will germinate good for both conquerors and con-quered; but also the germs will infect the place to which they are taken, and the infection invades the men of conquest too. It was a perception the original readers, in their cultural and political context, could not easily accept. Conrad's task was to express it, which he did partly through the complex narrative structure, the uses of irony, and by starting from normative expectations and working away from them, presenting a challenging perspective to accepted views.

Just before reaching Kurtz' stockade, bizarrely surrounded with its 'heads on the stakes' (p. 96), Marlow experiences a feeling of profound alienation:

> never, never before, did this land, this river, this jungle, the very arch of this blazing sky, appear to me so hopeless and so dark, so impenetrable to human thought, so pitiless to human weakness.
>
> (p. 94)

These thoughts are projected in too powerful a diction to be expressing the feelings of someone merely in a foreign place. The force of the passage comes partly from the staccato repetition – 'never', 'this', 'so' – and its unexpected inversion, the 'blazing sky' seemed 'dark', metaphorically of course. Ironically the arch of the sky does not liberate Marlow's spirit, taking it out to the furthest horizons, but oppresses it, closing down possibilities to despair and futility. The displacement is ontological. The whole purpose and meaning of Marlow's existence is called into doubt. He is in a sphere that lacks the philosophic essentials for human life: hope, pity, understanding. It brings out the dark and weak aspects of humanity: rapacious greed and a merciless uncaring for fellow creatures.

The hostile environment inevitably destroys Kurtz and the pil-grims. That fate can be avoided, however, through the restrained exercise of energy in work: 'No, I don't like work. I had rather laze about . . . I don't like work . . . but I like what is in the work – the chance to find yourself. Your own reality' (p. 59). This illustrates the kind of energy that is constructive, and it is why Marlow likes the writer of the naval manual, who has 'an honest concern for the right way of going to work' (p. 71). However, it is a personal salvation, not a collective one. Political ambitions are inevitably corrupted.

These factors are organised, and given specious validation, by imperialist ideology, but that could not occur if the germs of dark pitilessness did not already exist in individual humans. These are, for Conrad, the ultimately impenetrable features of mankind as a whole – which is the philosophic basis of Conrad's political thinking. He saw imperialism as a paradox: that it is simultaneously inevitable and futile. Stronger nations are always likely to conquer and exploit weaker ones, as the ancient Romans did the English; and such conquest contains the seeds of its own destruction. This was not a popular perception in a period of rapid colonial expansion – especially as it, paradoxically, touched a nerve of generally unacknowledged self-doubt in the British nation at a time of its greatest power.

5

The World Stage

The paradox of confidence and doubt occurred because as the British Empire expanded to cover the greatest area of the globe, and the largest number of people, of any imperial range known in human history, those very facts meant that it created more jealousy and was vulnerable to attack in more areas than ever before. Pride of achievement was tempered by anxiety about holding such an increasingly complex system together in the face of intensifying competition.

The dichotomy was expressed by Henry Norman in an article to commemorate the sixtieth year of Queen Victoria's accession. Examining the relationship of Britain and the world, it was significantly entitled 'The Globe and the Island'. British, and perhaps particularly English, attitudes seemed predominantly a mixture of isolationism – an island people separated from the corruption of the world at large – and mastery, that the world was there to be organised by, and critics would say for, the British. Norman noted the general flood of nationalistic pride that Victoria's jubilee provoked, and in asking why answered his own question:

> The British people knows that of late years its diplomatic prestige has diminished. It has sat still uneasily. . . . It has heard insults, even threats, bandied about against it. It has read that it is an octopus whose long tentacles are a fatal source of weakness. It has watched its neighbours discussing the possibilities of invading its Fatherland, and openly urging each other to rival its power on the sea. It has even listened to rumours that after the Jubilee a hostile combination was to be developed against it.
>
> (*Cosmopolis*, July 1897)

This expresses, from a British point of view, Britain's unpopularity amongst other European powers. The image of the octopus is revealing. It shows Britain to be predatory: the length of its tentacles, the size of its Empire, are both a symptom of its greed, from a rival's perspective, and an indication of its vulnerability. Norman's response to these implicit foreign criticisms is not a reasoned argument, or a plea for a return to isolationism, but a simple assertiveness: 'Britain is Imperialistic now. The "Little Englander" has wisely decided to efface himself. . . . We are Imperialists first, and Liberals or Tories afterwards' (ibid.). In the face of intensifying rivalry even party political differences become insignificant. It is significant, however, that Norman offers no rationale for imperialism, it is offered merely as a form of defence against hostile nations. The best defence of a large empire is an even bigger one, the argument goes, and so the purpose of imperialism becomes self-justifying: it has to expand in order to exist; its existence is justified by its expansion. There is no attempt to justify the imperialist adventure by arguing that Britain is civilising primitive natives, or converting the heathen to Christianity.

It was ironic that Norman's article was published in the same edition of *Cosmopolis* as the second part of Conrad's story *An Outpost of Progress*. This story explores the effect of the imperialist experience on two Europeans. When they are left alone at their outpost of civilisation in Africa:

> It was not the absolute and dumb solitude of the post that impressed them so much as an inarticulate feeling that something from within them was gone, something that worked for their safety, and had kept the wilderness from interfering with their hearts . . . out of the great silence of the surrounding wilderness, its very hopelessness and savagery seemed to approach them nearer, to draw them gently, to look upon them, to envelop them.
>
> (p. 101)

The result is that one of them murders the other over a dispute about sugar in coffee, and then hangs himself. This raises the kind of philosophical questions about the nature of empire that Norman assiduously avoids. To face such issues would be to admit their existence, allowing the possibility of self-doubt. In Norman's article the doubt is revealed by the obvious evasion. The very strutting bellicosity of the assertion reveals the anxiety behind it.

The African arena was to some extent a crucible for worldwide imperialist conflicts. The dark continent was a particularly volatile microcosm of macrocosmic colonial ambitions. The original Euro-

pean world powers such as Spain, Portugal, Holland had been
challenged since the eighteenth century by newer forces, of which
Britain was the leading example, but in the later nineteenth
century newly emergent nations joined the struggle for power,
territory, raw materials and markets. Germany, for instance,
sought a place amongst the colonial scramble; the USA began to
challenge western European countries; Russia and Japan expanded
their influence in the east. The larger Britain's empire became, the
more spheres of conflict it encountered, which is why pride in
expansionism was tempered by fear of over-reaching, especially
as that expansion triggered the jealousy of nations that were
increasing their own power potential.

From the early 1890s to the outbreak of the Great War, the period
in which Conrad began writing *Almayer's Folly* to the completion of
Victory, a new global dynamic began to emerge, which was in
many ways typified by the 1898 Spanish–US war. Spain had a
long-established colonial rule in Cuba that met with increasing
indigenous resistance in the last two decades of the nineteenth
century, an opposition that attracted the support of the USA. In
February 1898 the visiting US battleship *Maine* was blown up in
the harbour of the Cuban capital, Havana, with the loss of 260
American lives. Although the cause of the explosion was never
definitively discovered the US government blamed Spain, and
took the opportunity to proclaim the island independent despite
the objections of Spain. There were Spanish troops garrisoned on
Cuba, but the ensuing war consisted mainly of a series of naval
battles around the Spanish colonies in the Caribbean, and subsequently in the far east, where Spain had colonised the Philippine
Islands. The six-month war ended with the capitulation of the
Spanish forces in Manila, the capital of the Philippines. Spain
suffered a humilating defeat concluding with a peace treaty in
which that country conceded independence to Cuba, lost possession of Puerto Rico to the USA, and sold the Philippines also
to the USA.

The outcome was a clear sign that Spain was dwindling as an
imperial power, while the USA had entered the international
power struggle in earnest. In Britain the initial political response
to the war was in favour of the USA, perhaps because Spain was
a long-standing rival. There were some commentators, however,
who saw the potential danger of the USA on the world stage.
Blackwood's Magazine, in which *Heart of Darkness* subsequently

appeared, analysed the situation in a way that met Conrad's approval. Cedric Watts has summarised the article, which was printed in the August 1898 edition, with a succinctness that cannot be improved:

> the political commentator made a dispassionate and partly ironic survey . . . his main points being:
> (*a*) The Americans had glorified the war; yet it was a rather tawdry series of minor engagements.
> (*b*) At the outset, most English papers had urged Spain to sacrifice one or two colonies 'as a cheap means of peace'. But
> > 'now we have lately heard a great deal of the possibility, the not-unlikelihood, of a great European coalition to redistribute the colonial possessions of Great Britain . . . *At what point* would the beautifully accurate reasoning addressed to Spain be our own guide to giving in?'
> (*c*) The Americans had originally claimed that they were helping the rebels to attain independence, but now they claimed that the rebels were mere cut-throats: so that in Cuba and Manila
> > 'there is considerable likelihood that . . . the Americans will have to deal not with a population grateful to its liberators, but with a malcontent people well practised in rebellion who think themselves tricked into a change of masters.'
> (*d*) Therefore the war which had revealed the United States as a new imperialist power might well result in increased sympathy for Spain from other countries.[1]

Conrad wrote to Graham, using the common name of the magazine, 'I do like the attitude of the *Maga* on the Spanish business . . . Viva l'Espana!' (CL, vol. 2, p. 81). The paradox of Conrad's own attitudes is again revealed. He did not approve of colonialism, referring in the same letter to both Spain and the USA as 'thieves', but recognising the apparent inevitability of it, supported what he saw as the lesser of the two evils.

Conrad was suspicious of United States world ambitions, being aware that the globe was becoming a unified political stage rather than a collection of separate arenas. The fact that the Spanish-US conflict began in the Caribbean area and ended in the Far East was significant, for most previous wars had been geographically confined. Conrad also realised that imperialism was developing a more subtle aspect than the old form of simple military conquest.

Just as British involvement in the Belgian Congo is implied partly by the appearance of Martini-Henry rifles in *Heart of Darkness*, so too a US presence occurs. The 'pilgrims' specifically carry 'Winchesters' (p. 74), and Marlow has a vision of a 'row of pilgrims squirting lead in the air out of Winchesters held to the hip' (p. 106). Winchester rifles were manufactured in the USA, and they signify an economic involvement in the colonial activities.

After the Spanish-American war had led to Cuban independence, a feature of that country's economy, as Conrad suspected it would be, was large US investment. That input of capital was protected, as the historian J. H. Parry has noted, by a close political and military interest from 1898:

> Cuba, the largest and richest of the Caribbean islands, after a short period of North American occupation, became politically independent in 1902; but the United States retained a base . . . [and] a right to intervene in the event of serious disorder.[2]

Since the end of the American Civil War in 1865 the USA had become increasingly powerful economically. Relative political stability, enormous areas of rich agrarian land, newly developing industries and vast resources of raw materials, especially those such as oil that were just coming into industrial prominence, were all factors giving the USA an internal strength that by the turn of the century had begun to have external manifestations. D. W. Brogan has observed:

> Flushed with an easy victory over an impotent Spain, and moving into a new boom period, the American people was convinced that it was living in the best of all possible republics, and that it had nothing and no one to fear.[3]

The San Franciscan financier, Holroyd, expresses a similar view in *Nostromo*, referring to the USA as 'the greatest country in the whole of God's Universe' (p. 94). Parry observes that these attitudes led to 'a rising national feeling, a growing sense of power',[4] that initially took the form of attempting to lead a coalition of the new world. Pan-American conferences were organised in 1889 and 1901, but: 'Pan-Americanism was largely the product of North American policy; it was long suspected of being an instrument of North American political and economic power.'[5] For the first time in its existence the USA was becoming feared as a rival for world power.

Growing British distrust of the USA can be seen in the popular culture of the time. One of the reading public's favourite characters was Sherlock Holmes, and the Conan Doyle story 'The Dancing Men' provides a small, but specific, instance of the incipient anti-Americanism that existed by 1905. The victim of murder in this case was a stereotypical English squire: 'a tall, ruddy, clean-shaven gentleman . . . [with] clear eyes and florid cheeks'.[6] The perpetrator of the crime is described approaching the victim's manor house as a:

> swarthy fellow, clad in a suit of grey flannel, with a Panama hat, a bristling black beard . . . flourishing a cane as he walked. He swaggered up the path as if the place belonged to him, and we heard his loud, confident peal at the bell.
>
> (p. 534)

This brash, arrogant criminal is a citizen of the USA. His English victim has, as he had earlier explained to Holmes, a long pedigree: 'my people have been at Ridling Thorpe for a matter of five centuries, and there is no better-known family in the county of Norfolk' (p. 512). The wife of the Englishman is an American, but is trying to leave that background behind her, to adopt British culture and standards. It is in an attempt to prevent her achieving such a change of identity that the bristling, aggressive, swaggering and confident denizen of 'Chicago' (p. 523) interferes in the marriage and ultimately shoots the 'simple Norfolk squire' (p. 513). The story is set, perhaps with some significance, specifically in the year after Victoria's jubilee, 1898, the year of the Spanish-American war. It was, however, published in 1905, at a time when there was a great deal of international controversy over control of the Panama Canal. This became a vital shipping link between the Atlantic and Pacific oceans, and although not running through US territory was controlled from its inception by that country. In 'The Dancing Men' the villain's hat may be seen as an oblique reference to US imperialism in Latin America: his swaggering towards a quiet Norfolk manor house as though he owned it, certainly corresponds with a British perception of American global political assumptions.

It was against this kind of background that *Nostromo* was pub-

lished in 1904, and as might be expected from Conrad there is
more than a simple anti-American allegorisation. In the novel
the USA is represented by Holroyd, who is not presented as a
swaggering bully, but more as a respectable figure of commerce
and finance. Ultimately, such a man has far more power, and
operates on a vastly wider plane, than the mere individual mur-
derer. Conrad is not a political ideologue, he does not merely take
sides. In the novel he works through analysis of political realities,
exploring understandings of processes, rather than passing a
judgement on a particular event. About ten years later, around
1914, Conrad began to read the novels of Marcel Proust, and
especially admired the Frenchman's writing because, as he subsequently recorded in 1922: 'his is a creative art absolutely based
on analysis. . . . He is a writer who has pushed analysis to the
point when it becomes creative' (CD, p. 105). To some extent
Conrad was responding to a quality, although expressed in a
different way, in his own best fiction. The characteristic is evident
in *Nostromo*.

The USA is involved in Costaguana – which Conrad told
Graham 'is meant for a S. Am^can state in general' (CL, vol. 3, p.
175), because of the silver. The 'two wandering sailors' who
become folk legends haunting the Azuera mountains because
'Their souls cannot tear themselves away from their bodies mount-
ing guard over the discovered treasure' are '*Americanos*, perhaps'
(p. 40). The silver is not just a central material in the story, it is
also a key metaphor, as Conrad pointed out almost twenty years
after the novel's publication in a letter to the Swedish critic Ernst
Bendz:

> Silver is the pivot of the moral and material events, affecting
> the lives of everybody in the tale. That this was my deliberate
> purpose there can be no doubt. I struck the first note of my
> intention in the unusual form which I gave to the title of the
> First Part, by calling it 'The Silver of the Mine', and by telling
> the story of the enchanted lives of Azuera, which, strictly speak-
> ing, has nothing to do with the rest of the novel. The word
> 'silver' occurs almost at the very beginning of the story proper,
> and I took care to introduce it in the very last paragraph, which
> would perhaps have been better without the phrase which con-
> tains that key-word.
>
> (LL, vol. 2, p. 296)

The silver is a catalyst for both individual and collective greed. The exploitation of it involves other areas of economic capitalisation too: if the silver is attractive to international capitalists, it reciprocally attracts wealth into Costaguana. Sir John confirms this in conversation with the engineer-in-chief: 'I shall see Holroyd himself on my way back through the States . . . I've ascertained that he, too, wants the railway' (p. 68). If the Americans are involved in a form of imperialism in the novel it is clearly not a simple case of pillage. Conrad is aware of some of the complexities of international capitalism. Indeed, there is no pandering here to demotic prejudices against the USA as global rivals, for Britain is engaged with the US on this occasion. Sir John is English, and the railway is British-owned; Charles Gould too, the owner of the San Tomé silver mine, has an English background and wife.

The paradox of Britain recognising the USA as a rival for world power, yet cooperating in some respects, stemmed from the attitudes of other European nations. The joint venture that occurs in *Nostromo* reflects the political reality surrounding negotiations over the construction of the Panama Canal. The historian Maldwyn Jones has shown that the idea of a central trans-American canal had been in existence for over half a century:

> There were several difficulties to overcome. One was the Clayton–Bulwer treaty of 1850, which provided that any isthmian canal constructed by either the United States or Great Britain would be jointly controlled by them and would never be fortified. That obstacle was removed by the second Hay–Pauncefote Treaty of 1901. The Boer War had exposed Britain's isolation in Europe and she was eager for American friendship. So she agreed to exclusive American control of the canal and, by implication, to its fortification.[7]

Some official connivance with the USA, for these reasons, co-existed with a good deal of suspicion of an upstart nation. Doyle's fiction partly refracts the latter, *Nostromo* explores – although within Conrad's own deep distrust of US politics – the complexity and the apparent contradictions inherent in British metaphoric schizophrenia.

A slightly broader outline of the history of the USA provides the framework in which these factors and tensions came into existence. In 1823 the fifth president of the United States, James

Monroe, established a policy that became known as the Monroe Doctrine:

> The American continents . . . are henceforth not to be considered as subjects for future colonization by any European powers. . . . The political system of the allied [European] powers is essentially different . . . from that of America. . . . We should consider any attempt on their part to extend their system to any portion of this hemisphere as dangerous to our peace and safety.[8]

One of the limitations of the doctrine was that much of central and south America was still under European colonial domination or influence. The US itself had at that time been free of Britain for less than half a century. It was a form of political muscle-flexing that had little practical substance at the time, but as the USA grew in strength the Monroe Doctrine became an increasingly important principle of foreign policy.

That strength can be seen in, for instance, the fact that the population of the USA in 1810 was a little over 7 million, a hundred years later, by 1910, it was over 92 million and still rising dramatically. By the turn of the century industry was expanding enormously, overtaking European production capacities. Jones, for example, notes that in 1900 US: 'steel output . . . [was] more than the combined production of the two next most powerful industrial nations, Great Britain and Germany'.[9] When Conrad makes the railway a central feature of the development of Costaguana it is not by a casual, or coincidental, choice. Railways were the great symbol of scientific, technological and industrial progress in Europe during the nineteenth century, observed in such diverse novels as the English Dickens' *Dombey and Son*, the French Balzac's *Cousin Bette* and the Russian Tolstoy's *Anna Karenina*. The phenomenon was particularly important in the USA too:

> The distinctive characteristics of the new industrialization were most fully typified by the railroads. They were the key to post-Civil War economic growth and constituted the most important single economic interest in the country.[10]

In their painting at the end of the Civil War in 1865 the artists Currier and Ives portrayed the theme 'Westward the Course of

Empire' by depicting a train on a set of railway lines that run across a plain into the far horizon. That kind of sentiment is reflected in *Nostromo* when the railway is described as a 'progressive and patriotic undertaking', the very words in which: 'Ribiera, the Dictator of Costaguana, had described the National Central Railway in his great speech at the turning of the first sod' (p. 61). The scene is a satire on the portentousness of politicians and merchant bankers on such occasions. Capitalism is presented in the novel as dressing up its own interests so that they appear to be those of the common good. Sir John, for example:

> worked always on a great scale; there was a loan to the State, and a project for systematic colonization of the Occidental Province, involved in one vast scheme with the construction of the National Central Railway. Good faith, order, honesty, peace, were badly wanted for this great development of material interests.
>
> (p. 125)

Political stability is needed primarily in order to protect the investment of foreign capital. The virtues enumerated in this passage, in the form of free indirect speech from Sir John, are given an ironic tone by the context. 'Good faith, order, honesty, peace' are juxtaposed with 'material interests'; the bringing together of moral virtues and the pursuit of profit in the 'one vast scheme' creates an ambivalence in which lies a criticism of the practice of political economy. This is emphasised when the Goulds see the local people enjoying a native festival:

> from where the crowd was massed thickly about a huge temporary erection, like a circus tent of wood with a conical grass roof, came the resonant twanging of harp strings, the sharp ping of guitars, with the grave drumming throb of an Indian gombo pulsating steadily through the shrill choruses of the dancers.
>
> (p. 130)

The scene illustrates how the ordinary folk of the country are happy enjoying *im*material interests – music, song and dance. The description is immediately followed by Charles' sombre remark to his wife: 'All this piece of land belongs now to the Railway Com-

pany. There will be no more popular feasts held here' (p. 130).
The material interests being served by the railway are not those
of the common people, who must sacrifice their celebration days
and places for the progressive and patriotic undertaking. It is clear
from the juxtaposition of collective pleasure – related to a vibrating
sense of life, and a use of common land – and the possession of
land for private commercial use, that the faith, honesty and order
benefit the materialism of the Railway Company capitalists rather
than the mass of the people of Costaguana.

During the period in which *Nostromo* was written the economic
strength of the United States was translated into crypto-colonial
expansion through the twin forces of naval power and financial
investment. The former ensured political order, the latter led to
economic, and therefore political, control of the dominated
country's government. The US built its first battleship in 1890, and
throughout the decade expanded its naval capacity. The successful
campaign against Spain in 1898 appeared to validate this policy,
and Senator Albert Beveridge expressed the mood of the country:

> Fate has written our policy . . . the trade of the world must and
> can be ours. . . . We will cover the ocean with our merchant
> marine. We will build a navy to the measure of our greatness.
> Great colonies, governing themselves, flying our flag, and trad-
> ing with us, will grow about our ports of trade. . . . American
> law, American order, American civilisation and the American
> flag will plant themselves on shores hitherto bloody and
> benighted by those agents of God henceforth made beautiful
> and bright.[11]

The language carries a sense of inevitability. The USA is perceived
as the agent of Fate and God; American institutions will not be
imperially taken to the new colonies, but 'will plant themselves'
for the benefit of those people who resemble the 'benighted heathen' of Kipling's *Fuzzy-Wuzzy*. Holroyd reflects much of this feeling in *Nostromo* when he explains to Charles Gould:

> We shall be giving the word for everything: industry, trade,
> law, journalism, art, politics, and religion, from Cape Horn clear
> over to Smith's Sound, and beyond, too, if anything worth
> taking hold of turns up at the North Pole. And then we shall . . .
> take in hand the outlying islands and continents of the earth.

We shall run the world's business whether the world likes it or not. The world can't help it – and neither can we.

(pp. 94–5)

The imperatives here, the reiterated 'shall', build up a sense of an irrevocable process that culminates in the events happening whether anyone likes them or not. Even the North Americans themselves are caught up inevitably, without choice, as the agents of the Divine Fate that Beveridge described. In 1904 Holroyd's speech may have seemed slightly exaggerated in its ambitions for US world influence; in the event it provides an example of Conrad's prophetic political vision.

The US navy was the strong arm of its foreign policy, enabling a number of interventions in central and south American politics as unstable friendly governments needed support, or hostile ones were opposed by rebels inside a nation's boundaries. Captain Mitchell retails a significant detail that refracts this reality within the political verisimilitude of *Nostromo*:

there was 'in this very harbour' an international naval demonstration, which put an end to the Costaguana-Sulaco War . . . the United States cruiser, *Powhattan*, was the first to salute the Occidental flag.

(p. 405)

The Monroe Doctrine of 1823 had been an essentially defensive philosophy, but in 1904, the year of *Nostromo*'s publication, President Theodore Roosevelt added the more aggressive Roosevelt Corollary:

Chronic wrongdoing or an impotence which results in a general loosening of the ties of civilized society, may . . . ultimately require intervention by some civilized nation, and in the Western Hemisphere the adherence of the United States to the Monroe Doctrine may force the United States, however reluctantly, in flagrant cases of such wrong doing or impotence, to the exercise of an international police power.[12]

To some extent this was a rationalisation of attitudes already held, and actions taken, but it was also a statement of future policy. In *Nostromo* Holroyd insists to Gould that 'Europe must be kept out of this continent' (p. 96), by which he means physically, for he is not against utilising international finance. Holroyd echoes Roosevelt's sentiments, though in a curter language. Roosevelt's diction again has a tone of irrevocability – the US may be forced to act, by implication almost against its own better nature. Unless the unstable governments of Central and South America sort out their own problems the USA will inevitably be forced into the role of reluctant moral policeman. Doubtless there was some truly altruistic thinking behind this official statement, but the kind of feature Conrad held in suspicion was the lack of definition: 'wrong doing', 'impotence' and 'civilized' are all complex concepts – and no writer was more aware of the ambiguities of language than Conrad – which may be given different meanings in diverse circumstances.

International negotiations over a trans-oceanic canal illustrate a specific example of the rationalisation, and the potential ambiguities. Once Britain had made concessions to the US in the Hay–Pauncefote treaty it was decided, mainly for economic reasons, to site the canal in Panama, through the central American isthmus, which was territory controlled by the South American country of Colombia. A rebellion of Panamanians against Colombian imperialism resulted in the formation of the state of Panama, which was under US influence, or control, depending on interpretations of history. The role of the USA in the rebellion and subsequent settlement as a whole has been interpreted differently by different historians. Brogan has argued, for instance, that the Panamanian rebellion 'conveniently' broke out at the right time, and that 'American complicity in the convenient revolution was never proved'.[13] Jones, although fundamentally agreeing, stresses the active nature of the American strategy:

> Roosevelt did not actually foment the insurrection but let it be known that, if one occurred, he would be sympathetic . . . he ordered the cruiser *Nashville* to prevent Colombian forces from suppressing the revolt.[14]

A difficulty of interpreting history is illustrated by the analysis of the same events by Jenny Pearce:

> The Americans encouraged and helped finance a Panamanian independence movement and the new Panamanian government immediately signed a treaty with the United States . . . [the US]

assumed the maintenance of public order in the country. It sent troops into Panama in 1908, 1912 and 1918.[15]

This interpretation obviously sees the USA in a much more Machiavellian light, deliberately replacing an unfriendly government with one that was independent in theory, but dependent in economic and military fact.

One of the reasons for constructing the canal was to enable warships, as well as merchant vessels, to have easy passage to both the east and west coasts of Central and South America, an access the US had every intention of controlling. The US warship that turns up in Sulaco harbour clearly had its parallel in political reality. As Conrad suggests in *Nostromo* the US did have widespread financial investments in the region. He was certainly aware of the Panamanian situation, and US involvement in it, writing to Graham on Boxing Day 1903 expressing his disapproval: 'What do you think of the Yankee Conquistadores in Panama? Pretty, isn't it?' (CL, vol. 3, p. 102). The ironic, satiric tone is partly expressed by the use of the term Yankee, and its linking with the Conquistadores, the original Spanish ruthless conquerors, suppressors and exploiters of the region. It is not flattering to Roosevelt and the US politicians. Conrad was not specifically a political writer, but his analytical approach always leads the novels into an exploration of facets that are beneath the surface of events and apparent motives. His method is often elusive, rather than directly polemical, and therefore sometimes difficult to appreciate. The name of the fictional cruiser *Powhattan*, for example, is a reference to the early seventeenth century Chief Powhatan, an Indian who helped the original English settlers in America to survive, and whose daughter was the first Indian woman to marry an English settler. The hopes and ideals of those early days were soon lost in the bloody wars that were caused by the European urge for conquest, and the Indians' consequent defence of their livelihood. The implication is that any idealism in Roosevelt's foreign policy may well also fall into the reality of conquest and greed.

Captain Mitchell proudly tells visitors that 'the United States, sir, were the first great power to recognize the Occidental Republic' (p. 403), but he does not understand that the political relationship rests on the financial links between the San Tomé silver mine and the bankers, especially Holroyd, of San Francisco. Charles Gould, who begins the adventure as an idealist, who believes that from 'material interests. . . . A better justice will come' (p. 100), becomes the connection between capital and politics through his ownership of the silver mine: 'with a credit opened by the Third Southern Bank (located next door but one to the Holroyd Building), the Ribierist party in Costaguana took a practical shape under the eye of the administrator of the San Tomé mine' (p. 145). It is a more civilised form of colonialism than that occurring in Africa, but is ultimately, within the struture and tone of the novel, no less exploitive.

Conrad's fiction accurately mirrors the politico-economic reality of the time and region. In 1897 the United States direct investment in Central American countries was just over 11 million US dollars, by 1908 that amount had almost trebled, and at the outbreak of the Great War had reached virtually 77 million dollars.[16] To many observers Roosevelt's Corollary seemed designed to provide military protection for that financial investment. In Conrad's sceptical 1904 novel, as in the earlier *Heart of Darkness*, the experience of colonisation is corrupting to all parties. The silver in *Nostromo* is enough 'to make everybody in the world miserable', an 'accursed treasure' (pp. 458–9). It is a philosophical rather than a mere political corruption, fundamental to human life rather than a simple matter of ideological organisation.

The depth of Conrad's perception is easily recognised when seen in the context of more popular literature. He was not the only writer to see the literary possibilities for adventure in South America. A fairly typical demotic example appeared in a 1903 magazine. 'Called to Arms!' by Paul Herring was subtitled 'A Stirring Story of the Venezulan Blockade', and although not based on a specific historical episode it partly refracts, by representing the tensions in different circumstances, an earlier dispute between Britain and the USA over the Venezulan border with British Guiana – a South American part of the British Empire. The US government claimed that the Monroe Doctrine had been breached, and consequently: 'American belligerence almost provoked war with Great Britain . . . as Anglophobia swept the country, there were urgent demands for war.'[17] That catastrophe was averted by diplomatic international arbitration, but the fact that it almost occurred illustrates the nervousness of the situation.

'Called To Arms!' is a popular adventure story about a character who is: 'attached to the British Consulate, an officer of the Empire who guarded our interests in this wild-cat Republic of Venezula'

(*Union Jack*, XVIII, no. 459). The very title of the magazine is
indicative of its attitudes. It will not be portraying universal corruption, only the moral and political degeneracy of foreigners,
against which the Empire stands as a bastion of civilisation. The
'wild-cat' facet of South American republics is depicted by 'the
mad dreams of lawless and reckless revolutionists'. The President
is not unlike Costaguana's barbarous Guzman Bento, under whom
Monygham suffered, or the ambitious Monterist Sotillo who tor-
tured and murdered Hirsch. The Venezulan leader is: 'President
Castro, the adventurer, who had made himself President of Venezula by ingenious bluff and the rifles of swaggering soldiers'
(ibid.). But this character is not presented within the kind of
political analysis that occurs in *Nostromo*. Both stories utilise the
popular stereotype of South American republics' lawlessness and
recklessness, but where Conrad argues that is a reflection of a
profound human weakness Herring shows that it is merely the
result of foreign inadequacies. Since in the actual historical dispute
the USA supported an implicitly corrupt Venezulan government
the story implicates the US in lawless and reckless attitudes. In
this case the President's name is clearly Venezulan Spanish, and
therefore the European power is also involved in the political
thuggery.

The plot of 'Called To Arms!' is based on a triangular struggle
between the reckless Venezuelan government, Britain and Germany. President Castro of the story, as befits a swaggering South
American dictator, had: 'run up a bill of £3,000,000, mostly owing
to Germany'. In the ensuing adventurous conflict: 'Great Britain
wishes to protect her flag, that is all. The Germans want their debt
paid' (ibid.). However reasonable the Germans' desires are in
theory, in the context of the story they are a manifestation of
greed. The Germans happily persecute the innocent in their pursuit of the guilty; the Britons attempt to see fair play. Germany is
motivated by greed, Britain by honour – and those characteristics
are symbolised in the quotation above by the money and the flag,
which of course is the Union Jack after which the magazine is
named. All this is a popular, and populist, refraction of the fact
that Germany had become Britain's main European rival.

Germany had become a fully unified state only as recently as
1871, following victory in the 1870–1 Franco-Prussian war.
Wilhelm I became Emperor of the second *Reich* and Bismarck his
Chancellor, both holding aspirations of a great German Empire.

In pursuing these ambitions Germany became internationally disliked and distrusted. Bismarck's death in 1898 caused John Jay Chapman to write his 'Lines on the Death of Bismarck', part of which reads:

> Unity! Out of chaos, petty courts,
> Princelings and potentates – thrift, jealousy,
> Weakness, distemper, cowardice, distrust,
> To build a nation: the material –
> The fibres to be twisted – human strands.
> One race, one tongue, one instinct. Unify
> By banking prejudice, and, gaining power,
> Attract by vanity, compel by fear.
> Arm to the teeth: your friends will love you more,
> And we have much to do for Germany.
> Organized hatred, *that* is unity.[18]

Obituaries are usually complimentary to their subjects, so the title in this case emphasises the criticism of the former chancellor of Germany. The fact that the poet was American, and the unalleviated bitterness of this extract, indicate that it was not only Britons who hated the new Germany: a nation perceived to be based on economic and military power, and hatred of all non-Germans. This is also reflected in popular literature by Conan Doyle's story 'The Second Stain' in which Sherlock Holmes deals with 'the most important international case he has ever been called upon to handle' (p. 650). The story does not identify a particular country, and the secret agent in the plot lives in Paris, but there are indications that the nation Britain might 'be involved in a great war with' (p. 653) is Germany. The case concerns a stolen letter which 'is from a certain foreign potentate who has been ruffled by some recent colonial developments' (ibid.), suggesting Kaiser Wilhelm II, Emperor of the second *Reich*. Potentate was a term used of him, and his predecessor Wilhelm I, as Chapman's poem illustrates.

Doyle is perhaps also drawing on his readers' awareness of a relatively recent incident, which enabled him to encode the German Emperor into the story without risking an international furore by actually naming him. Throughout the two final decades of the nineteenth century there was increasing antagonism between new British settlers in southern Africa and the older established Boers (cf. chapter 4 above), and in 1896 a form of a

very small private army led by Dr Leander Jameson invaded the
Boer state of Transvaal. Although the British government repudi-
ated Jameson's Raid, as the incident was dubbed, the President of
Transvaal used it to create a maximum of international, diplomatic
embarrassment for London. The situation was worsened by
German intervention in the form of a telegram of congratulation
from Wilhelm II to the Transvaal President on his defeat of the
raiding party. News of this caused high dudgeon in Britain. Under
the headline 'Serious Action of the German Emperor', *The Times*
commented that the telegram:

> assumes . . . the character of a State document of the highest
> importance. . . . It is not surprising, therefore, that the Trans-
> vaal Government already draws from such powerful encourage-
> ment the conclusion that it can go a step further and denounce
> all its existing treaties with Great Britain . . . the occasion has
> been gladly seized 'to subject England to the well-deserved
> humiliation of a bitterly severe lesson'.
>
> (*The Times*, 4 January 1896)

The quotation within the newspaper article is a reference to a
German source, expressing the anti-English attitudes prevalent in
Germany. Although the episode did not have immediate reper-
cussions, when the Boer War broke out in 1899 the Kaiser's encour-
agement of Boer aspirations was perceived as a contributory factor.
'The Second Stain' was written shortly after that conflict and the
nature of the stolen letter in the story has connotations of the
German telegram. The fictitious 'Prime Minister' tells Holmes:

> the document in question is of such immense importance that
> [it might] . . . lead to European complications of the utmost
> moment. It is not too much to say that peace or war may hang
> upon the issue.
>
> (p. 651)

The early Edwardian reader could easily decode this as a reference
to general German belligerence, and the information that the
'document' – also *The Times*' term for the telegram – is:

> couched in so unfortunate a manner, and certain phrases in it
> are of so provocative a character, that its publication would

undoubtably lead to a most dangerous state of feeling in this country

(p. 653)

relates it clearly to the kind of expression quoted in *The Times'* article: 'the well-deserved humiliation of a bitterly severe lesson'. Germany was seen as ambitious, arrogant, bullying.

British attitudes were encapsulated by the new Poet Laureate's first publication, a few days after the Kaiser's telegram, and clearly a response to it. Alfred Austin's poem was entitled simply 'Jameson's Ride' and, significantly, published in *The Times*. The fictional narrative voice is that of Jameson:

> Wrong! Is it wrong? Well may be:
>   But I'm going, boys, all the same.
>   . . .
> I suppose we were wrong, were madmen,
>   Still I think at the Judgement Day,
> When God sifts the good from the bad men
>   There'll be something more to say . . .
>
> (*The Times*, 11 January 1896)

This is not an unrepresentative extract. The tone of acknowledged guilt is much less strong than that of defiance. God will support the raiders against the politicians, and the feeling of public school bravado carried here in the appeal to the judgement of the 'boys', as well as that of God, is emphasised in the spirit of adventure:

> So we forded and galloped forward,
>   As hard as our beasts could pelt,
> First eastward, then trending norward,
>   Right over the rolling veldt . . .
>
> (ibid.)

It is not the greatest poem ever written, but published a week after the article on the Kaiser's telegram it captured, and expressed, a populist mood of the repudiation of German interference. That fundamental unrepentance towards the Germans is perhaps more important than the original dispute with the Boers.

The national loathing of Germany sprang partly from well-founded fear. The Germans were seriously challenging Britain in both economic and naval strength, and although in the mid–1890s

Britain held its position as the world's leading power, it was not secure and therefore could not relax. Britain had been the power-house of the industrial revolution, but the historian David Thomson has argued that new materials and consequent technologies – such as oil and petrol, and the development of the internal combustion engine – changed the situation, and that by 1900: 'Germany led the world in the chemical and electrical industries . . . [by 1910] Germany and the United States were fast overtaking Britain's lead in total industrial production.'[19] In global terms this meant competition for raw materials in such areas of the world as Africa, and new markets for exports in slightly more wealthy regions such as South America. It is appropriate that in *Nostromo* Hirsch, 'the hide merchant' (p. 238) speaks German so naturally that when he is frightened he uses that language unconsciously. When Sotillo threatens Hirsch with torture the latter: 'repeated his entreaties and protestations of loyalty and innocence again in German, obstinately, because he was not aware in what language he was speaking' (p.284). A merchant in South America would speak German naturally because it was a major language of trade and commerce. It is implicitly understood in 'Called To Arms!' that German exports to the Venezulans are the reason they owe so much money to Germany.

World trade was conducted by sea, and therefore sea routes were vital for commerce, and also for military movement. The British had an enormous merchant navy, but in order to guarantee its freedom of the oceans a powerful fighting navy was necessary too. The USA had since 1890 expanded its fleet, with striking results, and Germany was following a similar policy as, for example, J. P. T. Bury has shown:

> The second German Navy Bill, introduced in January 1900, with its principle that 'Germany must have a battle fleet so strong that even the adversary possessed of the greatest sea power will attack it only with grave risk to herself', continued the potentially challenging policy inaugurated by Admiral von Tirpitz, who had become Minister of Marine in 1897.[20]

The quotation from a German source that Bury uses is obviously aimed at Britain. One British attitude to that kind of verbal ferocity was undaunted jauntiness, as illustrated by John Davidson's poem of the period, 'Song for the Twenty-Fourth of May':

The character and strength of us
  Who conquer everywhere,
We sing the English of it thus,
  And bid the world beware: –
  We bid the world beware
The perfect heart and will,
  That dare the utmost men may dare
And follow freedom still.
    Sea-room, land-room, ours, my masters, ours,
    Hand in hand with destiny, and first among
    the Powers!
    Our boasted Ocean Empire, sirs, we boast of
    it again,
    Our Monarch, and our Rulers, and our Women,
    and our Men![21]

The repetition of 'beware', 'dare', 'our', 'ours' and the boasting betrays a too strident tone, one of underlying anxiety rather than the self-confidence asserted on the surface. Here the British conquer by right of destiny, and this is close to Henry Norman's thoughts that were quoted earlier: working through assertion rather than a rationale. The title of the whole poem from which this extract is taken also reveals the centrality of imperialism to British strength and prestige. The 24th May had been Queen Victoria's birthday, and became designated at the end of her reign as Empire Day – a day on which specifically to celebrate the glories of the British Empire.

In 1904 a new first sea lord, Sir John Fisher, was appointed to regenerate British naval power. Ensor has summarised the situation as he sees it, from a historian's viewpoint, developing in 1904–5:

Fisher perceived plainly, as a professional man, that Tirpitz's fleet was built to fight the British; and, given the intense hatred and jealousy of England felt by the German classes engaged in shipping and foreign trade and their rapidly increasing influence over German policy, he could not believe that the plan would be easily diverted from proceeding to its conclusion.[22]

One relatively quick practical result of this philosophy was the introduction of a new, very much larger, battleship: the *Dread-*

nought class. The longer term effect was a British-German arma-
ments race, and a series of international confrontations culminat-
ing in the outbreak of the Great War in 1914.

In this atmosphere Conrad, especially given his personal,
Polish, dislike of Germany, might well have included villainous
Germans in *Nostromo*. The British reading public would not on the
whole have objected, and probably even expected such characters.
Artistic restraint, vision and honesty, however, prevented Conrad
from making the easy, simplistic point. The main German character in his fiction is Schomberg – Kurtz has a German name, but
he specifically represents all of Europe – who has a small role in
the early texts *Lord Jim* and *Falk*, but does not achieve major status
until *Victory*, the novel Conrad finished writing two months before
the outbreak of the Great War. Schomberg is a bullying, inter-
fering, stupid, egoistic liar, and in his 'Note to the First Edition'
of *Victory* Conrad stresses what he sees as the character's endemic
Germanic qualities:

> his deeper passions come into play, and thus his grotesque
> psychology is completed . . . I don't pretend to say this is the
> entire Teutonic psychology; but it is indubitably the psychology
> of a Teuton . . . far from being the incarnation of recent ani-
> mosities, he is the creature of my old, deep-seated and, as it
> were, impartial conviction.
>
> (pp. 45–6)

Conrad's conviction that the essence of the Teutonic character is
malevolent, grotesque to the truly civilised sensibility, was certainly deep-seated, and not merely related to the European disintegration of 1914; but whether or not a Pole could be impartial
about either Germany or Russia is a moot point. In *Victory* the
relationship between Schomberg being German and untrust-
worthy is emphasised: 'a big, manly, bearded creature of the
Teutonic persuasion, with an ungovernable tongue which surely
must have worked on a pivot. . . . He was a noxious ass'
(pp.69–70). The description 'creature of the Teutonic persuasion'
rather than the more straightforward term, German, draws attention to itself through free indirect speech. It is the kind of pompous
rhetoric Schomberg might use of himself, making reference to an
ancient race rather than a new, perhaps upstart, nation. He is
described too as 'malicious' and 'Satanic' (p. 131), which were

popularly perceived as Germanic characteristics. Narrational generalisations are also made, as when Schomberg complains that Heyst does not spend much money in the hotel: 'for which Schomberg wished him nothing less than a long and tormented existence. Observe the Teutonic sense of proportion and nice forgiving temper' (p. 75). The narrator's sardonic tone here is closer to popular literature than Conrad's most subtle style, but in terms of the period it is by no means vicious.

By 1914 the vast majority of British readers would have accepted a German villain without question. Even as early as 1897 Kipling had looked forward to a European conflagration in which the foreigners would be put in their place by the armed forces of the British Empire. In his story 'Slaves of the Lamp' the schoolboy character Stalky plays a trick on an unpopular teacher and a local tradesman to set them against one another, and divert attention from himself and his miscreant friends. As a young army officer in India Stalky plays the same trick in order to divert attention from his troop, and set two indigenous tribes against one another. The story concludes with the other characters discussing the events:

'Practically he duplicated that trick over again. There's nobody like Stalky.'

'That's just where you make the mistake,' I said. 'India's full of Stalkies – Cheltenham and Haileybury and Marlborough chaps – that we don't know anything about, and the surprises will begin when there is a really big row on.'

'Who will be surprised?' . . .

'The other side . . . Just imagine Stalky let loose on the sunny side of Europe with a sufficiency of Sikhs and a reasonable prospect of loot. Consider it quietly.'

(*Cosmopolis*, May 1897)[23]

It is interesting that although Kipling made his reputation partly as a demotic writer, one who sang the praises of the otherwise unsung common soldier, the emphasis in this story is strongly on the role and importance of the public schools and the officer class in the coming war. In this context the Indian imperial adventure is seen as a training ground for the real conflict, in which the loyalty of some of the colonised people will be to their colonisers, providing there is 'loot' to be had. Stalky's original trick in a sense taught the unpopular schoolmaster a lesson, it served him right, and the same moralising attitude is taken to 'the other side'. The European enemy will be punished for being so nasty – by implication and contemporary encoding, for threatening the prosperity, power and prestige of Britain.

Conrad's work is never that simplistic, and *Victory* repeats the fundamental pattern of the earlier texts. Complexities are introduced that made the novels difficult reading by denying the expectations of the readers. Although Schomberg, for instance, is the catalyst of the evil that overtakes Heyst and Lena, the actual agents of it are not Teutons. Pedro was 'picked . . . up in Colombia' (p. 136), South America; Ricardo Martin is in some ways English, though his 'ambiguous name' (p. 142) perhaps suggests part Spanish or Italian connections. The leader of this rather international trio – 'plain Mr Jones . . . a gentleman' (p. 139) – is certainly English, and ultimately Jones is the most evil character in the novel. Moreover, although Lena is English she is an accidental victim of the final bloodshed; the intended target, Heyst, is Swedish. This pattern does not suggest that Conrad had overall fallen into simple-minded prejudice. He was still concerned with a world perspective.

In *Nostromo* Costaguana is depicted as an international community. There are South American Indians, European Costaguanans and European immigrants. The Goulds are a mixture of the last two categories; Giorgio Viola is 'a Genoese'; and Nostromo an Italian 'a countryman of his' (p. 48); Teresa Viola 'was an Italian, too, a native of Spezzia' (p. 49); Decoud 'imagined himself Parisian' (p. 152) and is 'the adopted child of Western Europe' (p. 155). The Avellanos family are one of the representatives of the older, original colonists, the 'Spanish-American' (p. 150) community, although in fact Antonia Avellanos had a somewhat cosmopolitan background, 'born in Europe and educated partly in England' (p. 143); and the politicians and power-seekers have Hispanic names: Bento, Montero, Sotillo, Ribiera. The novel reflects an international reality in South America, rather than utilising a set of simple stereotypes that might please a xenophobic British readership. If the British were largely concerned with their rivalry with the USA and the other major European powers, and the vast majority of writers were mainly interested in stressing the differences between Britain and the rest of the world, Conrad was interested in exploring the connections and similarities the imperial nations shared. He believed there were differences too, but most other writers dealt only with them; Conrad was the main voice of global perspective in literature in his time.

The complexity is signalled in the character of Holroyd. Despite being the international capitalist who heralds the new, economic, form of colonialism that Conrad prophetically sees as replacing sheer military conquest, and which is perceived as perhaps even more damaging, Holroyd is not presented as an innately evil character. Although he is ironically described as 'the millionaire endower of churches' (p. 94) that activity is not interpreted as simple hypocrisy, for one of the most astute characters in the novel accepts it as harmlessly amusing: 'his lavish patronage . . . of church-building amused Mrs Gould' (p. 97). Despite being the great US financier, Holroyd, like Kurtz, is also associated with the whole of Europe:

> his massive profile was the profile of a Caesar's head on an old Roman coin. But his parentage was German and Scotch and English, with remote strains of Danish and French blood, giving him the temperament of a Puritan and an insatiable imagination of conquest.
>
> (p. 94)

It is that 'insatiable imagination of conquest' that motivates Holroyd to perceive himself, and the United States – as Roosevelt did – as an agent of fate, sent to conquer and organise the world for its own benefit. It is a misplaced energy, for the two redeemed characters in the novel both exercise the energy of personal renunciation. Monygham is considered 'scornful and soured', yet: 'The truth of his nature consisted in his capacity for passion and in the sensitiveness of his temperament' (p. 430). These characteristics are manifested in his love for Mrs Gould, and his restraint of it. Mrs Gould herself renounces the power of her husband's wealth: 'I, too, have hated the idea of that silver from the bottom of my heart' (p. 460). Her renunciation is of the demands of egoism in order to direct her energy altruistically, for she is 'full of endurance and compassion' (p. 458). A few individuals are able to evade the fate of materialism; political states, it seems, cannot.

Conrad is not so much interested in the mere exercise of political power, whether military or economic, by nations on the world stage, as in exploring the nature of power itself, in both nations and individuals. He used existing international tensions and concerns, but eschewed easy nationalistic points. Conrad was certainly a writer of his time, aware of contemporary issues, but always taking a universal perspective. His geographic perception was global rather than national, and his involvement with the crises of the day informed by a time perspective that allowed him to see that particular empires come and go, but that the imperialist urge is ever-present. For Conrad the concepts and actualities of power and conquest were more than the result of immediate rivalries, they were manifestations of ageless struggles and conflicts.

6

The Domestic Dynamic

In addition to the hostilities that existed between nations every country also experienced internal tensions. The paradox inherent in Britain's foreign policy and attitudes – pride in strength and expansionism existing simultaneously with an insecurity bred of fear – was mirrored on the domestic, social front. There has been a cultural tendency to romanticise the period in which Conrad began writing up to the Great War. The historian Anthony Wood has summarised, and commented on, that propensity:

> To those who looked back on it with nostalgia . . . Edwardian England seemed like some splendid sunset, a time of limitless security, peace, and pleasure.
>
> Security, however, lay only on the surface. The ultimate crash of this world in 1914 was not a sudden catastrophe. . . . New social forces and growing discord had already begun to undermine it long before that date.[1]

The processes of history often operate through a dialectic: in this case, security and threat. The former was as real as the latter, and if one of the forces becomes submerged, or ignored, in the retelling of events historical falsification occurs. Conrad's life as an Englishman, until the Great War, did see increasing wealth in Britain, greater educational provision, an expansion of trade unionism, and ultimately the beginning of welfare services in such ways as the introduction of Labour Exchanges and an old age pension. But against those aspects he saw a widening of social gaps between classes, greater inequality in the distribution of wealth, proliferation of trivial newspapers, and an increase in social disorder. Conrad's novels do not necessarily incorporate all these factors overtly, but they do refract his society's concerns. Conrad's fiction, as that of any great writer, was produced around the tensions of his time.

In Britain these arose partly from the economic and social dynamism created by over a hundred years of industrial revolution.

Governments often thought that changes were occurring too quickly, whilst diverse groups within the society felt they were happening too slowly, or even not at all. Some organisations, such as trade unions, operated generally within the legal system, although the laws were changed from time to time, sometimes ambiguously, and it was not always certain whether specific actions were within the law or not. The subsequent formation of the Labour Party was another constitutional manifestation of the urge towards greater social equality and political democracy. Other groups deliberately acted against the law because they perceived that to be the most effective form of publicity and protest. The Irish Home Rule movement and the Women's Suffrage supporters were two such collections of activists. For the society in which Conrad was writing these pressures dated from the mid–1860s, and had become central political and intellectual concerns by the late-Victorian/Edwardian period. Conrad's fiction does not simply mirror his society's concerns, and he very rarely deals directly with topical events, but the themes are refracted in the fiction, and the social dynamic of the period informs, in particular, *The Secret Agent*.

The gradual expansion of democracy was partly linked in the late-Victorian/Edwardian mind with an increasing breakdown in social order. The build up to the Second Reform Act of 1867 had been characterised by mass public meetings. A demonstration in favour of franchise reform in the summer of 1866, for instance, ended in considerable disorder and damage to property, including the uprooting of almost a mile of iron railings that surrounded London's Hyde Park. This caused a general distrust among the ruling classes of wider political democracy, and a concomitant fear of mob rule. These deep suspicions were not allayed by subsequent extensions of voting rights, and the re-erection of the railings revealed the insecurity of those inside them.

When similar disturbances occurred twenty years later there were immediate references back to the Hyde Park riots. In 1886 the Tory-dominated Fair Trade League called a political meeting in London's Trafalgar Square in favour of higher trade tariffs, and the Social Democratic Federation – which had been formed as the Democratic Federation five years earlier as the first large specifically Marxist-orientated political body in Britain – organised a counter-demonstration against high unemployment. There was some violence on the latter group's march to Hyde Park through the wealthy area of Pall Mall, and after the meeting a great deal more. *The Times* editorial of the following day reflected both fear and indignation:

> there occurred the most alarming and destructive riot that has taken place in London for many years . . . the most destructive that has taken place within living memory. The destruction of the Hyde Park railings in 1866 was in some respects a more threatening affair, as being the work of a bigger mob; but that, unlike the present business, was not accompanied by the whole-sale destruction of property and the looting of shops . . . a mob some thousands strong . . . smashing windows, wrecking private carriages, and robbing jewellers' and other shops, ulti-mately unchecked by the police. . . . An ugly feature of the affair was the attacks upon private carriages . . . broughams containing ladies were invaded, the windows broken, the paint maliciously spoilt, the doors half wrenched off, and sometimes the occupants robbed of their valuables.
>
> (*The Times*, 9 February 1886)

Some of these claims were subsequently challenged as exagger-ations, but there is no doubt that the events did have a profound impact on social attitudes for a long time. This editorial's reference to the 1866 railings episode illustrates just how long memories were in cases of mass violence. There was, however, a more alarming aspect to this 1886 incident: its apparent political motiv-ation. The actual facts are less important in understanding the mood of the times than the contemporary perception of events. The image of the unemployed working classes wrenching doors off private horse-drawn carriages, then robbing and threatening respectable higher class ladies is a powerful one of lawlessness, perhaps evoking the French Revolution in the late-Victorian mind. In conjunction with the attacks earlier in the day on the gentle-men's clubs in Pall Mall the violence was seen to be directed specifically against wealth, against the whole social order and hierarchy. This continued to be a fear even after any rational grounds for it had passed. The powerlessness of the police to protect individuals and private property under unusual circum-stances remained a spectre throughout the period. On the surface law and order reigned, but underneath there was an awareness of the volcanic threat of mob rule – a favourite phrase of the day

– and of the tenuousness of the security the privileged classes appeared to enjoy.

Early in *The Secret Agent*, when Verloc is on his way to the Embassy in his role of *agent provocateur*, he looks across Hyde Park:

> Through the park railings these glances beheld men and women riding in the Row, couples cantering past harmoniously, others advancing sedately at a walk, loitering groups of three or four, solitary horse-men looking unsociable . . . Carriages went bowling by, mostly two-horse broughams, with here and there a victoria . . . a peculiarly London sun – against which nothing could be said except that it looked bloodshot – glorified all this by its stare. It hung at a moderate elevation above Hyde Park Corner with an air of punctual and benign vigilance.
>
> (p. 51)

This was a typical scene of the initial reader's day. The time of the novel's setting is mainly somewhat vague. The actual explosion known as the Greenwich Bomb Outrage, on which the novel is generally accepted to have been based, occurred in 1894. The textual evidence, however, puts the action earlier than that. Winnie's wedding ring is engraved '24 June 1879' (p. 267) and she speaks of having been 'seven years a good wife' (p. 244), bringing the date, perhaps significantly, to 1886 – although the novel's concerns are certainly those of 1907. All this requires very careful reading and the deliberate ambiguity allows Conrad to achieve both a historical perspective and immediacy, effects which are emphasised by the novel's curious narrative time structure. In this scene the respectable, peaceful surface of society is presented: the privileged classes enjoying their public leisure. Contemporary readers could have recognised the verisimilic description without difficulty. The tone, however, undercuts the complacency. The comments on the sun are apparently facetious, but 'bloodshot' and 'stare' are also words carrying a hint of menace, especially in relation to Hyde Park, the venue of mass meetings and scenes of past mob violence. Bloodshot eyes and hard stares may be related to unemployed, perhaps even drunken, labourers who cannot be trusted. Yet the sun also glorifies the picture and is 'moderate', 'punctual', 'benign' and vigilant – all attributes of the stereotypical police constable. There is a tension between the conflicting characteristics – a method not uncommon in Conrad's work – of the sun.

Ultimately the thing is merely itself, the attributes are being read in by a perceiver. A central irony here is that the perceiver, the character who projects himself as the potential protector of privilege, is not a homely constable, for they have been proved inadequate against the mob. This observer of the upper classes is a devious secret agent who deals in mild pornography: 'photographs of more or less undressed dancing girls . . . books, with titles hinting at impropriety' (p. 45). Conrad is juxtaposing two fundamental Edwardian concerns: the facade of respectability, security and stability with the corrupt foundations on which it is built. The tension in the society sprang partly from its implicit, although infrequently articulated, consciousness of this truth that the novel expresses. Beneath the casual social and political confidence there existed a nervousness about the maintenance of order.

The relationship of facade and foundation is brought out further in a passage that moves subtly from diegesis to free indirect speech, from description of Verloc to an expression of his thoughts:

> He surveyed through the park railings the evidences of the town's opulence and luxury with an approving eye. All these people had to be protected. Protection is the first necessity of opulence and luxury. They had to be protected; and their horses, carriages, houses, servants had to be protected; and the source of their wealth had to be protected in the heart of the city and the heart of the country; the whole social order favourable to their hygenic idleness had to be protected against the shallow enviousness of unhygenic labour.
>
> (pp. 51–2)

This recalls the mood expressed in *The Times* editorial quoted above: wealth has to be free to take its leisure behind the railings in Hyde Park, and if necessary it must be protected from the jealous working classes. But Conrad is satirising such attitudes, and the satire is articulated by the structure and tone of the passage. These are the views of Verloc, whose employment as an *agent provocateur* means that he is professionally involved in deceit, and who sees protection as an easy form of employment, for he had at an early age 'embraced indolence' (p. 52). Verloc is literally, and metaphorically, the dubious outsider looking in, 'through the

park railings'. The idle rich are dependent on that socially excluded
pornographer.

The ironic and satiric tone is also expressed linguistically. It is
not mere wealth that Verloc looks at, but 'opulence and luxury',
ownership that goes beyond inanimate property to include horses
and, implicitly in the context, servants. At the time of the novel's
publication Conrad wrote to Graham: 'I would like to go for . . .
the millionaire. Then you would see the venom flow. But it's too
big a job' (CL, vol. 3, p. 491). The venom here flows through such
phrases as 'the whole social order favourable to their hygenic
idleness'. Hygenic is used both metaphorically as moral idleness
– a concept impossible to attain in Conrad's terms – and physically,
because at a time when most houses did not have bathrooms the
rich could afford to be clean and often thought of the poor as
dirty, whether they were or not. George Orwell retrospectively
wrote of a pervasive Edwardian attitude of the privileged classes:
'It is summed up in four frightful words . . . which were bandied
about quite freely in my childhood. The words were: *The lower
classes smell.*'[2] Orwell's memory confirms the validity of Conrad's
contemporary comment. In the extract the cleanness of the
wealthy is juxtaposed with their concept of the enviousness of
labour, which they see as both literally and metaphorically dirty;
and shallow because labour does not understand the complexities
of the unequal division of wealth. The free indirect speech is not
just the narrative discourse being projected in the terms Verloc
would have used, but even further, in the language the wealthy
themselves would have used to justify their privilege. By presenting those attitudes in this context – through the approving mind
of the disreputable and dishonest Verloc – Conrad is able to show
their shallowness.

Although the period of recurrent mass violent demonstrations
occurred while Conrad was still a seaman the ethos lingered on:
The Times' 1886 reference to an event of 1866 indicating the length
of social and political memories. Also Conrad had first hand
reports of the most famous, or infamous, of the subsequent demonstrations: Bloody Sunday of 13 November 1887. The social
Democratic Federation had frequently held meetings in Trafalgar
Square, some of which had led to confrontations with the police.
In that November the SDF organised another mass meeting and
the government vetoed the venue. When the organisers determined to attempt to hold the meeting anyway it became an issue

of freedom of speech and assembly, attracting a great many more people than the original cause would have. The government decided to defend the Square, and under the headline 'The Defence of Trafalgar-Square', *The Times* described its version of events:

> Around Trafalgar-square over 2,000 constables were massed. A cordon had been drawn along its four sides. . . . The thick black line [of constables] encircled the square completely . . . the groups of people around Trafalgar-square became large and numerous, and the mounted police commenced to show considerable activity. . . . Soon after 4 o'clock things were at their height . . . and a desperate and concerted attempt was made to break through the police into the centre. About 200 men headed it is said, by Mr Cunninghame Graham, M.P., rushed across from the corner of the Strand . . . and went full tilt at the police, who were drawn up four deep . . . there was a hand-to-hand tussle and fists were to be seen. . . . Some of the attacking party had sticks. . . . Reinforcements of police were hurried up and staves were drawn . . .
>
> (*The Times*, 14 November 1887)

It was clearly a pitched battle, although without the modern weapons of war. Nevertheless, there were over a hundred casualties and two deaths as a consequence. It was not a day that was forgotten, and partly inspired William Morris to write his great socialist utopian novel *News From Nowhere*. Graham who, paradoxically, eventually became one of Conrad's closest friends, served six weeks in Pentonville Prison for his involvement in the proceedings. Conrad was well aware of both the fear of social discord and its origins.

The fear of mob rule lingered on despite having no real rational basis by the time of *The Secret Agent*. The undermining of the threat's reality had occurred mainly because of economic changes. The period of numerous mass political meetings, with occasional violence, had been one of economic depression. By the middle of the Edwardian period trade and productivity, despite the competition from other countries, was well into a cycle of expansion and the working classes in general felt themselves *relatively* well off. Mass radical political activity had, on the whole, moved off the streets and into support for constitutional organisations such as the Labour Party and trade unions. In the 1906 general election the Labour Party had its greatest success so far in its short history, winning 53 seats. Membership of trade unions increased consistently during the period, resulting in more than a doubling of numbers between 1896 and 1912.

The relative affluence and economic strength of the working classes created its own problems for those who were concerned with the maintenance of the social order, so that the fear of its disintegration remained although the menace had changed its nature. The spectre became the hooligan, a word coined towards the end of Victoria's reign to describe the lawless youth who refused to accept the conventions and behaviour of respectable society. At the turn of the century *The Times* felt the issue important enough for an editorial:

> Every week some incident shows that certain parts of London are more perilous for the peaceable wayfarer than remote districts of Calabria, Sicily, or Greece, once the classic haunts of brigands. Every day in some police-court are narrated the details of acts of brutality of which the sufferers are unoffending men and women . . . systematic lawlessness of groups of lads and young men who are the terror of the neighbourhood in which they dwell. . . . Our 'Hooligans' go from bad to worse.
>
> (*The Times*, 30 October 1900)

The source of this admonition reveals how seriously the establishment took the challenge to law and order. The fact that *The Times* editorial used the word 'Hooligans' illustrates how pervasive the phenomenon had become, yet the quotation marks indicate that it was still a comparatively new term. The whole tone of the passage – the adverse comparison with Sicily, and so on, the insistence on the innocence of the victims, the assertion that the lawlessness is systematic, the use of words such as 'brutality' and 'terror' – illustrates the depth of the establishment's fear of social anarchy.

The fact that the hooligans had no political interest or motivation made no difference: they threatened the social fabric as a whole. The issue did not disappear or lessen, and eight years later Baden-Powell, hero of the Boers' siege of Mafeking, linked physical and moral degeneration, suggesting that the newly founded Boy Scout movement could help overcome the problem in the long run:

Recent reports on the deterioration of our race ought to act as a warning to be taken in time before it goes too far . . . much PREVENTABLE deterioration is being allowed to creep in among the rising generation . . . [there is] a great amount of illness resulting from self-abuse and venereal disease, as well as from drink. . . . The training of Boy Scouts would be therefore incomplete if it did not endeavour to help in remedying these evils.[3]

This amounted to a quasi-military solution on the equation healthy bodies make healthy minds, which create respectable citizens. In the context respectable becomes synonymous with acquiescent, so that the social fabric is not endangered.

The problem arose partly because increased relative affluence gave the working-class young male greater independence, and the economic boom meant there was plenty of menial work. It was the unskilled, uneducated, uninterested youth who was able to exploit the circumstances, shiftlessly moving from job to job, without roots or social responsibility, always able to pick up money from somewhere. As the sociologist Geoffrey Pearson has commented:

[There was] increasing demand in the job market for boys to do all sorts of simple work in the sphere of communications and transport: van boys, errand boys, messenger boys, boys to answer telephones, boys to hold horses' heads and other kinds of trivial but essential work . . . respectable England required various other, if less essential, fetch-and-carry amenities: hotel pages, uniformed door-openers, billiard-cue chalkers, boy golf caddies.[4]

The social paradox was that such a subclass was necessary, but was necessarily subversive in that it had no lasting stake in the social hierarchy. Living on the edge of society, these lads could treat rules, laws and proprieties with impunity.

They were of the kind of 'very young men' (p. 45) who slipped into Verloc's shop to purchase:

some object looking obviously and scandalously not worth the money which passed in the transaction: a small cardboard box with apparently nothing inside, for instance, or one of those carefully closed yellow flimsy envelopes, or a soiled volume in paper covers with a promising title.

(p. 46)

This passage is not simply part of the atmosphere of seediness that pervades the London of the novel, although it does contribute to that; more importantly it links Verloc's secret role as an agent of stability – as he sees himself, and for which the shop is his cover – with one of the groups in society that were perceived as a threat to social order. Ironically Verloc is serving the needs of the members of two opposing groups: those that need protecting, and those perceived as the potential subverters of the social fabric, with their desire for illicit pleasure.

One of Conrad's concerns in the novel is the interconnectedness of the diverse elements in modern society. The societal framework is conceived less in terms of a pyramidical hierarchy – although differences in class, wealth and power obviously exist – more as a web. The rich and the poor, the peaceful and the violent, the sane and the insane, the just and the unjust, the clean and the dirty, cannot simply be separated out from one another. Razumov discovers that in *Under Western Eyes*. Having attempted, successfully as he imagines, to cut himself off from the mainstream of society he suddenly becomes involved when the assassin Haldin appears in his room:

> The police would very soon find out all about him. They would set about discovering a conspiracy. Everybody Haldin had ever known would be in the greatest danger. . . . Razumov, of course, felt the safety of his lonely existence to be permanently endangered.

(pp. 68–9)

Razumov is trapped by the network of relationships it is impossible for even a deliberately 'lonely existence' to avoid. The police 'would set about discovering a conspiracy' whether or not one actually existed. The act of one man puts everybody 'in the greatest danger'. Russian and English societies, whatever their political differences, are alike in that interlocking characteristic. No individual, or group, is ultimately isolated from any other.

In London the railings behind which the opulent exercise their privilege were once torn up by a mob, and although the barrier has been replaced it is not a definitive defence. The means of protection, the railings themselves, need protecting. It is an implicit argument any Edwardian reader could appreciate.

Stevie sees the social and moral connections and their overlapping. His obsessive drawing of circles manifests this almost inarticulable perception:

> the innocent Stevie, seated very good and quiet at a deal table, drawing circles, circles, circles; innumberable circles, concentric, eccentric; a coruscating whirl of circles that by their tangled multitude of repeated curves, uniformity of form, and confusion of intersecting lines suggested a rendering of cosmic chaos, the symbolism of a mad art attempting the inconceivable.
>
> (p. 76)

The people inside the circle of the Hyde Park railings are linked to other people who are excluded from the particular circle because the various, 'innumberable circles' of the social cosmos 'whirl', tangle and intersect. The simple-minded, 'innocent' Stevie perceives that there is a relationship but can express the concept only symbolically. The confused moral chaos of society drives him almost to madness because he is unable to make the effective connections. Winnie explains that after her brother had read a story in an anarchist tract about cruelty in the German army:

> I couldn't do anything with Stevie that afternoon. The story was enough, too, to make one's blood boil. But what's the use of printing things like that? We aren't German slaves here, thank God. It's not our business – is it? . . . I had to take the carving knife from the boy. He was stamping and shouting and sobbing. He can't stand the notion of any cruelty.
>
> (p. 87)

Stevie's reaction is that cruelty must have a perpetrator, and can therefore be ended by personal retribution. Winnie, however, like Razumov, is content with comparative isolation. In this case although the story makes her angry too England isn't Germany, and Winnie has no wider responsibility than for Stevie – which is one she takes extremely seriously.

While Winnie would like to stay inside the circle of her own family Stevie realises that it intersects with others. In political terms the perimeters, the lines, of the circles, their boundaries, are occupied by the police – that is the body whose function it is to keep the circles separate. As *The Times* reported in 'The Defence of Trafalgar-square' a 'thick line [of constables, 'four deep'] encircled it'. It was, however, a role in which success could not always be guaranteed. In the period in which Conrad's earlier novels were written and published the police appeared not only to be losing the battle against the hooligan in some areas, but had incurred a more general unpopularity. Some contemporary reports contradict the later nostalgic view of the period of friendly and respected constables, and a peaceful rule of law, which is perhaps based on projections of late Victorian/Edwardian wish fulfilment. The Commissioner of the Metropolitan Police regularly reported that approximately a quarter of the capital's police were assaulted each year; while respectable journals and newspapers deplored the state of proletarian rebelliousness. There were, for instance, an increasing number of incidents in which the police were attacked by crowds when making an arrest:

> There are two cases in the papers this morning of assaults on policemen. The really disgraceful part of these cases, however, is the sympathy which the crowds showed to the prisoners. The constable in certain districts is apparently looked upon as the common enemy whom it is right to kick and beat whenever that can be done with safety.
>
> (*Pall Mall Gazette*, 19 February 1901)

The police's function in the social dynamic was in question. Many people remembered that the discontented population of impoverished east London was capable of demonstrating its feelings in the wealthy districts of west London, and that the railings of Hyde Park were not an adequate protection. If that was true of the largest city it was certainly also applicable in the smaller towns where rich and poor lived in closer proximity.

The ambiguity of the police's role, as both guardians of the oppressed, and potential oppressors themselves when called on to defend opulence and luxury, is reflected in *The Secret Agent*. Stevie's anger is roused by the social cruelty of the poverty of the cabman and his horse, but on this occasion there appears to be no one specifically to blame: 'It was a bad world. Bad! Bad! . . . Somebody, he felt, ought to be punished for it – punished with

great severity' (pp. 168–9). After some agitated thought Stevie
reaches a logical conclusion about the connection between moral
wrongs and punishment:

> Like the rest of mankind, perplexed by the mystery of the uni-
> verse, he had his moments of consoling trust in the organized
> powers of the earth.
> 'Police,' he suggested, confidently.
> 'The police aren't for that,' observed Mrs Verloc . . .
> 'Not for that?' he mumbled, resigned but surprised. 'Not for
> that?' He had formed for himself an ideal conception of the
> metropolitan police as a sort of benevolent institution for the
> suppression of evil. The notion of benevolence especially was
> very closely associated with his sense of the power of the men
> in blue. He had liked all police constables tenderly, with a
> guileless trustfulness. And he was pained. He was irritated, too,
> by a suspicion of duplicity in the members of the force.
>
> (p. 169)

In this passage the simple-minded Stevie expresses a basic Edwardian ambivalence. The 'organized powers' of punishment, of law
enforcement, are not necessarily concerned with morality. Law
and justice may be theoretically equated, but they are not always
so in practice. Stevie's innocent 'ideal conception' of the police's
function is one that many Edwardian readers might actually have
subscribed to, or like to have. But the educated initial reader is
put into a dilemma because in the novel the ideal view is held by
a simpleton. Either the reader must come to an uncomfortable
accommodation with a character who draws circles as a hobby,
and is too immature to look after himself, or accept the inadequacy
of the conventional – privileged-class – view. The ambivalence for
the open-minded reader concerns the ideal conception of society,
and its appointed guardians, as essentially just and moral; and
the reality of the knowledge of injustice and potential police
oppression. This is the 'duplicity' that Stevie cannot quite grasp,
and which pains him. It may also have been painful for the reader
to admit. Winnie summarises the position in answer to Stevie's
demands to know the police's real social function:

> 'Don't you know what the police are for, Stevie? They are there

so that them as have nothing shouldn't take anything away from them who have.'

'What?' he asked at once, anxiously. 'Not even if they were hungry?'

'Not if they were ever so,' said Mrs Verloc.

(p. 170)

This is why the *Pall Mall Gazette*'s honest constable is considered 'the common enemy' in some areas of poverty and hunger. It is the reason 'opulence and luxury' need 'to be protected against the shallow enviousness of unhygenic labour' (p. 52). Although these issues are not dealt with as a specific contemporary polemical debate, they are matters at the heart of the period's social and political thinking. The ironic tone raises them in a manner that is designed to challenge the reader's preconceptions about the nature of society, and its inter-relationships of wealth and poverty.

Conrad dealt with the crucial issues of his time, but he is not that kind of social critic who argues that if the privileged classes are morally wrong their opponents must necessarily be right. He eschewed that type of simplistic dichotomy, partly on the grounds that all social systems are, and must be, unfair. In one of Conrad's 1904 essays the French novelist Anatole France is praised because he: 'perceives that political institutions, whether contrived by the wisdom of the few or the ignorance of the many, are incapable of securing the happiness of mankind' (NL, p. 33). The old systems, both autocratic and relatively democratic, have clearly failed to prevent deprivation and misery. The most powerful of the new, 'Socialism' is 'too materialistic' and is characterised by: 'the stupidity of the dogma and the unlovely form of the ideal' (ibid., pp. 37–8). It is a satiric condemnation of Verloc that he is even less worthy than the practitioners of this political philosophy: 'He was too lazy even for a mere demagogue, for a workman orator, for a leader of labour' (p. 52). Conrad's scepticism emanated, not entirely from his innate conservatism, but from a distrust of language. The 'demagogue', the 'orator', can too easily move people and therefore can move them for his, or her, own benefit rather than for their collective good.

Whilst Conrad despised political movements he had great compassion for deprived and oppressed individuals. He admired Anatole France's Socialistic 'profound and unalterable compassion' (NL, p. 33), and embraced the feeling if not the political commitment. Stevie has great compassion, and demands that quality from the reader, but he is also a victim of the power of language: 'the mere names of certain transgressions filled him with horror. He had been always easily impressed by speeches' (p. 170). It is to Stevie's compassion that Verloc appeals with impressive words, leading not to the liberation of mankind but to the violent annihilation of the boy, 'blown to small bits' (p. 196).

Explosions are at the heart of the plots of both *The Secret Agent* and *Under Western Eyes*. Again they refract central concerns of the period. Although Edwardian England itself was free of explosions there was, as in the case of mass demonstrations, a memory of Victorian outrages; and an awareness of continued political violence on the continent of Europe – with a consequent fear that it might spread across the channel.

In Britain the memory was linked to the Irish Home Rule movement. Political independence for Ireland was a very old demand, but in the 1860s it took a new direction with the activities of the group commonly known as Fenians. Some Fenians believed that peaceful and constitutional arguments and methods were not efficacious, and in 1867 a number of illegal episodes occurred. Under the headline 'Atrocious Fenian Outrage' *The Times* reported a disturbing development in London:

an attempt was made to obtain the release of the Fenian prisoners Burke and Casey by blowing up with gunpowder the outer wall of the House of Detention at Clerkenwell. . . . Upwards of 40 innocent people – men, women, and children of all ages . . . were injured. . . . The explosion . . . was heard for miles round . . . it blew down houses and shattered windows of others in all directions.

(*The Times*, 14 December 1867)

The numbers injured were later reported as much higher, and twelve people subsequently died as a result of the explosion. The tone of indignation is evident in the diction: 'innocent people', 'women, and children of all ages' emphasises their vulnerability. Effects of the explosion rippled through London 'for miles . . . in all directions'. Even the innocent miles away are affected by this kind of act. Stevie might well be 'occupied by drawing circles . . . with great industry' (p. 50).

As with the mass demonstrations the Clerkenwell event sank

deep into the collective political memory, to resurface when a series of explosions in 1884 caused immense alarm:

> dynamite outrages . . . at Scotland-yard . . . [and] St. James's-square . . . the explosions appear to have been similar to those that occurred at the Government offices in Whitehall and at Victoria Railway Station. A black bag of dynamite, with a fuse attached, has fallen into the hands of the police. This, it is stated, was placed against the Nelson Monument in Trafalgar-square.
>
> (*The Times*, 31 May 1884)

One reason for the consternation was the targets chosen by the terrorists. The bomb at Scotland Yard did comparatively little damage, mainly blowing up a toilet, but the audacity of the attack was something new. The other targets were very public places and could have killed or injured many people; and the toppling of Nelson's Column would have been a symbolic gesture of enormous impact. Another significant factor in that campaign was the move from gunpowder to dynamite. The latter was a relatively new invention, a compound of nitro-glycerine that was very much more powerful than its forerunner. Dynamite was, from this time, to become the main explosives material used by revolutionists. It had, however, greater volatility than gunpowder and many anarchists were blown up by their own bombs. The Professor's obsessive, quasi-scientific, quest for the 'perfect detonator' (pp. 93ff) reflects this development.

By the Edwardian period the militant element of the Irish Home Rule movement had stopped causing explosions in England, and British anarchists had generally been more active in theorising about violence than committing it. The Irish and the anarchists were quite distinct groups with virtually no common ground, but their propensity to discuss the use of terrorism as a valid political activity tended to compound them in the public mind. The last major political explosion in England before the writing of *The Secret Agent* was the one Conrad is thought to have based the novel around, the Greenwich Park blowing up of an anarchist by his own bomb. The specific background to this has been extremely well detailed by Norman Sherry and Ian Watt in their respective articles republished in the Macmillan Casebook series.[5] It is, however, clearly more than a novel about an explosion. It deals with a profound anxiety regarding the fragile stability of Edwardian society. There remained a fear of the possibility of the recurrence of terrorism, or its importation from the continent, which informed the attitudes of many people during the period, and kept the issue one of contemporary concern.

Even whilst Conrad was writing *The Secret Agent*, for instance, there was an incident in Madrid that created widespread interest in Britain. On 31 May 1906 Princess Ena, who was related to the British royal family, married King Alfonso of Spain, and the event attracted an anarchist assassination attempt. In Britain it was seen as an indirect attack on the royal family, with *The Times* headlining its report 'Bomb Thrown at the Royal Carriage: Serious Loss of Life' (1 June 1906). The following day's report concentrated on the general carnage and the police response:

> The bomb caused terrible destruction . . . 20 were killed and 60 wounded . . . 800 Anarchists of whom the international police possess records [were arrested]. . . . An Englishman named Robert Hamilton has been detained . . . the public attempted to lynch him.
>
> (*The Times*, 2 June 1906)

The combination of a royal connection, the large number of anarchists alleged to be involved, and the apparent presence among them of an Englishman, all created anticipation of a widespread plot. It is possible that the number of anarchists was exaggerated, and ultimately, in any event, no network of conspirators was uncovered. Even Hamilton was released with an official admission that he had been arrested in error. However, all of that transpired later, and the immediate excitement revealed a raw nerve in Britain.

The self-styled anarchists in *The Secret Agent*, apart from the Professor, are not a threat because they are simply talkers, but unlike the dangerous demagogues they do not speak with effect. It is their presence that constitutes the danger, for that allows the foreign embassy to use Verloc to organise the terrorist outrage. The explosion that kills Stevie occurs because Vladimir wants to discourage the British government from allowing anarchists to seek refuge:

It would be much more to the point to have them all under

lock and key. England must be brought into line. The imbecile bourgeoisie of this country make themselves the accomplices of the very people whose aim is to drive them out of their houses to starve in ditches. . . . I suppose you agree that the middle classes are stupid? . . . What they want just now is a jolly good scare.

(p. 64)

Vladimir's speech certainly expresses a view prevalent amongst many of the middling classes who did not think of themselves as stupid. There was an increasing concern over the number of émigrés in the country, which at that time had no rigid emigration laws and was known to be relatively liberal.The two most famous Russian revolutionaries, for instance, Lenin and Trotsky, were both known to have visited London to attend political conferences in the early years of the century.

The novel published in 1907 embraces these contemporary concerns, but is also prophetic in that during December 1910 the activities of some London Russian anarchists led to the event called the Siege of Sidney Street. An almost full-scale military operation was conducted against three Russian exiles, one of whom – thought by some commentators to be Stalin – escaped. The siege was personally supervised by the Home Secretary, Winston Churchill, who used the emotions roused in order to pass, in the following year, an Act restricting emigration. The tone of parliamentary debate is illustrated by the speech with which A. E. Goulding opened the second reading of the Aliens Bill in the House of Commons:

this country was shocked, indeed, the world was amazed, at the siege which took place in the very heart of London . . . alien desperadoes held at bay for six hours a thousand of our police and military armed with a machine gun, magazine rifles and revolvers. At the end of the siege the house was wrecked, and the charred remains of two aliens were found. This result was achieved at considerable expense and loss of lives of two of our brave police and the wounding of others . . . for too long England, and London more particularly, has been . . . the sink of foreign refuse and also for foreign criminality.

(*Hansard*, 28 April 1911)

The fictional Vladimir would have been happy had he been able to persuade Verloc to achieve as great an outrage, with such political consequences. Extremism, whatever its source, leads to repression, a political truth the Polish Conrad knew well. It is Conrad's profound understanding of the very nature of politics that makes the novel not merely contemporary, but prophetic.

Another concern of the period related to the role of the police in these cases. In 1910 the politician Churchill overruled the professional judgement of his senior policemen, an almost unprecedented action that manifested the growing distrust between politicians and police. This is foreshadowed in *The Secret Agent* in the interview between the Assistant Commissioner and Sir Ethelred, 'the great Personage' with 'princely ancestors' (p. 143), who complains that the police do not keep the politicians fully informed: 'your idea of assurances . . . seems to consist mainly in making the Secretary of State look a fool' (p. 142). This was a topical issue that linked Edwardian events with those of the 1880s, and Fenian terrorism with anarchism in the public mind. In 1906 Sir Robert Anderson, a former police commissioner, published his memories of terrorists, secret agents and his own relations with his political head:

> [secrecy] was always a sore point with Sir William Harcourt, 'Anderson's idea of secrecy is not to tell the Secretary of State,' he once said to one of his colleagues, fixing his eyes on me as he spoke. And it was quite true. The first Fenian who ever gave me information was murdered on his arrival in New York. I had given his name to no one but Lord Mayo; and he assured me that he had mentioned it only to the Lord Lieutenant . . . at the Viceregal Lodge. But there happened to be a servant behind the screen. . . . Never again would I give an informant's name to any one, and no man who afterwards gave me information was ever betrayed.[6]

In his 1920 Author's Note to *The Secret Agent* (p. 40) Conrad drew attention to Anderson's book as a partial source for the novel. All sides involved used secret and double agents, and infiltration of governments into potentially revolutionary sects was common. The historian Walter Laquer has observed the paradox: 'a considerable proportion of the terrorist journals of the 1880s and 1890s were in fact founded or maintained by secret police money.'[7] The extract from Anderson's memoirs, especially taken in the context of later developments, confirms that the conflict between anarchists, police and politicians in the novel represents a working out of past, present and future relationships in Conrad's own society. Organisations and institutions, as well as individuals, had to come to terms with new and changing circumstances. *The Secret Agent* reworks those issues.

Another strong impetus for social and political change came from organised women's groups. The origin of these too occurred in the 1860s. The Kensington Society was formed by a group of women in 1865, and one of their first acts was to petition an MP for limited female suffrage. The issue continued to gain support throughout Victoria's reign, a National Union of Women's Suffrage Societies being founded in 1897, for example. Unfortunately successive governments did not subscribe to the idea of female franchise. In 1903 the Women's Social and Political Union was formed, and that eventually led to the increasing militancy shown by suffragettes, or suffragists, during the period.

Although he never dealt directly with the issue of the franchise Conrad was aware of the female dynamic, and the questioning of the traditional, and largely passive, roles of women. There was continuous agitation for women's suffrage whilst Conrad was writing *The Secret Agent*, but the prolonged campaign of violence did not fully begin until 1909, two years after the novel's publication. A mass march to Parliament in the summer of that year led to confrontation with 3000 policemen. The ensuing fracas was reported under such newspaper headlines as '116 arrests', 'Women's Raid on Parliament', 'A Horse Stabbed' (*Daily Mail*, 30 June 1909). The description 'Raid' was used partly because a great many windows were also broken as a conscious act of political destruction. The report of the horse stabbing reflected the generally hostile view of the press, providing an emotional example of suffragette callousness. In fact the horse was attacked by a male sympathiser of the women.

The June demonstration was followed in September by an assault on the prime minister, Herbert Asquith. In the subsequent court case the new mood of violent militancy was confirmed, one of the defendants being quoted as defiantly stating: 'I had the opportunity, had I chosen to take it, of seriously injuring Mr Asquith. I am now sorry I did not do it' (*The Times*, 23 September 1909). Many of the women were given prison sentences as a result of these disturbances, and hunger strikes became another major weapon in the war of attrition, to which the authorities at first replied by forced feeding. That was continuing in 1913 when the Secretary of State for the Home Department declared in Parliament:

> Fifteen suffragist prisoners are now in prison . . . three are being fed by tube, and one by cup, and one, who was received into prison last night, is refusing to take her food. Seven are in the prison infirmary . . . suffragist prisoners received into prison since the beginning of the year . . . number fifty five.
>
> (*Hansard*, 6 March 1913)

But this did not stop the violence. For instance, the women's suffrage societies had embarked on a campaign of posting incendiary letters, and Herbert Samuel's report in the House of Commons became typical:

> I am sorry to say that five postmen . . . suffered painful injuries from flames caused by chemicals which had been placed in thin glass tubes among the correspondence in letter-boxes.
>
> (*Hansard*, 10 February 1913)

The escalation of violence was ended only by the outbreak of the Great War in the following year.

Although the specific issue was the franchise the enormous publicity and concern generated led also to wider matters. Edwardian society's whole perception of women began to be radically changed, and this broader aspect is reflected in Conrad's fiction even before the dramatic events outlined above had taken place. His earliest work is little concerned with female characters. In *Nostromo*, however, Antonia Avellanos emerges as a politically aware woman, although still one who takes a relatively passive role. Natalia Haldin is to some extent an extension of this, being described by the narrator of *Under Western Eyes* as 'the perfection of collected independence' (p. 342). Flora in *Chance*, Lena in *Victory* and Catherine in *The Rover* are all later female characters who aspire to an active role – but as individuals, not within any political organisation.

Winnie, in *The Secret Agent*, with her elderly widowed mother to care for, is in a classic Victorian/Edwardian situation, trapped into a social fate over which she has no apparent control. It is intensified because she also accepts responsibility for her simple-minded brother. The obvious way of accomplishing her aims, in the social context, is marriage to someone who will accept Winnie's responsibilities. In the mind of Winnie's mother Verloc is: 'ideal . . . [he] inspired her with a sense of absolute safety. Her daughter's future was obviously assured, and even as to her son Stevie she need have no anxiety' (p. 48). Winnie is placed in a position of subservience in order to fulfil her dutiful role. Even worse, as she later explains to the bewildered Ossipon, in order to get into that position of submission Winnie has had to forego the possibility of a happy marriage:

> 'I was a young girl. I was done up. I was tired. I had two people depending on what I could do, and it did seem as if I couldn't do any more. Two people – mother and the boy. He was much more mine than mother's. I sat up nights and nights with him on my lap, all alone upstairs, when I wasn't more than eight years old myself. . . . There was a young fellow –'
>
> The memory of the early romance with the young butcher survived, tenacious, like the image of a glimpsed ideal . . .
>
> 'That was the man I loved . . . his father threatened to kick him out of the business if he made such a fool of himself as to marry a girl with a crippled mother and a crazy idiot of a boy on her hands. But he would hang about me, till one evening I found the courage to slam the door in his face. I had to do it. I loved him dearly.'
>
> (pp. 243–4)

The passage makes clear that Winnie's fate is to sacrifice everything for the sake of others. She became a quasi-mother whilst still a child, and in a sense becomes a metaphoric mother and protector to both her own mother and her brother. A woman of Winnie's social class could do that at the time only through a marriage of convenience. Yet she ultimately murders Verloc, her apparent benefactor. It is an irrevocable declaration of individual independence: an act of assertive energy. As she conceives the action of a 'free woman' her features take on 'a new and startling expression' (p. 233). When Winnie frees herself of her social fate she does not act as a mere individual:

Into that plunging blow . . . Mrs Verloc had put all the inheritance of her immemorial and obscure descent, the simple ferocity of the age of caverns, and the unbalanced nervous fury of
the age of bar-rooms.

(p. 234)

Winnie's energy springs partly from her being an archetype of
female repression.

Thematically Winnie does not murder her husband because he
has caused the death of Stevie. Winnie's final image of Stevie's
'decapitated head' leads her to temporarily regain the control of
her own destiny that she had lost:

her wits, no longer disconnected, were working under the control of her will. . . . She had become a free woman with a
perfection of freedom which left her nothing to desire and absolutely nothing to do, since Stevie's urgent claim on her devotion
no longer existed.

(pp. 233–5)

It is, paradoxically, the final acceptance of her brother's death that
gives Winnie freedom to act. The murder is her first action as a
free woman, not simply as revenge for Stevie's demise but because
there is no longer any emotional or social constraint on her. It is
precisely because she has 'nothing to desire . . . nothing to do'
that Winnie is able to take an irrevocable step.

That state of being, however, cannot last in an organised society,
and it elides into fear: 'Mrs Verloc was afraid of the gallows . . .
the last argument of men's justice' (p. 237). It is that fear – specifically of 'men's justice' – which, ironically, propels her into the
power of another man. When Ossipon also betrays her trust
Winnie can take the only free action left to end 'the blind, mad
fear of the gallows' (p. 267).

The character of Winnie projects an image of very many ordinary
Victorian and Edwardian women caught in a socio-economic trap:
of dependency on a husband. In an unhappy marriage, one in
which the husband treated the woman badly, divorce was
extremely difficult in law and often impossible to contemplate
financially. The woman had to live with the problem. The movement for suffrage, and the violent direction it eventually took, was

a manifestation of female frustration at a gender-determined lack of independence.

Winnie's husband behaves decently towards her up to the point of causing Stevie's death, but that selfish carelessness can be seen as a metaphor for any cruelty. Her response of murder is extreme, but again it is metaphorically, and prophetically, an expression of that frustration which caused a suffragette to effectively commit suicide by throwing herself in front of the king's horse during the Derby, six years after the publication of the novel, as a gesture for female emancipation. In his 1920 Author's Note Conrad wrote: 'I have never had any doubt of the reality of Mrs Verloc's story' (p. 41). He did not mean the simple verisimilitude of the plot, which was of course fictional, but the essential veracity of a woman's life that 'doesn't stand much looking into' (ibid). Whatever view our own time has come to of that period it was, at least in part, unjust, repressive and consequently violent.

Conrad was completely aware of the social dynamic through which he lived, and although not writing in an overtly topical manner nevertheless dealt with the issues of the period. They were in many ways uneasy times, with confidence and prosperity being undermined by uncertainty and doubts about the future. These had a physical basis in the political and social dynamic, but there were also metaphysical concerns that caused philosophic anxieties.

7

The Entropic Labyrinth

The roots of most of the anxieties, physical and metaphysical, of the late-Victorian/Edwardian period can be found earlier in the nineteenth century. Many of the philosophic concerns of Conrad's writing lifetime emanated from the advance of science, and the popular interest which it gradually created. It is not insignificant that three of the most widely read novelists of Conrad's period all dealt, in some way, with the ideas of science, in a demotic form. Robert Louis Stevenson's *The Strange Case of Dr Jekyll and Mr Hyde* explored duality of personality in relation to scientific chemistry; Conan Doyle's character Sherlock Holmes was a gentleman scientist who used the deductive method to solve mysteries; H. G. Wells wrote a number of novels in what has subsequently been categorised as the science fiction genre.

Although Conrad was not a scientist he was interested in the concepts. He admired Wells sufficiently, for instance, to dedicate *The Secret Agent* to him. Conrad engaged in his own form of science fiction too, in his collaboration with Ford Madox Ford, on *The Inheritors*, written whilst *Lord Jim* was also in process of composition. Some of the philosophic extensions of current scientific interests are worked through the novel Conrad completed immediately before the outbreak of the Great War fatally ruptured the course of history: the ironically titled *Victory*.

In so far as any generalisation has validity, and acknowledging the limitations of its truth, it might be said that at the beginning of the nineteenth century the state of both religion and science in Europe was *comparatively* static. There were diverse forms of Christianity, but all based on an acceptance of Biblical theology: one God had created all matter, and retained ultimate control over it. Interpretations of the detail varied but fundamental doubt of belief on a large scale was excluded. The perception of the physical universe was basically that outlined by Newton and Galileo over a hundred years earlier. While it was accepted that not everything in physics and astronomy was known, it was believed, however, that all things could be understood, and would be in time: a lack of actual knowledge was admitted, but no profound epistemological doubt existed.

During the course of the nineteenth century both these pillars of belief were profoundly challenged. The scientists who caused the intellectual challenge did not necessarily want to attack religion, it was rather that over a period of time earlier concepts of God's creation and those of science were seen as incompatible. Some examples of the widespread build up of interest in evolutionary theory can be seen in the French naturalist Lamarck's *Philosophie zoologique*, published in 1809, the British geologist Sir Charles Lyell's 1830 *Principles of Geology*, and an 1844 popular summary of the ideas in Robert Chambers' *Vestiges of the Natural History of Creation*. The catalystic, and possibly cataclysmic, work of evolutionary theory was Charles Darwin's *Origin of Species*, published in 1859. The implications of Darwinist Natural Selection reverberated throughout Conrad's lifetime. The ideas of the discrete creation of Adam and Eve, and of a gradual ascent of mankind from lower species were difficult to reconcile.

Other work threw doubt on the state of traditionally accepted knowledge and perceptions. European mathematicians such as Gauss, Lobachevski and Bolyai began to present theories that refuted the accepted classical axioms of Euclid. The permeation of this into British scientific thought is illustrated by the fact that in 1869 J. J. Sylvester expounded an understanding of the new mathematics to the British Association for the Advancement of Science:

> mathematical analysis is constantly invoking the aid of new principles, new ideas, and new methods, not capable of being defined by any form of words, but springing direct from the inherent powers and activity of the human mind, and from continually renewed introspection of that inner world.
>
> (*The Times*, 20 August 1869)

The speech emphasised that the whole subject was being radically reperceived, rather than simply being developed along traditional lines. Sylvester also insisted on the creative nature of mathematics, which draws on 'inherent powers' and the 'inner world' – it is not an isolated cerebral activity, but an expression of the introspective, contemplative world, with its forms not in common language but in that of mathematics: symbols.

The theories were disseminated into the broader intellectual world by such journals as the *Fortnightly Review*, which many years later also published some of Conrad's work. Joan Richards, approaching the subject from the perspective of the discipline the History of Science, has stated that the innovative ideas were presented not merely in a mathematical context, but: 'as a massive threat to the authoritarian approach to knowledge' [1] because they attacked the very basis upon which the understanding of mathematics had been founded for over 2000 years.

The wider, philosophic implications of this have been explicated by Robinson:

> Euclidean geometry has stood for a long time as the exemplar of a kind of knowledge which was absolute and true. Particularly in British writings, you could find statements like: It is as certain that God exists as it is that the sum of the angles of a triangle is equal to 180°. This was knowledge which was not merely mathematically consistent but was both mathematically true and descriptive of reality . . . that kind of knowledge was characterized by the inconceivability of its opposite . . . non-Euclidean geometry can be regarded as the notion that the sum of the angles of a triangle might not be 180°. All of a sudden, the whole superstructure of ethics, religion, and hope for finding true knowledge . . . collapses. That hope had rested on the belief that there was already at least one piece of such knowledge, but, now, it was no longer certain.[2]

The mathematical change occurred because the new theorists conceived of triangles on curved rather than flat planes – it is interesting that at the beginning of the twentieth century Einstein's revolutionary theories were partly based on the concept of the curvature of space – and the framing of the hypotheses, lines on flat or curved planes, became a determinate in the conclusion achieved. The solution to questions became in part a matter of how the question itself was perceived.

This concept moves away from the monolithic notion of objective perception, that any event or problem can be seen in only one correct way. During the 1860s the German scientist, Helmholtz, wrote his *Treatise on Physiological Optics*, the seminal work on the relationship between visual seeing and psychological perception, the interpretation of what is thought to have been

seen. His theory of Unconscious Inference – or Inductive Conclusion – was concerned with the extent to which new information
is interpreted, perceived, in the light of previous experience and
expectation. This is another area in which the notion of objective
truth was questioned: if each individual perceives the same
phenomena differently there cannot be a single indivisible reality.
The novelist, critic and essayist Walter Pater expressed the scientific mood of the decade in his 1865 essay on Coleridge:

> Modern thought is distinguished from ancient by its cultivation
> of the 'relative' spirit in place of the 'absolute'. Ancient philo-
> sophy sought to arrest every object in an eternal outline, to fix
> thought in a necessary formula, and the varieties of life in a
> classification by 'kinds', or *genera*. To the modern spirit nothing
> is, or can be rightly known, except relatively. . . . The philo-
> sophical conception of the relative has been developed in
> modern times through the influence of the sciences of obser-
> vation. Those sciences reveal types of life evanescing into each
> other by inexpressible refinements of change. Things pass into
> their opposites by accumulation of undefinable quantities.[3]

This is not simply a scientist's perception of the newly emerging
world, but an articulate general intellectual view that illustrates a
unity of thought between the artistic and scientific worlds which
has perhaps since been lost. Pater went on to specifically link the
physical discoveries with their metaphysical extensions:

> The moral world is ever in contact with the physical, and the
> relative spirit has invaded moral philosophy from the ground
> of the inductive sciences. There it has started a new analysis of
> the relations of body and mind, good and evil, freedom and
> necessity. Hard and abstract moralities are yielding to a more
> exact estimate of the subtlety and complexity of our life.[4]

The process was gradual and cumulative, with the issues growing
more urgent in the time between Pater's observations and Conrad's great novels. They became increasingly critical, with some
people clinging to the traditional religious beliefs, while others
looked for new certainties, such as socialism, or scientific progress
itself, or materialism. Conrad observed these responses, whilst
himself retaining a sceptical mind. He was clearly aware of philo-

sophic and ethical conflicts, and of the sources that had provoked them. Conrad knew and admired, for example, Pater's work. When Garnett sent him a copy of Pater's novel *Marius the Epicurean* in 1897 Conrad wrote in thanks, 'I am licking my chops in anticipation' (CL, vol 1, p. 355).

Just as Darwin culminated thinking on evolution in regard to the natural world, Einstein's work epitomised the application of relativity to time and space: his Special Theory of Relativity being published in 1905. The ideas of Quantum Mechanics began to emerge very slightly earlier, applying, in a sense, the notions of the relative to physical matter; indeed carrying them to a logical conclusion. Nothing can be known ultimately, for the observer changes what is being observed by the nature of observing it. Richard Gregory, both an academic and an experimental scientist, has summarised the position:

> Quantum Mechanics is based on uncertainties. . . . Since information is transmitted by discrete energy changes, there is a strict limit to the precision of observations, and so to knowledge . . . there is an essential interaction between the observation and what is observed.[5]

The world had come a long way from the certainties and absolute values that, in broad terms, existed a hundred years earlier, when it was believed that knowledge of all things was at least possible. It is no longer possible to know the physical universe completely, for it is constantly changing, being transformed even by the action of watching it. This was the crux of the epistemological crisis.

Although Conrad was not actually a scientist his intellectual circle was concerned with such ideas, and Conrad was aware of them in essence if not in detail. His interest in perception has been touched on in chapter 4 above; and Marius the Epicurean, whom Conrad had looked forward to reading, for instance, mused that: 'all that is real in our experience [is] but a series of fleeting impressions . . . we are never to get beyond the walls of this closely shut cell of one's own personality'.[6] In some respects this might be seen as an unconsciously prophetic statement of the position of Quantum Mechanics. When Conrad first encountered an X ray machine, which was in fact one of the first such instruments ever used, he became very excited by the scientific prin-

ciples involved, writing to Garnett in 1898 a description of the
evening spent with the pioneer radiologist John McIntyre:

> talk about *the* secret of the universe and the nonexistence of, so
> called, matter. The secret of the universe is in the existence of
> horizontal waves whose varied vibrations are at the bottom of
> all states of consciousness. If the waves were vertical the uni-
> verse would be different . . . there is nothing in the world to
> prevent the simultaneous existence of vertical waves, of waves
> at any angles; in fact there are mathematical reasons for believ-
> ing that such waves do exist. Therefore it follows that two
> universes may exist in the same place at the same time – and
> not only two universes but an infinity of different universes –
> if by universe we mean a set of states of consciousness; and
> note, *all* (the universes) composed of the same matter, *all matter*
> being only that thing of inconceivable tenuity through which
> the various vibrations of waves (electricity, heat, sound, light,
> etc.) are propagated, thus giving birth to our sensations . . . and
> there is no space, time, matter, mind as vulgarly understood,
> there is only the eternal something that waves and an eternal
> force that causes the waves.
>
> (CL, vol. 2, pp. 94–5)

There is a degree of science fiction fantasy-thinking in this passage.
There are, however, a number of substantial points: the linking of
scientific activity and thought with philosophy, for example; and
the idea that the meaning of the universe is scientific rather than
religious was an important extension of the intellectual impact of
the biological concept of evolution, reflecting the accelerating pace
at which the perception of life and the cosmos was changing.

This continued, both scientifically and philosophically, throughout Conrad's lifetime. In 1911 Ernest Rutherford proposed that
atoms consisted of a nuclear, rather than indivisible, structure; a
concept of the physical world that the physicist Sir Arthur Edding-
ton referred to as: 'the greatest change in our idea of matter since
the time of Democritus'[7] again illustrating a rupture from 2000
years of intellectual tradition. Rutherford's model also implied that
if atoms did not have a monolithic structure the different elements
in them could be divided. In 1919 he achieved a transmutation of
atomic elements, opening up the possibility of the whole subsequent field of atomic and nuclear physics. By the Edwardian

period it was not merely writer-intellectuals who were concerned
with a philosophy of science, but the scientists themselves had
become involved. Under the heading 'Matter and its Structure' a
journal of Rutherford's (and Conrad's), time typically reported:

> Modern science, which depends upon observation and experi-
> ment, has shown an odd tendency to revolve about metaphys-
> ical ideas . . . the physicist or chemist of today finds himself
> compelled by each characteristic line of inquiry to formulate
> some hypothesis of the basic stuff of the material world.
>
> (*The Nation*, 17 March 1917)

This indicates that the integration of scientific concepts and philosophical ideas was a general intellectual activity, and one in which
Conrad was again working at the centre of his age's consciousness.

The opening sentence of *Victory* clearly places the novel in that
nucleus: 'There is, as every schoolboy knows in this scientific age,
a very close chemical relation between coal and diamonds' (p. 57).
The common element is carbon, but the significant feature of this
comment to begin the narration is the assumption – whether or
not 'every schoolboy' should be taken literally – that the reader
will have some passing appreciation of the importance of scientific
ideas. This is emphasised in the second paragraph when an ironic
analogy between the worlds of commerce and science is drawn:

> The Tropical Belt Coal Company went into liquidation. The
> world of finance is a mysterious world in which, incredible as
> the fact may appear, evaporation precedes liquidation. First the
> capital evaporates, and then the company goes into liquidation.
> These are very unnatural physics, but they account for the per-
> sistent inertia of Heyst. . . . An inert body can do no harm to
> any one.
>
> (ibid.)

In his Notes to this edition of *Victory* Robert Hampson succinctly
explains:

> 'Liquidation' is the process of winding up a company. The nar-
> rator plays on the word to bring in two processes from the
> natural sciences: 'liquefaction' (the conversion of a solid or gas
> into a liquid) and 'evaporation' (the conversion of a solid or

liquid into vapour). A similar scientific humour hovers about the phrases 'unnatural physics' and 'inert body'.

(p. 389)

These reiterated references to the laws and language of science, especially at the very beginning of the narrative, certainly create an expectation that readers will fully appreciate the novel only if they are able to comprehend the thematic value, if not the exact meaning, of the scientific concepts.

In addition to the advances in the fields of physics and chemistry other areas of scientific achievement also affected the ways in which reality was perceived and expressed. The intellectual groundswell emanating from the 1860s ideas on natural selection and perception was given an additional impetus by the publication of Freud's seminal works. *The Interpretation of Dreams* and *The Psychopathology of Everyday Life* – which were originally published in German in 1900 and 1901 respectively, although not appearing in English until 1913 and 1914 – for instance, provided a popular quasi-scientific basis for many concepts that imaginative writers were already exploring. Redmond O'Hanlon has pointed out that both Conrad and Freud:

> thought about the problem of man's behaviour within his society in terms of the same contemporary scientific ideas. The theory of the evolution of a moral sense leads at once to the theory of a conflict of instincts.[8]

Freudian philosophy is indeed based on the idea that reality exists beneath, rather than on, the surface of actions and apparent motives. Although Conrad was not a Freudian he did explore the covert in human nature.

Also, in the field of perception it had become clear that reality was not merely a monolithic, indivisible entity. Science and art were again in accord, and of an exhibition of post-impressionist paintings that opened in November 1910 Vanessa Bell commented in a Memoir: 'It is impossible . . . that any other single exhibition can ever have had so much effect'.[9] In 1924 her sister, Virginia Woolf, claimed of the same event: 'in or about December, 1910, human character changed'.[10] It was not that human character had actually changed, but perception of reality as a whole had certainly become more complex over a period of time.

Victory explores this concern with reality, illusion and self-delusion. Schomberg's hatred of Heyst, for example, is intensified by the action of Alma/Lena:

> He could not believe that the creature he had coveted with so much force and with so little effect, was in reality tender, docile to her impulses . . . Nothing would serve Schomberg but that she must have been circumvented by some occult exercise of force or craft, by the laying of some subtle trap.
>
> (p.132)

Schomberg does not merely misunderstand the other two characters involved, but actually constructs untrue personalities for them. It is not the real Alma/Lena he covets, rather an image of her of his own creation that he has projected onto an innocent victim. Similarly Schomberg cannot perceive that Heyst is essentially honest and straightforward, the very qualities Lena trusts in him. Schomberg constructs Heyst in his own image of cunning and deviance. When Schomberg confides to Alma of his wife, 'We'll soon get rid of the old woman' (p. 131), he does not realise how much of his own egoism and ruthlessness that sentiment reveals. He goes beyond simple inability, or refusal, to perceive the truth of Heyst, but actually brings himself to believe the validity of his prejudices: 'Schomberg believed . . . firmly in the reality of Heyst as created by his own power of false inferences' (p.184) and the strength of those preconceptions extends into the character's view of himself. Fundamentally Schomberg misunderstands, and recreates, the personalities of the other protagonists because he also fails to perceive his own true nature:

> His wounded vanity wondered ceaselessly at the means 'that Swede' had employed to seduce her away from a man like him . . . as though those means were bound to have been extraordinary, unheard of, inconceivable.
>
> (p. 132)

He is unable to see either his own vanity or the fact that he frightened Alma/Lena: 'how I hated, hated, *hated*, that man! . . . I wished I could die of my fright' (p. 211), as she later confirms to Heyst. The repetition in the diction emphasises the power of

Lena's feelings, and her desire to die reflects the strength of the need for escape.

Schomberg may live in his own world, but he does not, of course, live in the world on his own. He imposes his perception of reality onto other characters' realities, and by doing so destroys them: of the six characters most involved with Schomberg's machinations – Heyst, Lena, Jones, Ricardo and Pedro being the others – he is the only one literally to survive. The finality of the conflict illustrates the importance of the theme, and is part of the novel's tragedy: perception is not a merely abstract concern.

The imposition of one character's perception on another's is aided by the willingness of the duped to be deluded. Jones' greed leads him into accepting the hints of Heyst's wealth; and also into disregarding the possible hazards of the murder and robbery: 'That hotel-keeper tried to talk to me once of some girl he had lost, but I told him I didn't want to hear any of his beastly women stories' (p. 364). Heyst points out the irony inherent in Jones' lack of perception 'Of the only effective truth in the welter of silly lies' (p. 365). Learning of that truth, Lena's presence, is a catastrophic revelation for Jones, which leads, cataclysmically, to his murder of Ricardo.

Martin Ricardo also believes in the treasure, sufficiently to take the risk of deceiving Jones by not informing him of the woman's presence on the island. It is again Heyst who perceives the element of self-delusion in Ricardo's perception:

> I should think he wanted very much to be convinced . . . he must be the most credulous brigand in existence. . . . If the story of my riches were ever so true, do you think Schomberg would have imparted it to you from sheer altruism?
>
> (p. 363)

Although Jones answers the question with a rationalisation – that Schomberg was afraid – it is clearly an uncomfortable situation for him. If Ricardo is 'the most credulous brigand' Jones is also implicated, for he has believed his secretary. Linguistically Heyst puts Jones into a paradoxical position. If Jones accepts that Ricardo is *the* most credulous man, he also denies that characteristic to his servant; for Jones has also believed the story, taking it from a credulous source, which makes Jones himself *the* most credulous brigand. The possibility of Ricardo's betrayal of Jones sprang from the latter's own failure to perceive Schomberg's fundamental motive. Jones admits that Schomberg 'wanted to get rid of us' (p. 364), but did not see the German's hatred of Heyst. It is essentially an egoistic perception – Jones sees himself as the centre of Schomberg's reality, whereas he is comparatively peripheral in that character's jealous sexual obsession with Lena and Heyst.

Heyst was right in surmising that Ricardo had been a willing victim to the delusion of riches, but more than that Ricardo is like Schomberg in that he too egotistically perceives other characters in the light of his own personality and experience: Ricardo fails to understand Heyst 'because he created for himself a vision of him in his own image' (p. 349). In a relativistic world such attitudes inevitably lead to disaster. When, for instance, Ricardo is discomposed by Heyst's activities: 'He concluded that a man up with a cigar in the middle of the night must be doing a think' (p. 265). The free indirect speech indicates that Ricardo suspects Heyst of hatching a plot, and therefore urges Jones to do so too. In fact Heyst is 'irritated' because 'The outer world had broken upon him' (p. 261). The misperception leads to an action that is ultimately, and literally, fatal to all of them.

The characterisation of the island's visitors has attracted some adverse critical attention. Even the sympathetic biographer Jocelyn Baines dismissed the characters as 'figures of melodrama . . . mere abstractions' portrayed in 'imagery which . . . is obvious and repetitive'.[11] These characteristics certainly exist, and looked at in terms of nineteenth century realism may leave something to be desired. They serve a genuine artistic purpose, however, in this novel.

Where the mid-Victorians' main concern about Darwinism related to theology, by the late-Victorian/Edwardian period it had moved on to the nature of humanity. If humanity had evolved upward from the lower species, the argument ran, it might be possible for it to regress back down the evolutionary scale into savagery. In a relativistic universe the moral guidelines to behaviour were more difficult to discern than in previous ages. The individual had to rely more on personal ethical values. Jekyll and Hyde was a literary illustration of the breakdown of both social rules, and the individual psyche into a brute state. Conrad's friend Wells considered the phenomenon from a different perspective in his 1896 novel *The Island of Doctor Moreau*. The narrator describes meeting some strange characters with:

elfin faces . . . faces with protruding lower jaws and bright eyes.
They had lank black hair, almost like horse-hair . . . their bodies
were abnormally long, and the thigh-part of the leg short and
curiously twisted . . . an amazingly ugly gang.[12]

These are not brutalised humans, but 'humanized animals'.[13] The
philosophic concern is the same: the problematic relationship
between humanity and its origins.

The philosopher Schopenhauer had expressed a bleak vision of
humanity as early as 1851: 'Man is at bottom a dreadful wild
animal.'[14] Conrad expressed a similar view in 1899 in a letter to
Graham: 'L'homme est un animal méchant' [Man is a vicious
animal] (CL, vol. 2, pp. 159–60). Galsworthy commented in his
1924 *Reminiscences of Conrad*: 'Of philosophy he had read a good
deal . . . Schopenhauer used to give him satisfaction twenty years
and more ago.'[15] There are Schopenhauerean influences in *Victory*,
although perhaps the slightly older Conrad had a more sceptical
approach to them.

The nineteenth century pessimism of Schopenhauer, contemporary concerns with Darwinism, and the confirmations from
Freudian thought of the latent darkness and deviousness of
human nature, all contribute to the characterisation, revealing the
way in which Conrad used characters in order to explore urgent
intellectual issues. In this purpose, even if he differs in the details
of technique, Conrad is like all great novelists.

Heyst explicates the emblemism of the island's visitors to Lena:
'the envoys of the outer world. Here they are before you – evil
intelligence, instinctive savagery, arm in arm. The brute force is
at the back' (p. 318). Jones and Ricardo are metaphorically, as well
as perhaps literally, arm in arm – just as Pedro is both physically
and metaphysically behind them. In the inverse terms of natural
selection evil with a civilised veneer regresses towards animalistic
savagery. It is a corruption of the mind, reasoning used for
immoral ends, linking with instinct for self-preservation and
advancement. The dialectic between reason and instinct – often
posed as that of head and heart – was a central concern for Conrad's contemporaries. In broad terms Wells advocated the advance
of reason as humanity's salvation, Lawrence thought instinct the
true path, Forster wanted to connect the two aspects. Conrad
recognised that inherent within the dialectic of head and heart
there were two dichotomies: that both reason and instinct had an

impetus for good and ill; that they are, arm in arm. Sheer brute force has no moral dimension, it merely acts without thought or consciousness of possible consequences. In evolutionary terms it is necessary to regress far back in order to reach it. The characters are associated with abstractions, but the concepts have some complexity, and raised extremely vital questions for the era.

In fact there is also some complexity in those characters, in addition to the ideas they help explore. In some ways Conrad's technique is not unlike the approach of the post-impressionist painters who so excited the intellectual/artistic world in the 1910 exhibition referred to above. One of the post-impressionists, Van Gogh, for example, explained in a letter to a friend how he painted a portrait. Having initially produced a traditional representation he continued the process:

> I exaggerate the fair colour of the hair, I take orange, chrome, lemon colour, and behind the head I do not paint the trivial wall of the room but the Infinite . . . the public will see nothing but caricature in this exaggeration.[16]

Van Gogh was interested in bringing out the essence of the sitter, an inner reality, aspects not perceived purely by the outer eye or the superficial mind. This is character-study rather than mere caricature, linking the portrait to a wider, 'Infinite' concept.

Baines' objection, and he is not alone in it, to the characterisation in *Victory* is on the lines that it is not traditionally representational. For instance, Pedro is indeed several times described in brutish terms, and Heyst confirms the narrative view in speaking of him as: 'A creature with an antediluvian lower jaw, hairy like a mastodon, and formed like a prehistoric ape' (p.342). But Pedro cooks too, and has 'laid this table' with its 'immaculate cloth' (ibid.). The character is not a simple regression, but has a latent, if tiny, ability to advance, a reminder of a very early stage in the process that created Heyst, Lena and all true civilisation.

Ricardo is at a higher stage, but the civilised veneer is still thin, as when prowling in Heyst's bungalow he catches a glimpse of Lena:

> The self-restraint was at an end: his psychology must have its way. The instinct for the feral spring could no longer be denied. Ravish or kill – it was all one to him.

(p. 287)

This feral character too has a human weakness, and after Lena has physically fought him off she is able to charm him into sub-mission, in his own terms, to 'tame' (p. 158) him, an achievement manifested in her gaining possession of Ricardo's murderous knife: 'She had done it! The very sting of death was in her hands' (p. 375).

Jones has evolved in intelligence and social status as far as he can go, but quintessentially he is dead. This is suggested by the recurring imagery of death associated with him: 'spectre' (pp. 148, 277), for instance. He is also dead, in the sense of being sterile, of having reached the end of his line, in the suggestions of homo-sexuality. This was a delicate theme in 1915, which could be approached only circumspectly. He has fled from England for an unnamed reason, although he is a gentleman, and claims to Heyst: 'that we belong to the same – social sphere . . . Something has driven you out – the originality of your ideas, perhaps. Or your tastes' (p. 359). Heyst is a baron, so Jones is claiming membership of a high social stratum – a claim Ricardo substantiates – and it is possible he is suggesting to Heyst that the 'tastes' for which the baron was driven out were homosexual, the same reasons, per-haps, for Jones' own hasty departure from England. At this stage Jones does not know there is a woman on the island. His powerful aversion to women is known to Ricardo, who related it to Schom-berg: 'He funks women' (p. 183); and when Jones discovers the presence of Lena he reacts in a 'fury' (p. 365). Then, too, Jones' own appearance has female attributes: 'his long, feminine eye-lashes were very noticeable' (p. 138), 'Mr Jones languidly . . . lifted his delicate and beautifully pencilled eyebrows' (p. 144). This is not a lot of evidence, but these details are significant in the context of Jones and his companions travelling around the eastern seas somewhat disreputably. Jones is a representative of that part of the species which, in terms of natural selection, would breed itself out.

More urgently, however, the sterility of Jones, his lack of a potent future, is symptomatic of the whole cosmic condition. There was a notion, which gained strength throughout the latter part of the nineteenth century, and ran into the twentieth, that the known universe was doomed to extinction as the heat of the sun ran out. The demotic Wells expressed this bleak vision in his uturistic 1895 novel *The Time Machine*. The time traveller reveals the future:

I cannot convey the sense of abominable desolation that hung over the world. . . . A bitter cold assailed me. . . . The darkness grew apace. . . . A horror of this great darkness came upon me.[17]

This represented a real fear during Conrad's lifetime, not because it was felt to be imminent, but because it appeared to be scientifically verifiable. The inevitability of the process seemed to subvert moral and ethical ideas, rendering all life ultimately pointless.

The concept was an extension of the Frenchman Carnot's ideas expressed in 1824, and became embodied in the Second Law of Thermodynamics, which itself became the basis of the idea of entropy. Gregory states these scientific concepts as:

Second Law: heat cannot by itself pass from a cold body to a warm body . . .
Entropy: loss of energy, which can no longer do useful work, through increasing randomness.[18]

A crude summation of these theories applied to the sun is that its heat is finite, unrenewable, and must therefore eventually become too weak to be 'useful'.

It was a theory of considerable scientific repute. In 1862 Professor William Thomson – the later Lord Kelvin, and one of the most eminent of Victorian physicists – wrote 'On the Age of the Sun's Heat':

The second great law of Thermodynamics involves a certain principle of *irreversible action in nature* . . . there is a universal tendency to its dissipation, which produces gradual augmentation and diffusion of heat, cessation of motion, and exhaustion of potential energy through the material universe. . . . As for the future, we may say . . . that inhabitants of the earth cannot continue to enjoy the light and heat essential to their life.

(*Macmillan's Magazine*, March 1862)

That this was not an individualistic, eccentric view is illustrated by a professor of a later generation, Alexander Winchell, in 'The Sun Cooling Off':

The conviction cannot be resisted that the processes going forward before our eyes aim directly at the final extinction of the solar fire. Helmholtz says: 'The inexorable laws of mechanics show that the store of heat in the sun must be finally exhausted.' . . . The treasury of life and motion from age to age is running lower and lower. The great sun which, stricken with the pangs of dissolution, has bravely looked down with steady and undimmed eye . . . is nevertheless a dying existence.

(*Scientific American*, 10 October 1891)

This bringing together of the ideas of Thomson and Helmholtz indicates how different areas of scientific thought reinforced one another.

The epistemological crisis created by doubt about the nature of knowledge and learning was intensified by an ontological crisis in which humanity's purpose in the vast cosmic scheme was difficult to assert. Conrad caught the pessimistic philosophic connotations in a letter to Graham in 1898: 'The fate of a humanity condemned ultimately to perish from cold is not worth troubling about' (CL, vol. 2, p. 17). Conrad made this entropic statement in the context of rejecting Graham's socialism, using scientific reality to rebut political idealism. It highlights the dichotomy in Conrad's thinking about humanity, as he oscillates between affirmative admiration and dismissive pessimism.

Heyst is much affected by his father's philosophy of despair: 'Man on this earth is an unforeseen accident' (p. 213), he tells Lena. It was because of such thoughts that Heyst 'perceived the means of passing through life' to be one of 'solitary . . . restless wandering . . . invulnerable because elusive'. He is entropic man, wandering a segment of a universe that is perceived to be destined for extinction, not understanding the purpose of the experience that leads to 'universal nothingness' (p. 230).

The idea that Heyst is entropic man, representing all humanity that is conscious of its ultimate collective fate, is reinforced by his eventual resting place. His island 'is but the top of a mountain', and the closest mountain:

his nearest neighbour . . . was an indolent volcano which smoked faintly all day with its head just above the northern horizon, and at night levelled at him, from amongst the clear stars, a dull red glow, expanding and collapsing spasmodically like the end of a gigantic cigar puffed intermittently in the dark. Axel Heyst was also a smoker; and when he lounged out on his

verandah with his cheroot . . . he made in the night the same
sort of glow and of the same size.

(p.58)

Heyst's 'nearest neighbour' has a double metaphoric value. It is
an extension of Heyst himself – in the dark it is not possible to
distinguish between the glows created by the character and the
volcano – and he might be 'perched on it' (p. 57), since both island
and volcano are simply mountains. The volcano in fact becomes
a beacon to the island. Schomberg convinces Ricardo of the ease
of finding Heyst by the Biblical description: 'What do you think
of a pillar of smoke by day and a loom of fire at night?' (p.189).
This passage not only emphasises the connection between Heyst
and the volcano, it prefigures his eventual death by fire at night
too. The volcano's other metaphoric function is related to the sun,
the source of solar heat and energy, for that mountain is also a
manifestation of primeval energy and fire. Amongst 'clear stars' it
emanates 'a dull red glow, expanding and collapsing' in the
manner of the sun's own predicted end. The idea of heat and
energy emanating from primal sources is expressed too by another
narrative description:

the volcano, a feather of smoke by day and a cigar-glow at night,
took its first fiery expanding breath of the evening. Above it a
reddish star came out like an expelled spark from the fiery
bosom of the earth, enchanted into permanency by the mysterious spell of frozen spaces.

(p. 341)

The reiteration of the 'cigar-glow' image emphasises the thematic
links between the volcano and Heyst; whilst the repetition of
'fiery', with its second occurrence specifically related to the 'bosom
of the earth', reinforces the concept of a primal source of heat and
energy. The connection between volcano and sun is also stressed
by the juxtaposition of the 'reddish star' and the fiery 'expelled
spark', which are both images of the universal centre. The terms
'enchanted' and 'spell' echo the initial description of Heyst (pp.
59–60). The diction indicates that the passage is clearly more than
atmospheric, and that the volcano has a thematic purpose more
profound than a mere plot function.

The concept of entropy is also expressed metaphorically in the narrator's description of the secret meeting between Heyst and Alma/Lena: 'While she was growing quieter in his arms, he was becoming more agitated, as if there were only a fixed quantity of violent emotion on this earth' (p. 123). The fixed quantity of solar energy will, in fact, run out for the Earth. Heyst anticipates that time when he refers to himself as 'a man of the last hour – or is it the hour before last?' (p. 343). His own time is certainly nearing an end.

Heyst has sought refuge from the 'calumny' and 'snares' (pp. 226–7) of life in the entropic universe in 'detachment' (p. 128), but even so cannot escape: 'I've said to the Earth that bore me: "I am I and you are a shadow." . . . But . . . I am on a Shadow inhabited by Shades' (p. 335). All people are metaphorically dead, since they are not only fated to die individually but as a species that cannot be repeated, because the whole cosmic system is doomed. The central Shade for Heyst is the 'spectral' (pp. 360, 361, 363, 370) Jones, already metaphysically dead himself and bringing physical death to the island of detachment. Jones embodies entropy; inevitable and necessary decay into chaos, or randomness. He describes himself emblematically to Heyst, 'I am a sort of fate' (p. 359). The catalytic confrontation between Heyst and Jones is accompanied by cosmic disruption and menace: 'the doorway incessantly flickered with distant lightning, and the continuous rumble of thunder went on irritatingly' (p. 364). It is as though the universe itself is coming to an end. Heyst does have a premonition of the episode's conclusion: 'This diabolical calumny will end in actually and literally taking my life from me' (p. 360). For entropic man fate is indeed diabolic.

The idea of an ultimately malevolent fate ran through the period. In 1922, for example, Sir James Frazer concluded the abridged edition of his anthropological study *The Golden Bough* with a warning concerning the historical development of humanity:

> But a dark shadow lies athwart the far end of this fair prospect. For however vast the increase of knowledge and of power which the future may have in store for man, he can scarcely hope to stay the sweep of those great forces which seem to be making silently but relentlessly for the destruction of all this starry universe.[19]

The reason is that outlined by Thomson in the 1860s: it is impossible to 'rekindle the dying fire of the sun'.[20] During the particular time in which *Victory* was being written – 'October 1912 – May 1914' (p. 385) – the philosophy of pessimism emanating from the idea of entropy had a more specific base too in the feeling of the impending catastrophe of war. The Great War broke out within weeks of Conrad completing the novel, and that conflagration had been threatened since the 1890s (cf. chapters 4 and 5 above).

He, however, was not a simple pessimist. In 1905 Conrad had written in *Speaker* an article entitled 'Books', which argued that of the artist he: 'would require . . . many acts of faith of which the first would be the cherishing of an undying hope' (NL, pp. 8–9). This idea recurs in *Victory*. Although Heyst deliberately seeks detachment from life, to 'Look on – make no sound' (p. 194), because 'all action is bound to be harmful' (p. 98), he is compelled to act: 'Action – the first thought, or perhaps the first impulse, on earth!' (p. 193). Heyst cannot simply avoid action because it is ultimately purposeless, because of entropic pessimism, for it may have meaning at the time. This is expressed in the paradox of his feelings at the very moment he decides upon a course of detachment: 'he was irrationally moved by this sense of loneliness' (p. 110).

In fact both Heyst's major acts, the salvation of Morrison and of Alma/Lena, are achieved in moments of unreflecting spontaneity and break his isolation. A further paradox is that a character who is intelligent and visionary enough to see the ultimate fate of the universe, must necessarily also perceive the unjustified sufferings of others: 'Heyst was not indifferent . . . to the girl's fate. He was the same man who had plunged after the submerged Morrison whom he hardly knew' (p. 118). He 'was temperamentally sympathetic' (p. 113) and 'his sceptical mind was dominated by the fulness of his heart' (p. 123). The central paradox of Heyst's existence is encapsulated in the fact that his attachment to Lena creates both a limitation to his life and a strength. Lena's presence prevents him from dealing with the intruders: 'only three months ago I would not have cared. I would have defied their scoundrelism . . . But now I have you!' (p. 315). But her presence also defines his own life for him: 'that human being so near and still so strange, gave him a greater sense of his own reality than he had ever known in all his life' (p. 215). This reflects a view argued by the contemporary philosopher James Ward. He quoted, and commented on, the work of Edward Caird:

'It may be truly said that we find ourselves in others before we find ourselves in ourselves, and that the full consciousness of self comes only through the consciousness of beings without us who are also selves' . . . experience from the outset involves both subject and object, both self and other.[21]

It is an attempt, in the face of cosmic fragmentation, to assert the value of union within humanity.

It is Heyst's compassion, an emotion that does unify him with others, that generates the spontaneous energy which causes him to act, ironically, as 'an agent of Providence' (p. 214). Heyst transcends the hostile fate of entropy, and its agent, Jones, bringing natural chaos, by not being cowardly or pessimistic. Heyst embraces death – just as Lena did: 'by the exertions of her tremendous victory, capturing the very sting of death in the service of love' (p. 380). He avoids the fate of having death thrust unexpectedly upon him by means of 'an energetic act of renunciation' (NL, p. 18) (cf. chapter 1 above). In renouncing his own life through the natural element of fire – 'and fire purifies everything' (p. 384) – he affirms his control over his own destiny: that is his paradoxical and ironic Victory.

It is the only way out of the entropic labyrinth. In 1905 in writing on 'Henry James' in the *North American Review* Conrad had asserted his own faith in hope. On the universe's last day, he argued of the 'artist', 'the imaginative man':

[if] there is a group alive, clustered on his threshold to watch the last flicker of light on a black sky, to hear the last word uttered in the stilled workshop of the earth. . . . I am inclined to think that the last utterance will formulate, strange as it may appear, some hope now to us utterly inconceivable. For mankind is delightful in its pride, its assurance, and its indomitable tenacity. . . . It will not know when it is beaten. And perhaps it is right in that quality. The victories are not, perhaps, so barren as it may appear from a purely strategical, utilitarian point of view.

(NL, p. 14)

In this context Heyst's death is not a barren negation. It is a form of victory, an active action positively embracing the inevitable, rather than a passive submission to it. Heyst asserts the value of

Lena, and would rather leave life with her than merely exist without her. His final words affirm the necessity of 'hope', 'love', 'trust' (p. 383).

The novel begins with an assertion of epistemological certainty, 'every schoolboy knows' (p. 57), and ends with the ontological 'sadness' of 'Nothing' (p. 385). The certainty has been challenged, for all the individual characters actually know less than they realise, falsely perceiving events and information in the light of their own needs. Part of the ontological crisis entails facing that fact, recognising that knowledge will always be incomplete, and accepting that existence still has to be confronted – either by living or *choosing* to die – rather than avoided by inertia.

Conrad provided his own conclusion to the contemporary debate in the 'Note to the First Edition' of *Victory*, which significantly celebrated:

> the obscure promptings of that pagan residuum of awe and wonder which lurks still at the bottom of our old humanity.
>
> (p. 45)

Humanity may be on the brink of evolutionary regression, the sun may be going out, but Heyst's three acts – the salvation of Morrison, the rescue of Alma/Lena, and his choice of final renunciation – are all affirmations of faith, energetic affronts to an uncaring fate. Humanity's paradox is that its own efforts to understand its cosmic environment, the very pursuit of knowledge itself, led to the discovery of the abyss, the hollow core of the volcano; but the power of the energy that motivated the search ensures the continuance of the quest.

8

Conradian Criticism

There are two basic reactions to most new writers: either reviewers and critics recognise some value, or they are dismissed as worthless. Conrad was treated like other authors in this respect – except that both the recognition and the dismissals were rather warmer or more frigid than most initiates experience. His somewhat different prose style, and critical confusion with Kipling, did not help Conrad to become accepted quite on his own terms in the early days, although many reviewers were at least sympathetic to a new writer who obviously had much originality. Norman Sherry, though, has commented:

> But from the beginning there was recognition also of those characteristics which would prevent Conrad becoming a 'popular' writer. The curious aspect of his reputation may be said to lie largely in an extraordinary and late flowering of his popularity.[1]

His reputation certainly blossomed late but emphatically, as the interest of early film makers, and episodes such as the sale of his manuscripts (cf. chapter 3 above) illustrate.

The Far East and sea books published in the 1890s attracted attention because of the unusualness, at that time, of the settings and treatments. They seemed so attractive that Arthur Waugh feared a spate of imitators:

> The only hope is that the wily brotherhood of novelists, hunting about for new material, may not suddenly involve us in a torrent of Bornean fiction.
>
> (*Critic*, 11 May 1895)

This kind of sentiment establishes just how unexpected such settings were. The originality of setting and style exasperated a few readers, such as the anonymous reviewer of *Almayer's Folly*:

> a dreary record of a still more dreary existence . . . life is monot-

onous and sordid, and the recital thereof is almost as
wearisome . . . the book is as dull as it well could be.

(World, 15 May 1895)

However, that peevish tone was not common and the same novel
drew such praise as:

> a remarkable book . . . its scene of action lies in regions as yet
> little, if at all, visited by novelists. . . . The story is a sad one;
> but it has nothing depressing in its sombreness. It will be read
> by many with interest and admiration.

(Scotsman, 29 April 1895)

The argument about the sombreness of Conrad's material was
to become, and of course remains, a central feature of readers'
responses. Another anonymous reviewer appeared to have an
original response of his/her own:

> one of the most charming romances that it has been our fortune
> to read . . . a romance in all senses of the word.

(Guardian, 3 July 1895)

Conrad's works have rarely been described as charming, and it is
difficult to see how charm, sombre and dreary can all be applied
validly to the same novel. It is a useful lesson in not taking for
granted any particular interpretation, and assuming no other is
possible.

Conrad's eschewing of popular literary conventions was
remarked with general approval in regard to *The Nigger of the
'Narcissus'*. The absence of a cause and effect related plot, and of
romantic interests, indeed the fact that the novel has no female
characters, and lacks a hero in the ordinary sense of the word,
were considered by some critics as welcome deviations from the
formula writing they mainly had to read. The idea of Conrad
searching for a new kind of structure had been noted with appreciation in respect of his first novel:

> [he] is content with an idea rather than a plot, and he is well
> advised . . . he shows the emasculating and despair-breeding
> effect of the tired but scheming East upon a weak neurotic
> Western organisation. This is done in no set piece of description,

but the knowledge of it is built up in the reader's mind by a
hundred touches. . . . The scenery does not appear behind the
characters . . . it mingles with them.

(Daily Chronicle, 11 May 1895)

This is very perceptive criticism, understanding the way in which
the structure of the novel works through the juxtaposition of
incidents and characters, and the way in which the visible, physical world – the scenery in this case – gains a metaphysical value.
It is now possible to see how basic these techniques are to Conrad's
whole output; to see it from the beginning is an example of fine,
and in this case unfortunately unsigned, reading.

The early books brought Conrad to the admiring attention of
two writers who were themselves novelists of some contemporary
stature. H. G. Wells wrote anonymous reviews of Conrad's first
two books, the second of these reviews ending as follows:

> Only greatness could make books of which the detailed work-
> manship was so copiously bad, so well worth reading, so con-
> vincing, and so stimulating.

(Saturday Review, 16 May 1896)

The criticism – Wells objected in detail to aspects of Conrad's style,
'Conrad is wordy . . .' – gave the praise more value, and this
review motivated Conrad to write to the critic, whom he did not
at that time know. The correspondence led to personal friendship,
although eventually Wells' optimistic belief in the efficacy of socialism and science was too much for Conrad and the warmth of over
ten years cooled. However, just after the publication of *The Nigger
of the 'Narcissus'*, Arnold Bennett wrote to Wells:

> I owe you a good turn for pointing out Conrad to me. . . .
> Where did the man pick up that style, & that *synthetic* way of
> gathering up a general impression . . . ? He is so consciously
> an artist.[2]

Conrad's method of synthesising diverse impressions, which so
impressed a fellow novelist, by-passed another reader who
enjoyed the characterisation and:

> only regrets that they never do anything else than their mere

commonplace duties, and that they are not connected with a story.

(Daily Mail, 7 December 1897)

Although Conrad sometimes professed to ignore reviews, he more usually read them, and occasionally, as in this case, became irate. He wrote to Graham complaining of this criticism, pointing out 'There are twenty years of life, six months of scribbling in that book' (CL, vol. 1, p. 418). On the whole Conrad was appreciated by people who understood the purposes and problems of writing. The minor novelist James Payn commented that even the lack of a heroine is not a defect, because 'such is his skill . . . as a descriptive writer of high rank and also as a (hitherto unsuspected) humorist', going on to eulogise the style:

> Never in any book within which I am acquainted has a storm at sea been so magnificently yet so realistically depicted; the description extends over many pages with a dreadful but far from wearisome monotony.

(Illustrated London News, 5 February 1898)

To express monotony without inducing it presents the writer with an extremely challenging task. It is significant that someone professionally aware of that could appreciate the way Conrad had overcome the problem.

The first actual book of Conrad's with an extended narrative complexity to be published, in 1900, was *Lord Jim* – although *Heart of Darkness* had already been printed in serial form, it was not published in a volume edition until 1902. The strangeness of the narrative structure of *Lord Jim* bewildered some readers:

> The mechanism of the story is curious, and it includes a convention which may be attacked. . . . The narrative is taken up by a ship's captain who happened to be present at the inquiry. Some years afterwards he tells the strange story to an after-dinner party of men . . . the night must have been artificially prolonged to contain it . . . there is something distracting in a convention physically impossible.

(Manchester Guardian, 29 October 1900)

All art, of course, is artificial, and based on artistic conventions.

The desire that literature should obey the rules of life is a critical difficulty from which many authors have suffered. Conrad's insistence on exploring the conventions of art has always caused the sort of misreading – though with a kind of Conradian paradox this reviewer did like the novel – evident in the case of the anonymous writer quoted above.

Although the overall response to the novel was congratulatory many critics were puzzled by the narrative structure. J.B.P. summarised the situation accurately:

> Conrad works it out . . . in his own peculiar fashion. If he keeps on writing the same sort, he may arrive at the unique distinction of having few readers in his own generation, and a fair chance of several in the next.
>
> (*Critic* (USA), May 1901)

If the critics were willing to accept the form of narration as a merely irritating idiosyncrasy, holding back a good story unnecessarily, the public as a whole were less tolerant.

So far Conrad had in the main assaulted only the artistic conventions of the accepted literary canon. Any ideological challenge had been largely, although not entirely, glossed over in the reviewers' concern with the unusual form of Conrad's fiction; and also for many critics in the admiration for a powerful new talent. His books had been set at sea or in exotic areas of the world, and his work was placed with that of Kipling, who was considered a great celebrant of imperialism, or Robert Louis Stevenson, the writer of such adventure stories as *Treasure Island* and *Kidnapped*.

In 1902, however, *Heart of Darkness* became available in book form. The impact of it was somewhat diluted by its appearance as the middle part of a trilogy published under the title: *Youth: A Narrative and Two Other Stories*. *The End of the Tether* was the final story. In a letter to his American publisher Conrad much later referred to the volume as 'the three ages of man' (LL, vol. 2, p. 338). Perhaps because *Youth* was the first story in the collection it received much attention, and a good deal of praise.

Heart of Darkness presented difficulties artistically and ideologically, and his/her failure to confront those problems – despite seeing the story as 'strangely interesting' – led to the Daily Mail reviewer misreading even the title as 'The Haunt of Darkness' (25 November 1902). The most articulate dismissal of the story came

from John Masefield, a writer of considerable contemporary reputation who actually admired much of Conrad's work enormously
but who was a bastion of establishment attitudes, subsequently
appointed Poet Laureate, and found the profound criticism of
colonialism unacceptable. He described *Heart of Darkness* in particular as:

> fine writing, good literature, and so forth, but most unconvinc-
> ing narrative. His narrative is not vigorous, direct, effective,
> like that of Mr. Kipling. It is not clear and fresh like that of
> Stevenson. . . . It gives one a curious impression of remoteness
> and aloofness from its subject.
>
> (*Speaker*, 31 January 1903)

Masefield avoids the uncomfortableness of the subject matter by
concentrating on the style, and displaying his confusion by his
lack of comprehension. The old comparison with Kipling and
Stevenson by now infuriated Conrad, and he later wrote to Pinker:

> I know how the minds of professional critics work. They live on
> comparisons, because that is the easiest method of appreciation.
> Whereas I hate them, even if made in my favour.
>
> (LL, vol. 2, p. 250)

Masefield was really asking for an African adventure story in the
Victorian popular tradition, with its implicit ideological affirmation
of the validity of imperialism. He appreciates that the story does
not meet either of those criteria, that the narrative is not direct or
clear, that it is remote from the subject, but he cannot make the
critical judgement to understand why, to appreciate the purpose
of the technique. It is easier to assert the unconscious inadequacy
of the author than to approach the text as a conscious attempt to
create something new, a work that is in some ways artistically and
ideologically subversive.

Garnett did see the immense worth of the volume, and *Heart of
Darkness* especially. He also appreciated the difference between
reading that work in three one-monthly instalments and its impact
as an entity:

> on its appearance in *Blackwood's Magazine* our first impression
> was that Mr. Conrad had, here and there, lost his way. Now

that the story can be read, not in parts, but from the first page to the last at a sitting, we retract this opinion and hold 'Heart of Darkness' to be the high-water mark of the author's talent . . . a piece of art, fascinating and remorseless.

(*Academy and Literature*, 6 December 1902)

Not every reader may be able to manage *Heart of Darkness* literally 'at a sitting', but the point is very shrewd – and as virtually all Conrad's major fiction was first serialised it is an important one. Much of his work involves an intensity of concentration on the reader's part, and that is obviously diffused over a long period of reading with many interruptions.

After *Typhoon*, in 1902, Conrad's creative talent inevitably extended beyond those areas with which he had become associated: the sea, the Far East and Africa. However, *Nostromo* also has a relatively exotic setting, in South America, and is not entirely devoid of a sea background; nevertheless a number of reviewers were disappointed with the novel, perhaps because it did not conform to their expectations. One unknown critic summed up a common response in writing that Conrad:

has made a novel of a short story . . . the publication of this book as it stands is an artistic mistake. . . . The first third of *Nostromo* should have been compressed into a few pages . . . in *Nostromo* there are moments when it is impossible to feel sure whether the past or the present is being described . . . *Nostromo* is disappointing. It is not on a level with Mr. Conrad's best work.

(*The Times Literary Supplement*, 21 October 1904)

This reviewer, like Masefield earlier, sees some of the main points of the novel without understanding them, attributing them to error rather than comprehending that those facets have a conscious artistic purpose, and then attempting to understand the work as it stands. Conrad suffered more than most from this kind of reader, one who brings preconceptions to the text and blames the author if they are not confirmed.

Another example of this type of reading is again anonymous, and concerns a comparison of *Nostromo* with *The Nigger of the 'Narcissus'*:

Only here and there does he now catch anything of the terrible mystery of the sea . . . the descriptive passages themselves are not marvellous.

(Black and White, 5 November 1904)

The idea that a writer might want to break new ground, might desire to develop his/her techniques, style, themes seems impossible for these critics to grasp. Everything new is referred back to some known point. Even the reviewer who thought it 'the great achievement in fiction of the year' also considered 'that it is formless' (*Illustrated London News*, 26 November 1904). The reception of *Nostromo* was Conrad's greatest disappointment to date, and later in thanking Bennett for his praise he recollected that 'With the public it was the blackest possible frost' (LL, vol. 2, p. 143).

Conrad's bitterness was the greater because he knew the novel had value, telling Pinker 'the book is no mean feat' (CL, vol. 3, p. 178). It was three years before his next novel was published in volume form – *The Secret Agent*, which Conrad told Graham was 'a new departure in genre' (CL, vol. 3, p. 491). Again the reviews were mixed, the ambivalence perhaps encapsulated by the anonymous reviewer who observed of Conrad:

Englishmen cannot be too grateful that this alien of genius, casting about for a medium in which to express his sympathy and his knowledge, hit upon our own tongue.

(The Times Literary Supplement, 20 September 1907)

The recognition of Conrad's genius is genuine, but the tone is a distrustful superciliousness. Conrad did not cast about for the English language, he was a naturalised Briton before he began to write serious fiction, and the reviewer's confusion seems to be caused by his or her recognising an exceptional writer without having the critical ability to quite understand why s/he has just read a great novel. The criticism of *The Secret Agent* reveals this confused state:

it lacks the free movement of 'Youth' and the terrible minuteness of *Lord Jim*, while it offers no scope for the employment of the tender and warm fancy that made 'Karain' so memorable; but it is, we think, an advance upon *Nostromo*.

(ibid.)

Such readers were not able to follow Conrad's work into its increasingly complex ideas; they simply wanted more of the earlier atmospheric story-telling – which, of course, also denies the fundamental value of a story like *Youth*.

There were, however, as always, the discerning reviewers. A. N. Monkhouse recognised that *The Secret Agent* 'breaks fresh ground', and although he too regretted the loss of the 'memorable experiences' he appreciated an aspect of Conrad's work largely unnoticed, perhaps because unexpected: 'the grim comedy . . . a nimble and even whimsical humour . . . rich in comic types and detail' (*Manchester Guardian*, 12 September 1907). Relatively few readers in 1907, however, were willing to accept a treatment of anarchism that included comedy, even if grimly presented. Conrad was caught between his artistic instincts and the need for a readership that was wider than a coterie. Four months after the reviews quoted above he wrote to Galsworthy:

> what an inspiration-killing anxiety it is to think: 'is it saleable?' There's nothing more cruel than to be caught between one's impulse, one's act, and that question, which for me simply is a question of life and death.
>
> (LL, vol. 2, p. 65)

The problem had in fact been identified by an unnamed reviewer of *The Secret Agent* who realised both its worth and its difficulty for readers of the time:

> The subtlety of his mental processes, the keenness of his artistic senses, have placed him further away from the great reading public – if infinitely nearer to the select few who have trained faculties of literary appreciation – than many a writer of far less worth.
>
> (*Athenaeum*, 28 September 1907)

That remained a difficulty for several years, for the next novel created a similar mixture of qualified admiration and bewilderment.

An anonymous reviewer of *Under Western Eyes*, for example, began by reporting that 'The story itself is fresh and full of the bitter irony of life', but concluded: 'Possibly Mr. Conrad allows his own dislikes and prejudices to pierce through a little too much . . . and thus injures the effect of his own work' (*Daily Mail*, 13 October 1911). The review revealed no appreciation of the narrative subtlety, although s/he was not alone in that. W. L. Courtney caught the general tone of reviews when he linked the Russian background of *Under Western Eyes* with the great nineteenth century novelists of that country:

> a piece of work that we think will endure, because the impression which it leaves bites as deep as Turgenieff's *Father and Sons* or the great novel of Dostoieffsky.
>
> (*Daily Telegraph*, 25 October 1911)

Such comparisons did not entirely please Conrad, as he thought the Dostoevsky references in particular were inappropriate (the reasons for which are outlined in chapter 3 above). This novel in particular caused a furore within the Conrad circle. His old friend and champion, Garnett, had sympathetic connections amongst Russian revolutionary exiles and, despite his overall approval of *Under Western Eyes*, fell into the same critical trap as the *Daily Mail* writer, taking exception to their treatment in the novel: 'There is something almost vitriolic in Mr. Conrad's scathing rejection of the shibboleths of humanitarian lovers of their kind' (*Nation*, 21 October 1911). Garnett also stated that Conrad 'bears affinities and owes a debt' (ibid.) to Turgenev and Dostoevsky. Conrad objected to that, and to the idea that anarchists are in fact lovers of humanity. He also denied, in a letter to Garnett, that the book was simply anti-revolutionists:

> There's just about as much or as little hatred in this book as in the *Outcast of the Islands* for instance . . . it is hard . . . to be charged with the rather low trick of putting one's hate into a novel.[3]

Much later Garnett, with great honesty and generosity, retracted his view: 'after re-reading the story twenty-five years later, I own I was wrong'[4] – but at the time Conrad was not happy with the reception of the novel. In the following year, in the Author's Note to his next volume, he again recorded with regret that the book had 'found no favour in the public eye' (*'Twixt Land and Sea*, p. 3).

The first of Conrad's novels to achieve that favour, although on a limited level in comparison with thoroughgoing best-sellers, was *Chance*. It was his biggest selling work to date in both the USA and Britain. In its first two years the UK sales of *Chance* were treble those of *Under Western Eyes* for the comparative period. The reviews, of course, came before most of the sales, and they set a more hopeful tone for *Chance* than for any of Conrad's previous fiction, not just in simple praise for the book but in terms of the overall respect with which Conrad was treated as a novelist.

There were still the ambivalent responses, such as that of Robert Lynd, who commenting on the narrative structure and style concluded 'many readers will find *Chance* tedious', but nevertheless found it 'a book of magical genius' (*Daily News*, 15 January 1915); whilst another unattributed review proclaimed 'the whole thing is much nearer wizardry than workmanship' (*Punch*, 28 January 1914). Sir Sidney Colvin rhapsodised over the narrative technique, which he outlined, adding:

> Thus described, the method sounds highly complicated and involved; but it is employed with such cunning art and resource that even during a first reading we are never puzzled and almost always tensely held; while a second and a third reading bring out continual new points of which the full relevance and significance had at first escaped us.
>
> (*Observer*, 18 January 1914)

The reviewers appeared to have accepted the artistic validity of Conrad's complex and difficult structure and style.

Colvin's piece was a fairly detailed large column and a half consideration, rather than the usual two or three paragraph review. This was one of the most important aspects of the reception of *Chance*: many reviews were not of the conventional, superficial kind but tended to use the opportunity to survey Conrad's work as a whole. This new reputableness was epitomised by *The Times Literary Supplement*, which had not always recognised Conrad's literary achievements, in devoting the front editorial page to him in a substantial article that ran onto the second page. Under the generic heading 'The Novels of Mr. Conrad' the author affirmed:

> A writer who remains faithful to his conception of art and of life is seldom encumbered with a superfluity of worldly reward,

nor is humanity usually grateful for the loan of a truthful and searching looking-glass . . . [we] owe a debt past all payment to this stranger who has so nobly and generously made of himself a friend within our gates.

(*The Times Literary Supplement*, 15 January 1914)

This was high praise from the pinnacle of the establishment. The rhetoric perhaps displays a conscious recognition that Conrad had not received full, critical, payment for his earlier works.

Good, tending toward ecstatic, reviews must have helped to introduce Conrad's work to a wider readership. Garnett suggested retrospectively that:

it is probable that the figure of the lady on the 'jacket' of *Chance* (1914) did more to bring the novel into popular favour than the long reviews by Sir Sidney Colvin in *The Observer*.[5]

It was a very chaste figure, and not one to lead the reader into expecting anything even mildly salacious. Just before publication Conrad had written to Pinker that he hoped the novel would be something of a commercial breakthrough:

It's the sort of stuff that *may* have a chance with the public. All of it about a girl and with a steady run of references to women in general all along . . . It ought to go down.[6]

Suffragette activity had brought the social position of women into the headlines (cf. chapter 6 above), and that perhaps made the novel look more overtly involved, to the casual reader, with contemporary issues than most of Conrad's works – although for the diligent reader Conrad was always profoundly concerned with them – an impression strengthened also by the interest in large-scale fraud cases. Those factors may have helped to sell the book. As too, perhaps, did the chapter headings which appear as Conrad's concession to popular taste only in this novel; along with a relatively conventional happy ending. If *Chance* is Conrad's only serious attempt to compromise between art and commerce it succeeded in so far as the novel pleased both the reviewers and more of the reading public than any of his previous work.

By the publication of *Victory*, then, Conrad had a settled reputation. Lynd on this occasion wrote without ambivalence:

his work is an exaltation of all those beautiful things whose doom is so sure . . . it is the true gold of genuis.

(*Daily News*, 24 September 1915)

Walter de la Mare, himself a respected novelist and poet, summarised attitudes to Conrad's output at this stage in relation to *Victory*:

Either . . . the spell of the old familiar seduction instantly re-envelopes us . . . or we are irritated, shocked, repelled.

If fascinated we acquiesce; if repelled, we criticize.

(*The Times Literary Supplement*, 30 September 1915)

The consensus by now, although still in a limited market, appeared to be towards fascination.

The next major publication, *The Shadow-Line*, was greeted with enthusiasm by an anonymous reviewer who put Conrad's fiction in a wider perspective significantly entitled *The Great Conrad*:

It is childish to regard him as a brilliant teller of sea-stories, to point out what an oddity it is for a Pole to use the English language with such rich felicity. Until we recognize once and for all that Mr. Conrad is an artist of creative imagination, one of the great ones, not of the present, but of the world, critical words are wasted upon him.

(*Nation*, 24 March 1917)

Gerald Gould also linked the novel with the great creative tradition: 'The Shadow-Line suggests a comparison with *The Ancient Mariner*' (*New Statesman*, 31 March 1917).

Conrad's position with the reviewers had been secured, but they write in peculiar circumstances, generally shortly after a book's publication and usually with little time for rereading or serious reflection. They may influence the more immediate sales and reputation of a writer, but the judgements of posterity are not necessarily those of a novelist's contemporaries. In some cases reviewers also attained the status of critics. Garnett might be seen in this way, although his influence and interests were commercial rather than academic or scholarly; the novelists such as Henry James, Bennett, Galsworthy, Wells, also had reputations as critics.

James passed one of the first scholarly critical judgements on Conrad, attempting to apply the perspective of posterity on a working writer. The essay, entitled 'The New Novel', was written just after the publication of *Chance* and so the Conrad section leans heavily on that novel, though the ambit of the article as a whole is much wider. In claiming that the new novel requires new methods James cites *Chance* as: 'an extraordinary exhibition of method by the fact that the method is, we venture to say, without a precedent in any like work'.[7]

Conrad's method of narrative complexity was not, however, to James' liking. Many authors following their own theory of art and/ or life become messianic, able to appreciate other writers in so far as they appear to be on the right path, but responding to variations as deviations from the truth. James used Conrad's work to validate new methods, but considered them taken too far:

> Conrad's first care . . . is expressly to posit or set up a reciter, a definite responsible first person singular, possessed of infinite sources of reference, who immediately proceeds to set up another, to the end that this other may conform again to the practice.[8]

Later in the essay James becomes actually satiric about this process:

> the Marlows and their determinant inventors and interlocutors, the Powells, the Franklins, the Fynes, the tell-tale little dogs, the successive members of a cue from one to the other of which the sense and the interest of the subject have to be passed on together, in the manner of the buckets of water for the impro-vised extinction of a fire, before reaching our apprehension.[9]

Conrad, not suprisingly, failed to be amused by the references to tell-tale little dogs, characters as buckets of water, or the overall tenor of the piece. James and Conrad were old friends, and James was probably the living novelist Conrad most admired. It is not surprising that Conrad felt the attack was unfair, and it does appear in part to be based on the idea that Conrad was not writing entirely Jamesean novels. It caused Conrad two years later to record it as 'the *only* time a criticism affected me painfully'[10] in a letter to the manuscript collector Quinn. No matter how much misunderstanding there was in James' essay there was enough appreciative comprehension in it for this study by an eminent intellectual to validate Conrad's importance in the larger critical canon.

D. H. Lawrence was another contemporary novelist, although of a younger generation, who read Conrad with both enthusiasm and messianic misunderstanding. In 1912 he wrote to their mutual friend Garnett:

> The Conrad, after months of Europe, makes me furious – and the stories are *so* good. But why this giving in before you start, that pervades all Conrad and such folks – the Writers among the Ruins. I can't forgive Conrad for being so sad and for giving in.[11]

E. M. Forster, too, whose own *A Passage to India* might appear to contain echoes of *Heart of Darkness*, had difficulty with Conrad's work. In a 1920 essay, later reprinted, Forster commented of Conrad:

> What is so elusive about him is that he is always promising to make some general philosophic statement about the universe, and then refraining . . . he is misty in the middle as well as at the edges . . . the secret casket of his genius contains a vapour rather than a jewel . . . we need not write him down philosophically, because there is, in this particular direction, nothing to write.[12]

Virginia Woolf made a scathing attack in 1924, in *Character in Fiction*, on novelists who still used traditional, basically Victorian, narrative methods. Among the guilty were in particular Bennett and Galsworthy who, she argued, did not help younger writers to find a new direction. In passing she dismissed Conrad's importance to the debate:

> the men and women who began writing novels in 1910 or thereabouts had this great difficulty to face – that there was no English novelist living from whom they could learn their business. Mr. Conrad is a Pole; which sets him apart, and makes him, however admirable, not very helpful.[13]

This is a curious attitude, especially in view of Conrad's influence on the development of English fiction and the admiration in which both Galsworthy and Bennett held him. A little before 1910, for example, Galsworthy claimed of Conrad's fiction:

There is no other living English novelist that so reveals the comfort and the beauty of the mystery in which we live . . . probably the only writing of the last twelve years that will enrich the English language to any great extent.

(Fortnightly Review, 1 April 1908)

A little after 1910 Bennett complimented Conrad in a letter, expressing his 'intense satisfaction in seeing a thing truly *done*, mixed with anger because I know I can never do it as well myself'.[14] Neither of these novelists are worried by Conrad's native Polishness, both realise they cannot imitate him. Indeed, despite his immense general influence Conrad's style has been too elusive, and varied, to spawn specific imitators.

Conrad's status appears to have been involved in a Conradian paradox: he was admired and respected by traditional writers, who might have been expected to find him incomprehensible and obtuse; but basically unappreciated by modernistic authors who were using similar techniques, or exploring similar ideas, and in the main building on the foundation Conrad above all had helped to create. Each of the latter group – Lawrence, Forster, Woolf – had a strong notion of what novels should be, and how they must be written, and could not quite embrace Conrad's difference. These critics, who were fine authors themselves, illustrate the problems that occur when a reader approaches a text with preconceptions. They wanted to find something that wasn't in the fiction – and was never intended to be – and therefore deemed it a failure, without fully appreciating the qualities that were in it. Perhaps the most important task of academic criticism is to find common, objective ground on which to explore texts to discover what is actually there.

Academic criticism has been very industrious, although not always completely successful, in the terms just outlined, since the Second World War. In 1948 the influential Cambridge critic F. R. Leavis published *The Great Tradition*, which was a study of George Eliot, Henry James and Conrad. It firmly established Conrad at the centre of subsequent debates about the development of the novel. In fact – and despite his reservations about *Heart of Darkness* (quoted in chapter 1 above) – Leavis begins his essay by acknowledging Conrad's status at that time: 'He has, of course, long been generally held to be among the English masters'.[15] He concludes by affirming 'that Conrad is among the very greatest novelists in the language – or any language'.[16] Leavis' primary criterion for this assertion:

> is the achievement in work addressed to the adult mind, and capable as such of engaging again and again its full critical attention.[17]

Although the relative values of different books of Conrad's have been debated with everyone having their favourite loves and hates – the centrality of his position in the mainstream of literature has not been fundamentally questioned since Leavis' acclaim.

The variability of quality in Conrad's output has, for many critics, been more than offset by the breadth of the canon. Douglas Brown put this case succinctly in 1961:

> Conrad's art has its limitations . . . it lent itself to a good deal of plainly inferior work, and two or three even among the masterpieces are flawed . . . But there is no point in making much of the limitations, for Conrad's astonishing *range* of achievement is part and parcel of them.[18]

Since then Conrad's work has been subjected to many different types of critical scrutiny, generating a diversity of interpretations.

The narrative techniques, in particular, have been closely examined. Approaching *The Secret Agent*, for example, from a poststructuralist postion Jakob Lothe observes that the novel:

> is one of the most illustrative examples in the Conrad canon of a fictional text in which the narrative method both generates, complicates, and sets at odds dissimilar thematic and ideological elements.[19]

Stephen Land has concluded, of the same novel, that the main purpose of the narrative complexity is the 'presentation of the hero as attempting neutrality between conflicting worlds'.[20] Hero is used here in the technical sense of main protagonist, and Land applies the idea to Verloc, who:

is forced, by the inherent paradox of his position, to accept an undesirable course of action which promises to bring him to his goal, but . . . in the end deprive[s] him of what he seeks.[21]

Terry Eagleton pushes the notion a little further, seeing an unconscious paradox:

neutrality in the narrator's sense of avoiding evaluative judgements can, of course, be as much a mode of commitment as explicit partiality: by withholding judgement at a crucial point, it can silently endorse a questionable attitude.[22]

This interpretation is based on the Marxist idea that non-protest implicitly supports the *status quo*. However, in the context the theory is linking *The Secret Agent* and *Under Western Eyes* without acknowledging the different narrative forms of the two novels. Writing in this extract mainly although not exclusively of *The Secret Agent*, William Bonney attempts to get beyond purely political considerations:

wisdom is the exclusive possession of Conrad's narrative voices, which must express it in a negative manner by stating what characters do *not* know and implying thereby what these characters might be able to comprehend could they move outside Western dyads. The 'high official' in *The Secret Agent* seems unaware of the mutual attraction exerted by opposites, but the narrative voice makes such awareness available in the abstract by suggesting that, if it were not his 'official kind' of 'wisdom', 'he might have reflected . . . that in the close-woven stuff of relations between conspirator and police there occur unexpected solutions of continuity.'[23]

Against this kind of philosophical exploration of duality and epistemology the novel also still provokes political responses. Jacques Berthoud finds the politics muted, but nevertheless recognises that it is present:

So far as conservatism in *The Secret Agent* finds political expression at all, it is in the form of a national policy of moderation. Such a policy must not be taken as a symptom of weakness of the body politic; on the contrary, it is a mark of its stability, its cohesiveness, and its confidence in itself. The British government's toleration of revolutionary refugees from abroad smothers them in a demoralising embrace.[24]

This could be interpreted as revealing Conrad's moderate conservatism, or his penetrating Marxist, pre-Gramscian perception of the hegemonic nature of British democracy. Eagleton, however, tends to read the novel in neither of these ways:

> The complexity of the text is the product of certain contradictions between its component elements – contradictions which are in turn produced by the mutually conflictual relations of those elements to mutually conflictual aspects of the Conradian ideology *as that ideology is produced by the novel*.[25]

This reading is based on the idea that the fundamental conflicts are not within the novel's themes, but between Conrad's overt intentions and his involuntary ones. Conrad, child of fallen aristocracy, is seen as reproducing ruling-class ideology without realising it.

The novels have also been read as covert autobiography. In discussing *The Secret Agent*, for instance, Aaron Fogel notices that Stevie's remains are identified only by the label sewn into his coat, and connects that fact to a Biblical precedent. In *Genesis* chapter 37 Joseph is sold into captivity by his brothers, and his coat of many colours – a distinguishing piece of clothing – soaked in animal's blood so that his father is persuaded Joseph has been killed by a wild beast. Relating the ideas of identification by means of coats, of real and reported deaths, and noting the coincidence of names between Conrad and the Biblical character, Fogel argues:

> [Stevie's] death *mis*represents the comic fact that the young Jôzef Korzeniowski himself didn't die but survived the political destruction of his immediate family. . . . The pitying and laughing author has a secret stake in the work. He wrote the book as a Joseph, or exiled survivor of a family destroyed from within and without by politics. In the book itself, the family has no such survivor.[26]

This kind of argument interprets the novel as a form of encoded psychological confession. Conrad was in exile most of his life, and that is certainly a recurrent theme in his fiction.

The discussion here of the diversity of more recent debate, for reasons of space, has been mostly, although not entirely, around one novel – but all Conrad's profound work has caused similar academic argument. It is part of the greatness of Conrad's work that it can provoke such a diversity of critical progeny. Despite their enormous differences all of these views may have some validity. There is a *deliberate* ambiguity at the heart of great art that is based on, and inspires, philosophical conflict. Conrad is not a polemical writer within the tradition of simply communicating a message, or even a meaning – in the single, indissoluble sense; the critical debate has established his works as the highest form of art. This involves the exploration of ideas in a manner that requires, not the mere application of a predetermined hypothesis in order to elucidate them, but an open-minded reperception of the texts and the reality from which they were created.

Chronological Table

1857   Conrad born in the Ukraine, Poland, then occupied by Czarist Russia.

1859   Charles Darwin's *Origin of Species* published.

1860   Discovery of the source of the Nile.
Abraham Lincoln elected President of the USA.

1861   American Civil War begins.

1862   Conrad's father, Apollo, is exiled into a remote area of Russia for political activities against the Russian forces of occupation. Joseph Conrad and his mother accompany Apollo.

1863   Unsuccessful revolt in Poland against Russian occupation.

1865   Conrad's mother dies in exile, leaving Joseph to be brought up by his father – with visits to an uncle in Poland.
Lincoln assassinated.
The American Civil War ends.

1867   Karl Marx' *Das Kapital* published.
The British Second Reform Act extends the franchise.
Clerkenwell explosion caused by Irish Fenians.

1868   First meeting of the Trades Union Congress (TUC).

1869   Conrad's father dies. His uncle becomes Conrad's guardian.
The Suez Canal is opened.

1870   Forster's Education Act extends provision for schooling.
Franco-Prussian war in which the French are heavily defeated, and as a result of which Prussian militarism becomes the central force in the unification of Germany, and the creation of a new German State.

1872   Publication in serial form of George Eliot's *Middlemarch* comleted.
Secret Ballot introduced into the British electoral system.

1874   Conrad leaves Poland for Marseilles, France, where he has relatives.
British begin to colonise Malaya.

1875   Conrad enters the French merchant service.
Medical School for Women founded in London.

1876 Britain and France take an uneasy joint control of Egypt.
      Alexander Graham Bell invents the telephone.
1877 Turgenev's *Virgin Soil* published.
1878 Conrad works on a British ship for the first time. Becomes
      a sailor in the British merchant fleet, and begins a career
      that takes him all over the world in the following years.
      Many of Conrad's adventures during his sailing years later
      formed the basis of stories and novels.
      Tolstoy's *Anna Karenina* published.
      London University opens its degrees to women under-
      graduates.
      Introduction of electric street lighting in London.
1879 British–Zulu war in South Africa.
      Founding of the first women's college at Oxford University.
      Ibsen's *A Doll's House* produced.
1880 Dostoevsky's *The Brothers Karamazov* published.
      Mundella's Education Act introduces compulsory schooling
      for children between the ages of five and thirteen.
1883 The Incorporated Society of Authors founded.
1884 A series of explosions in London caused by Fenians.
      British franchise extended to most adult males.
1885 General Gordon killed in Khartoum, with consequent dim-
      inution of British influence in northern Africa.
      Maupassant's *Bel-Ami* published.
      Pater's *Marius the Epicurean* published.
1886 Conrad becomes a naturalised British citizen, and passes
      the examination to gain a master's certificate.
      Riot in London's fashionable West End.
1887 Bloody Sunday riot in Trafalgar Square.
1890 After briefly visiting his relatives in Poland Conrad attains
      an appointment in the Belgian Congo.
1891 Suffering from malaria and other sickness Conrad returns
      to London and the British Merchant Service.
1892 Three Independent Socialists elected as MPs.
1893 Conrad meets Galsworthy, and is himself working on
      Almayer's Folly.
1894 The novel is accepted for publication by Fisher Unwin, and
      Conrad meets Garnett.
      An anarchist attempts to blow up Greenwich Observatory.
1895 *Almayer's Folly* published. (Most of Conrad's novels were
      serialised before appearing in volume form, but the dates

given here are mainly those for book publication.)
Dispute with Venezuela almost causes British–USA armed
conflict.
X rays discovered.

1896   *An Outcast of the Islands* published. Conrad married to Jessie
George.
Hardy's *Jude the Obscure* published.
Daily Mail appears as the first mass publication daily news-
paper. Several others follow in the next four years.
Jameson's Raid into Transvaal.

1897   *The Nigger of the 'Narcissus'* published.
National Union of Women's Suffrage Societies founded.

1898   *Tales of Unrest*, which included *An Outpost of Progress*, pub-
lished.
Spanish–USA war.
Conrad's first son, Borys, is born.
Khartoum retaken by the British Army.

1899   *Heart of Darkness* is serialised.
Pinker becomes Conrad's agent.
Boer War begins.

1900   *Lord Jim* published.
Freud's *The Interpretation of Dreams* published.
Elucidation of Planck's Constant, an important stage in the
development of the theories of Quantum Mechanics.
Labour Party founded.

1901   Death of Queen Victoria.
Accession of King Edward VII.
Freud's *The Psychopathology of Everyday Life* published.

1902   Conrad receives a grant from the Royal Literary Fund.
Heart of Darkness published in a volume with *Youth* and *The
End of the Tether*.
Boer War ends.

1903   *Typhoon, and Other Stories* published.
Women's Social and Political Union formed.

1904   *Nostromo* published and Conrad writes his first play: *One
Day More*.
Henry James' *The Golden Bowl* published.
Britain begins programme of building *Dreadnought* battle-
ships in response to increasing naval power of the USA,
and more particularly of Germany.

1905   Conrad receives a grant from the Royal Bounty, and his play is performed without success.

British Science Guild founded.

Einstein's *Special Theory of Relativity* published.

Unsuccessful attempt at political revolution in Russia.

Moroccan crisis almost provokes war between France and Germany.

1906   *The Mirror of the Sea* published.

Conrad's son John is born.

Labour Party wins 53 seats in the general election.

1907   *The Secret Agent* published.

1908   *A Set of Six* published.

Old age pensions introduced, preceding other important social legislation.

1910   Sidney Street siege of Russian anarchists in London.

1911   Conrad is awarded a Civil List pension; Quinn, the American collector, begins to purchase Conrad's manuscripts.

Under Western Eyes published.

The physicist Rutherford proposes a new conception of the atom.

1912   *A Personal Record* published, under its original title *Some Reminiscences*; as is *'Twixt Land and Sea*.

1913   *Chance* published, the first of Conrad's novels to achieve any kind of public popularity.

1914   Conrad and his family visit Poland.

The Great War (First World War) breaks out.

Richard Curle's *Joseph Conrad, A Study* published.

1915   *Victory* published, and the stories entitled *Within the Tides*.

D. H. Lawrence's *The Rainbow* published.

1916   Conrad flies for the first time.

Einstein's *General Theory of Relativity* published.

1917   *The Shadow-Line* published.

Russian Revolution.

1918   The Great War finally ends after immense destruction and loss of life.

Limited female franchise granted in Britain.

1919   Conrad becomes one of the first major living authors to sell the film rights to his works. A film version of *Victory* is made.

The Arrow of Gold published.

Rutherford achieves a transmutation of atomic elements.

1920   Conrad completes two plays: *The Secret Agent* and *Laughing*

Anne. He writes the Author's Notes for a collected edition of his works, and *The Rescue* is published.

Works with Pinker unsuccessfully on a film version of 'Gaspar Ruiz'.

Lawrence's *Women in Love* published.
1921   *Notes on Life and Letters* published.
1922   *The Secret Agent* is performed on stage without critical or public success.

Joyce's *Ulysses* published.

Woolf's *Jacob's Room* published.
1923   Conrad visits the USA, and *The Rover* is published.

Quinn sells Conrad's manuscripts.
1924   Following the refusal of honorary degrees from several universities in previous years Conrad declines the offer of a knighthood. Conrad dies and is buried in Kent under his native Polish name.

Forster's *A Passage to India* published.
1925   *Suspense, Tales of Hearsay* and *The Congo Diary* are published separately.
1926   *Last Essays* published.
1934   *Three Plays* published.

Notes

Chapter 1 The Unique Background

1. H. V. Marrot, *The Life and Letters of John Galsworthy* (London: William Heinemann, 1935), p. 88.
2. Letter written 16 June 1862; printed in *Tygodnik Illustrowany*, No. 4, 1920; cited in Jocelyn Baines, *Joseph Conrad: A Critical Biography* (London: Weidenfeld & Nicolson, 1967), pp. 13–14.
3. W. D. Handcock (ed.), *English Historical Documents*, XII, 1874–1914 (London: Eyre & Spottiswoode, 1977), p. 191.
4. The letters written by John Pine are in the possession of Miss Alice Sheridan. They are taken from a compilation made by Alan Hankinson and broadcast on Radio 4 on 31 July 1989 (repeated 22 December 1989), in a programme produced by Gillian Hush for BBC Manchester.
5. Ibid.
6. George Macaulay Trevelyan, *British History in the Nineteenth Century and After (1782–1919)* (London: Longmans, Green, 1966), p. 372.
7. Charles Dickens, *American Notes for General Circulation* (Harmondsworth: Penguin, 1989), pp. 65–7.
8. W. H. S. Jones, *The Cape Horn Breed* (London: Jarrolds, 1968), pp. 115–16.
9. Albert Thys, *Au Congo et au Kassai* (Brussels, 1888), p. 7; cited in C. T. Watts (ed.), *Joseph Conrad's Letters to R. B. Cunninghame Graham* (Cambridge: University Press, 1969), p. 151. The original is 'on se croirant devant au pays maudit, véritable barrière qui semble créée par la nature pour arrêter le progrès'.
10. Edward Garnett (ed.), *Letters from Conrad: 1895–1924* (London: Nonesuch Press, 1928), p. xix.
11. Ford Madox Ford, *Joseph Conrad: A Personal Remembrance* (London: Duckworth, 1924), p. 201.
12. F. R. Leavis, *The Great Tradition* (Harmondsworth: Penguin, 1966), pp. 196–9.

Chapter 2 Conrad as Crucible

1. Ford, *Joseph Conrad*, p. 200.
2. Ibid.
3. Norman Page, *A Conrad Companion* (Basingstoke: Macmillan, 1986), p. 165.
4. Richard Curle (ed.), *Conrad to a Friend* (London: Sampson, Low, Marston, 1928), p. 114.
5. Ibid.

6.   Frederick R. Karl, *Joseph Conrad: The Three Lives* (London: Faber & Faber, 1979), pp. 764–5.
7.   Raymond Williams, *Culture and Society* (London: Hogarth Press, 1990), p. 161.

Chapter 3   Conrad in Context

1.   N. John Hall (ed.), *The Letters of Anthony Trollope*, II (Stanford, California: Stanford University Press, 1983), p. 715.
2.   Ibid.
3.   Peter Keating, *The Haunted Study: A Social History of the English Novel 1875–1914* (London: Secker & Warburg, 1989), p. 15.
4.   William Blackburn (ed.), *Joseph Conrad: Letters to William Blackwood and David S. Meldrum* (Durham, North Carolina: Duke University Press, 1958), p. 40.
5.   Baines, *Critical Biography*, p. 427.
6.   Karl, *The Three Lives*, pp. 881–2.
7.   Garnett, *Letters from Conrad*, p. 328.
8.   W. N. Medlicott, *Contemporary England 1914–1964* (London: Longmans, 1967), p. 81.
9.   Pauline Gregg, *A Social and Economic History of Britain 1760–1980* (London: Harrap, 1982) p. 514. The quotations within the passage are attributed to an official document: *Report of the Privy Council on Education for 1886*, XXVIII, pp. 262–3.
10.   G. D. H. Cole and Raymond Postgate, *The Common People 1746–1946* (London: Methuen, 1968), p. 454.
11.   David Daiches, *The Novel and the Modern World* (Chicago: University of Chicago Press, 1965), p. 58.
12.   Ford, *Joseph Conrad* p. 200.
13.   Guy de Maupassant, translated by Leonard Tancock, *Pierre and Jean* (Harmondsworth: Penguin, 1987), p. 25.

Chapter 4   The African Arena

1.   *Rudyard Kipling's Verse: Definitive Edition* (London: Hodder & Stoughton, 1986), p. 400.
2.   John Evelyn Wrench, *Alfred, Lord Milner: The Man of No Illusions 1854–1925* (London: Eyre & Spottiswoode, 1958), p. 213.
3.   Ibid., pp. 213–14.
4.   Ibid., p. 213.
5.   R. C. K. Ensor, *England 1870–1914* (Oxford: Clarendon Press, 1963), p. 347.
6.   Anthony Wood, *Nineteenth Century Britain 1815–1914* (London: Longman, 1982), p. 384.
7.   Ibid., p. 385.
8.   The general idea of the British presence in the Congo has been developed by Dr Valentine Cunningham in his Oxford lectures, and can be found in more detail in his forthcoming book: *In the Reading Gaol* (Oxford: Basil Blackwell).

9.   Roger Webster, *Studying Literary Theory: An Introduction* (London: Edward Arnold, 1990), p. 86.
10. H. Rider Haggard, *King Solomon's Mines* (London: Dent, 1975), p. 40. Subsequent page references to the novel are to this edition.
11. Brian V. Street, *The Savage in Literature* (London: Routledge & Kegan Paul, 1975), p. 123. This is a very useful introduction to popular literature in the period, despite misunderstanding Conrad's own purpose.

Chapter 5   The World Stage

1.   C. T. Watts, *Letters to Cunninghame Graham*, p. 97.
2.   J. H. Parry, 'Latin America, 1899–1949', in David Thomson (ed.), *The New Cambridge Modern History*, XII (Cambridge: University Press, 1960), p. 186.
3.   D. W. Brogan, 'The United States of America', in Thomson, ibid., p. 150.
4.   Parry, 'Latin America', p. 178.
5.   Ibid., p. 179.
6.   Sir Arthur Conan Doyle, *The Complete Sherlock Holmes* (London: Secker & Warburg, 1981), p. 512. All subsequent references to Doyle's stories are to this edition.
7.   Maldwyn A. Jones, *The Limits of Liberty* (Oxford: University Press, 1991), p. 407.
8.   Samuel Eliot Morison, Henry Steele Commager and William E. Leuchtenburg, *The Growth of the American Republic*, I (Oxford: University Press, 1980), p. 411.
9.   Jones, *Limits of Liberty*, p. 304.
10. Ibid., p. 300.
11. Jenny Pearce, *Under the Eagle* (London: Latin American Bureau, 1981), p. 9.
12. Ibid., p. 11.
13. Brogan, 'United States', p. 152.
14. Jones, *Limits of Liberty*, p. 408.
15. Pearce, *Under the Eagle*, pp. 11–12.
16. Ibid., p. 18.
17. Jones, *Limits of Liberty*, p. 399.
18. W. H. Auden and Norman Holmes Pearson (eds), *Poets of the English Language*, V (London: Eyre & Spottiswoode, 1971), p. 593.
19. David Thomson, 'The Transformation of Social Life', in Thomson, *New Cambridge Modern History*, XII, pp. 42–3.
20. J. P. T. Bury, 'International Relations, 1900–12', in Thomson, ibid., p. 312.
21. Andrew Turnbull (ed.), *The Poems of John Davidson*, I (Edinburgh: Scottish Academic Press, 1973), p. 184.
22. Ensor, *England 1870–1914*, p. 363.
23. The story is reprinted in part in Rudyard Kipling, *War Stories and Poems* (Oxford: University Press, 1990), pp. 105–22.

Chapter 6   The Domestic Dynamic

1.   Wood, *Nineteenth Century Britain*, p. 386.
2.   George Orwell, *The Road to Wigan Pier* (Harmondsworth: Penguin, 1989), p. 119.
3.   R. S. S. Baden-Powell, *Scouting for Boys* (London: Horace Cox, 1908), pp. 208–9.
4.   Geoffrey Pearson, *Hooligan: A history of respectable fears* (London: Macmillan, 1983), p. 59.
5.   Ian Watt (ed.), *Conrad: The Secret Agent* (London: Macmillan, 1983), pp. 202–51.
6.   Sir Robert Anderson, *Sidelights on the Home Rule Movement* (London: John Murray, 1906), pp. 89–90.
7.   Walter Laqueur, *Terrorism* (London: Weidenfeld & Nicolson, 1978), p. 99.

Chapter 7   The Entropic Labyrinth

1.   Philip J. Davis and Reuben Hersh, *Descartes' Dream* (Brighton: Harvester, 1986), p. 206.
2.   Ibid., pp. 207–8.
3.   Walter Pater, *The Complete Works of Walter Pater*, V (London: Macmillan, 1901), p. 66.
4.   Ibid., p. 67.
5.   Richard L. Gregory, *Mind in Science* (Harmondsworth: Penguin, 1984), p. 538.
6.   See C. T. Watts, *Letters to Cunninghame Graham*, pp. 67, 69, who makes a connection between Conrad's thought and this quotation in a slightly different context.
7.   Douglas McKie, 'Science and Technology', in Thomson, *New Cambridge Modern History*, V, p. 104.
8.   Redmond O'Hanlon, *Joseph Conrad and Charles Darwin* (Edinburgh: Salamander Press, 1984), p. 47.
9.   Frances Spalding, *Vanessa Bell* (London: Macmillan, 1984), p. 92.
10. Virginia Woolf, *Collected Essays*, I (London: Hogarth Press, 1966), p. 320.
11. Baines, *Critical Biography*, p. 398.
12. H. G. Wells, *The Island of Doctor Moreau* (Harmondsworth: Penguin, 1967), pp. 38–9.
13. Ibid., p. 101.
14. Arthur Schopenhauer, translated by R. J. Hollingdale, *Essays and Aphorisms* (Harmondsworth: Penguin, 1978), p. 138.
15. John Galsworthy, *Castles in Spain* (London: Heinemann, 1927), p. 91.
16. E. H. Gombrich, *The Story of Art* (London: Phaidon Press, 1966), pp. 428–9.
17. H. G. Wells, *The Time Machine* (London: Dent, Everyman's Library, 1969), pp. 95–7.
18. Gregory, *Mind in Science*, p. 150.

19. Sir James George Frazer, *The Golden Bough* (London: Macmillan, 1980), p. 713.
20. Ibid.
21. James Ward, *The Realm of Ends* (Cambridge: University Press, 1912), pp. 128–9.

Chapter 8 Conradian Criticism

1. Norman Sherry (ed.), *Conrad: The Critical Heritage* (London: Routledge & Kegan Paul, 1973), p. 1. A number of the reviews quoted in this chapter also appear in Sherry's invaluable anthology.
2. James Hepburn (ed.), *Letters of Arnold Bennett*, II, 1889–1915 (London: Oxford University Press, 1968), p. 94.
3. Garnett, *Letters from Conrad*, pp. 248–9.
4. *Conrad's Prefaces to his Works*, with an introductory essay by Edward Garnett (London: Dent, 1937), p. 27.
5. Garnett, *Letters from Conrad*, p. xx.
6. Baines, *Critical Biography*, p. 381.
7. Morris Shapira (ed.), *Henry James: Selected Literary Criticism* (Cambridge: University Press, 1981), p. 331.
8. Ibid., p. 332.
9. Ibid., p. 334.
10. Karl, *The Three Lives*, p. 746.
11. James T. Boulton (ed.), *The Letters of D. H. Lawrence*, I, 1901–13 (Cambridge: University Press, 1979), p. 465.
12. E. M. Forster, *Abinger Harvest* (Harmondsworth: Penguin, 1974), p. 152.
13. Andrew McNeillie (ed.), *The Essays of Virginia Woolf*, III, 1919–1924 (London: Hogarth Press, 1988), p. 427.
14. Hepburn, *Letters of Arnold Bennett*, p. 321.
15. Leavis, *Great Tradition*, p. 192.
16. Ibid., p. 248.
17. Ibid.
18. Douglas Brown, 'From *Heart of Darkness* to *Nostromo*: An Approach to Conrad', in Boris Ford (ed.), *The New Pelican Guide to English Literature*, VII (Harmondsworth: Penguin, 1990), p. 131.
19. Jakob Lothe, *Conrad's Narrative Method* (Oxford: Clarendon Press, 1989), p. 261.
20. Stephen K. Land, *Conrad and the Paradox of the Plot* (London: Macmillan, 1984), p. 148.
21. Ibid., p. 150.
22. Terry Eagleton, *Exiles and Emigrés* (London: Chatto & Windus, 1970), p. 23.
23. William W. Bonney, *Thorns & Arabesques* (Baltimore: Johns Hopkins University Press, 1980), p. 18.
24. Jacques Berthoud, *Joseph Conrad: The Major Phase* (Cambridge: University Press, 1978), p. 133.
25. Terry Eagleton, *Against the Grain: Essays 1975–1985* (London: Verso, 1986), p. 31.

26. Aaron Fogel, *Coercion to Speak: Conrad's Poetics of Dialogue* (Cambridge, Mass.: Harvard University Press, 1985), pp. 178–9.

Select Bibliography

Conrad's Main Fiction

Almayer's Folly (Harmondsworth: Penguin, 1988)
Arrow of Gold, The (London: Dent, 1972)
Chance (Oxford: Oxford University Press, 1990)
End of the Tether, The (Penguin, 1975)
Heart of Darkness (Penguin, 1989)
Lord Jim (Penguin, 1986)
Nigger of the 'Narcissus', The (Penguin, 1988)
Nostromo (Penguin, 1990)
Outcast of the Islands, The (Penguin, 1975)
Rescue, The (Penguin, 1950)
Rover, The (Dent, 1965)
Secret Agent, The (Penguin, 1990)
Set of Six, A (Dent, 1961)
Shadow-Line, The (Penguin, 1987)
Tales of Unrest (Penguin, 1977)
'Twixt Land and Sea (Penguin, 1988)
Typhoon and Other Stories (Penguin, 1990)
Under Western Eyes (Penguin, 1989)
Victory (Penguin, 1989)
Within the Tides (Penguin, 1978)
Youth (Penguin, 1975)

Other Main Writing

Conrad's Prefaces to his Works, with an introductory essay by Edward
    Garnett (Dent, 1937)
Last Essays (Dent, 1926)
Mirror of the Sea, The (OUP, 1989)
Notes on Life and Letters (Dent, 1970)
Personal Record, A (OUP, 1989)
G. Jean-Aubrey (ed.), *Joseph Conrad: Life & Letters*, vols 1 and 2 (London:
    Heinemann, 1927)
William Blackburn (ed.), *Joseph Conrad: Letters to William Blackwood and
    David S. Meldrum* (Durham, North Carolina: Duke University Press,
    1958)
Richard Curle (ed.), *Conrad to a Friend* (London: Sampson, Low, Marston,
    1928)
Edward Garnett (ed.), *Letters from Conrad: 1895–1924* (London: Nonesuch
    Press, 1928)
Frederick R. Karl and Laurence Davies (eds), *The Collected Letters of Joseph
    Conrad* (Cambridge: University Press):

Vol. I, 1861–1897, published 1983
Vol. II, 1898–1902, published 1986
Vol. III, 1903–1907, published 1988
Vol. IV, 1908–1911, published 1990
Zdzisław Najder (ed.), *Congo Diary and Other Uncollected Pieces by Joseph Conrad* (New York: Doubleday, 1978)
C. T. Watts (ed.), *Joseph Conrad's Letters to R. B. Cunninghame Graham* (Cambridge: University Press, 1969).

Critical Works

There are a great many biographical and critical books concerned with Conrad. This is necessarily a short list and the exclusion of any book from it does not imply disapproval. The journal *The Conradian* is a very useful source of new ideas and information.

Jocelyn Baines, *Joseph Conrad: A Critical Biography* (London: Weidenfeld & Nicolson, 1967)
Jacques Berthoud, *Joseph Conrad: The Major Phase* (Cambridge: University Press, 1978)
William W. Bonney, *Thorns & Arabesques* (Baltimore: Johns Hopkins University Press, 1980)
C. B. Cox (ed.), *Conrad: Heart of Darkness, Nostromo and Under Western Eyes* (Basingstoke: Macmillan, 1989)
Valentine Cunningham, *In the Reading Gaol* (Oxford: Basil Blackwell, forthcoming)
David Daiches, *The Novel and the Modern World* (Chicago: University of Chicago Press, 1965)
Terry Eagleton, *Exiles and Emigrés* (London: Chatto & Windus, 1970)
Aaron Fogel, *Coercion to Speak: Conrad's Poetics of Dialogue* (Cambridge, Mass.: Harvard University Press, 1985)
Ford Madox Ford, *Joseph Conrad: A Personal Remembrance* (London: Duckworth, 1924)
Gail Fraser, *Interweaving Patterns in the Works of Joseph Conrad* (Ann Arbor, Mich.: UMI Research Press, 1988)
Yves Hervouet, *The French Face of Joseph Conrad* (Cambridge: University Press, 1991)
Frederick R. Karl, *Joseph Conrad: The Three Lives* (London: Faber & Faber, 1979)
Owen Knowles, *A Conrad Chronology* (Basingstoke: Macmillan, 1989)
Stephen K. Land, *Conrad and the Paradox of the Plot* (London: Macmillan, 1984)
F. R. Leavis, *The Great Tradition* (Harmondsworth: Penguin, 1966)
Jakob Lothe, *Conrad's Narrative Method* (Oxford: Clarendon Press, 1989)
Marvin Mudrick (ed.), *Conrad: A Collection of Critical Essays* (Englewood Cliffs, N.J.: Prentice-Hall, 1966)
Ross C. Murfin (ed.), *'Heart of Darkness': A Case Study in Contemporary Criticism* (New York: St. Martin's Press, 1989)
Zdzisław Najder, *Joseph Conrad: A Chronicle* (Cambridge: University Press, 1983)

Redmond O'Hanlon, *Joseph Conrad and Charles Darwin* (Edinburgh: Salamander Press, 1984)

Norman Page, *A Conrad Companion* (Basingstoke: Macmillan, 1986)

Benita Parry, *Conrad and Imperialism* (London: Macmillan, 1983)

Martin Ray (ed.), *Joseph Conrad: Interviews and Recollections* (Basingstoke: Macmillan, 1990)

Norman Sherry (ed.), *Conrad: The Critical Heritage* (London: Routledge & Kegan Paul, 1973)

Norman Sherry, *Conrad's Eastern World* (Cambridge: University Press, 1977)

Norman Sherry, *Conrad's Western World* (Cambridge: University Press, 1980)

Ian Watt, *Conrad in the Nineteenth Century* (London: Chatto & Windus, 1980)

Ian Watt (ed.), *Conrad: The Secret Agent* (London: Macmillan, 1983)

Cedric Watts, *Joseph Conrad: A Literary Life* (Basingstoke: Macmillan, 1989)

Cedric Watts, *The Deceptive Text* (Brighton: Harvester, 1984)

Selected Background Bibliography

G. D. H. Cole and Raymond Postgate, *The Common People 1746–1946* (London: Methuen, 1968)

R. C. K. Ensor, *England 1870–1914* (Oxford: Clarendon Press, 1963)

Boris Ford (ed.), *The Edwardian Age and the Inter-War Years: The Cambridge Guide to the Arts in Britain*, vol. VIII (Cambridge: University Press, 1988)

Boris Ford (ed.), *The New Pelican Guide to English Literature*, vols 6 and 7 (Harmondsworth: Penguin, 1990)

Pauline Gregg, *A Social and Economic History of Britain 1760–1980* (London: Harrap, 1982)

Richard L. Gregory, *Mind in Science* (Harmondsworth: Penguin, 1984)

Maldwyn A. Jones, *The Limits of Liberty* (Oxford: University Press, 1983)

Peter Keating, *The Haunted Study: A Social History of the English Novel 1875–1914* (London: Secker & Warburg, 1989)

Walter Laqueur, *Terrorism* (London: Weidenfeld & Nicolson, 1978)

Jenny Pearce, *Under the Eagle* (London: Latin American Bureau, 1981)

Geoffrey Pearson, *Hooligan: A history of respectable fears* (London: Macmillan, 1983)

Brian V. Street, *The Savage in Literature* (London: Routledge & Kegan Paul, 1975)

David Thomson (ed.), *The New Cambridge Modern History*, vol. XII (Cambridge: University Press, 1960)

Raymond Williams, *Culture and Society* (London: Hogarth Press, 1990)

Anthony Wood, *Nineteenth Century Britain 1815–1914* (London: Longman, 1982)

George Woodcock, *Anarchism* (Harmondsworth: Penguin, 1986)

John Evelyn Wrench, *Alfred, Lord Milner: The Man of No Illusions 1854–1925* (London: Eyre & Spottiswoode, 1958).

Index

195

Index